Mastering Julia

From Basics to Expert Proficiency

Contents

Introduction

Julia is a high-level, high-performance programming language designed for technical and scientific computing. Its development was initiated by Jeff Bezanson, Stefan Karpinski, Viral B. Shah, and Alan Edelman. The language was officially released to the public in 2012 and has since grown into a mature platform for numerical and data-intensive tasks.

The need for Julia arose from a unique mix of performance requirements and the ease of use demanded by computational scientists, data scientists, and engineers. Traditional languages such as Python and R offer simplicity and a rich ecosystem but often lack the computational speed necessary for high-performance tasks. Conversely, languages like C and Fortran provide speed but are cumbersome for interactive use and require intricate management of data structures and memory. Julia was designed to bridge this gap by offering the ease of use associated with high-level languages while competing favorably with low-level languages in terms of performance.

Given this context, Julia's rise has been marked by significant speed advantages and a versatile ecosystem inclusive of packages for optimization, statistics, machine learning, and more. As a result, Julia has been widely adopted in academic research, data science, and various engineering fields.

This book aims to provide a comprehensive guide to mastering Julia, from the basic syntax to expert-level metaprogramming, performance optimization, and interfacing with other languages. Whether you are new to programming or an experienced developer, this text will equip you with the knowledge necessary to utilize Julia's capabilities to their fullest extent.

We begin by exploring the installation process for Julia and setting up the development environment. Following this, we delve into the language's syntax and built-in types, establishing a foundation upon which more complex concepts are built. The book proceeds to cover control flow, functions, and methods, offering a detailed understanding of these critical elements of any programming language.

The exploration of collections and data structures introduces you to Julia's versatile array handling, tuples, dictionaries, and other structures imperative for data management. With a solid understanding of these fundamentals, we move on to the ecosystem of Julia packages and modules, illustrated with practical examples to help you extend Julia's functionality effortlessly.

File I/O and data handling chapters will guide you through efficient manipulation of various data formats, including CSV, JSON, and database interfacing. As data operations are central to computing tasks, mastering these will be key to your success with Julia.

Metaprogramming, an advanced topic, opens a doorway to code generation, introspection, and the creation of domain-specific languages within Julia. Such capabilities can significantly streamline workflows and enhance code efficiency. This naturally transitions to the chapter on performance and optimization, where we delve into benchmarking, profiling, and optimizing Julia code for speed and efficiency.

Interfacing with other languages ensures that Julia can leverage existing codebases and libraries from languages like C, Python, and R. Understanding these interfaces broadens the scope of projects you can execute efficiently within Julia.

In conclusion, this book is structured to take you step-by-step from basic to advanced levels in Julia programming. It is designed to equip you with both theoretical knowledge and practical skills, ensuring you can tackle computational problems with ease and efficiency using Julia. Through in-depth discussions, code examples, and practical guidelines, you will gain the proficiency required to leverage Julia's full potential in diverse fields.

Chapter 1

Introduction to Julia Programming

This chapter provides an overview of Julia's purpose and evolution, guides through the installation and setup of the Julia environment, and introduces basic usage via the Julia REPL and Jupyter Notebooks. It covers the fundamental syntax and conventions, explores Julia's type system, and explains how to access help and documentation. Additionally, it outlines the Julia ecosystem, compares Julia with other programming languages, and directs readers to community resources.

1.1 The Evolution and Purpose of Julia

Julia is a high-level, high-performance programming language that was developed with the goal of combining the ease of use found in languages like Python, R, and Matlab with the performance of low-level languages like C and Fortran. The development of Julia started in 2009, and by 2012 the first public release was made available. The decision to create Julia was driven by the observation that in scientific computing and data analysis, many practitioners were using high-level languages for prototyping and then re-implementing the same algorithms in low-level languages to gain performance.

Julia was designed to address the "two-language problem," a situation that arises when developers use one language for prototyping and research (due to its simplicity and expressive nature) and another for production (due to its efficiency and speed). This problem can lead to inefficiencies, increased error rates, and longer development times.

One of the key features of Julia is its type system and just-in-time (JIT) compilation using LLVM (Low-Level Virtual Machine). This combination allows Julia to approach the speed of statically typed, compiled languages while maintaining the flexibility of dynamically typed languages. Here, we explore the key motivations behind the creation of Julia and its development trajectory.

Key Motivations:

- High-Level Syntax: Julia's syntax is designed to be as intuitive and easy to read as other high-level languages. For example, mathematical operations in Julia look very similar to their mathematical notation, which makes the language particularly attractive for mathematicians and scientists.

- Performance: Julia was designed to achieve performance comparable to statically-typed languages like C and Fortran. By leveraging LLVM for JIT compilation, Julia compiles functions just before they are executed, allowing it to optimize for performance at runtime.

- Multiple Dispatch: Julia's core programming paradigm is multiple dispatch, which allows the selection of functions to be based on the types of all of their arguments. This contrasts with single dispatch systems, such as those in C++ or Java, where the method to invoke is chosen based on the type of one receiver object.

- Metaprogramming: Julia's ability to generate and include code dynamically using metaprogramming (programs that write programs) allows users to abstract away repetitive coding patterns and creates more generic and reusable code.

- Community and Collaboration: Engaging the community was a significant focus for Julia's creators from the outset. By making it open-source and encouraging contributions, Julia rapidly evolved through collaborative innovation.

Development Timeline:

- 2009: Development begins. The creators, Jeff Bezanson, Stefan Karpinski, Viral B. Shah, and Alan Edelman, at MIT, start developing what would become Julia.
- 2012: Julia is publicly released on February 14. The creators publish a blog post introducing Julia to the world, outlining its advantages and inviting others to join in its development.
- 2015: Julia reaches version 0.4, introducing significant performance improvements, additional language features, and numerous standard library enhancements.
- 2018: The long-anticipated version 1.0 is released, signifying the language's readiness for production use. This version focused on stability and performance improvements, setting a foundation for the future.
- 2021: Julia version 1.6, considered the culmination of years of refinement, is released, optimizing the compiler and enhancing the overall performance and usability of the language.

Core Principles and Design Decisions:

- Homoiconicity: Julia programs are represented as data structures of the language itself (abstract syntax trees), similar to Lisp. This property allows powerful metaprogramming capabilities, such as macros that transform and generate code.
- Type Declaration: While Julia allows for optional type declarations, its type inference mechanism is powerful enough to optimize the code efficiently during compilation. This makes the language flexible for the user without compromising on performance.
- Package Ecosystem: Julia's package system is designed to be easy to use and manage. Packages are stored in a central repository, making it straightforward to share and distribute code.
- Global Scope Design: The scope design in Julia carefully strikes a balance between simplicity for interactive use (like in REPL) and performance considerations for larger programs. This includes detailed handling of variable scopes and namespace management.

Applications and Use Cases: Julia excels in fields that require high-performance numerical and scientific computing. Due to its dynamic nature and high-performance capabilities, it is particularly popular in areas like data science, machine learning, visualization, and computational biology. Its ability to seamlessly call C and Fortran libraries, run in parallel, and interface with Python makes it an attractive choice for diverse computational tasks.

```
# A sample Julia code snippet showcasing the language's advantages in matrix
    operations

# Define two matrices
A = [1 2; 3 4]
B = [5 6; 7 8]

# Perform matrix multiplication
C = A * B

# Print the result
println(C)
```

```
[19 22]
[43 50]
```

These features ensure that Julia is not only a modern, high-performance language but also one that is designed with future extensibility and adaptability in mind. This allows it to continually evolve, embracing new paradigms and optimizations as the world's computational requirements grow and change.

1.2 Installing Julia and Setting Up the Environment

In this section, we will guide you through the process of installing Julia on various operating systems and setting up a suitable development environment. This includes downloading and installing the Julia binaries, configuring the PATH environment variable, and introducing tools such as Visual Studio Code (VS Code) and Jupyter Notebooks for an enhanced coding experience.

Step 1: Downloading and Installing Julia

Julia can be downloaded from the official Julia website: https://julialang.org/downloads/. Julia provides installers for several operating systems, including Windows, macOS, and Linux. Select the appropriate installer for your operating system and follow the instructions below.

- **Windows:** Download the Julia installer (.exe) file. Double-click the downloaded file and follow the on-screen instructions. By default, the installer will place Julia in C:\Users\<YourUsername>\AppData\Local\Julia-<Version>. You can change this location if desired.

- **macOS:** Download the Julia .dmg file. Open the .dmg file and drag the Julia icon to the Applications folder. This will install Julia on your macOS system.

- **Linux:** Download the Julia tarball (.tar.gz). Open a terminal and use the following commands to extract and install Julia.

```
tar -xvzf julia-<version>-linux-x86_64.tar.gz
sudo cp -r julia-<version> /opt/
sudo ln -s /opt/julia-<version>/bin/julia /usr/local/bin/julia
```

This will extract Julia to the /opt directory and create a symbolic link, allowing the Julia executable to be accessible system-wide.

Step 2: Configuring the PATH Environment Variable

After installing Julia, it is essential to configure the PATH environment variable to include the Julia binaries. This ensures that you can run Julia from the command line or terminal without specifying the full path to the executable.

- **Windows:** Open the Start menu and search for "Environment Variables." Select "Edit the system environment variables." In the System Properties window, click on the "Environment Variables" button. In the Environment Variables window, locate the "Path" variable under System variables, and click "Edit." Add the path to your Julia installation directory (e.g., C:\Users\<YourUsername>\AppData\Local\Julia-<Version>\bin) and click "OK" to save the changes.

- **macOS:** Open a terminal and edit your shell configuration file (/.bashrc, /.zshrc, etc.) to include the Julia binaries in your PATH.

```
export PATH="/Applications/Julia-<Version>.app/Contents/Resources/julia/bin:
    $PATH"
```

Save the file and run source /.bashrc (or the corresponding command for your shell configuration file) to reload the PATH.

- **Linux:** Open a terminal and edit your shell configuration file (/.bashrc, /.profile, etc.) to include the Julia binaries in your PATH.

```
export PATH=”/opt/julia-<version>/bin:$PATH”
```

Save the file and run source /.bashrc to reload the PATH.

Step 3: Verifying the Installation

To verify that Julia is correctly installed and the PATH is configured, open a terminal or command prompt and type:

```
julia --version
```

You should see output similar to the following:

```
julia version 1.x.x
```

Step 4: Setting Up a Development Environment

To make the coding experience more efficient, it is advisable to use an Integrated Development Environment (IDE) or advanced code editors like Visual Studio Code (VS Code) or Jupyter Notebooks.

- **Visual Studio Code (VS Code):** VS Code is a popular code editor that supports Julia through the Julia extension. To install VS Code, download it from the official website: https://code.visualstudio.com/. After installing VS Code, open it and navigate to the Extensions view by clicking the Extensions icon in the Activity Bar on the side of the window. Search for the ”Julia” extension and click ”Install.”

- **Jupyter Notebooks:** Jupyter Notebooks provide an interactive environment for writing and running code in Julia. To use Jupyter Notebooks with Julia, you need to install the IJulia package. Open the Julia REPL and enter the following commands:

```
using Pkg
Pkg.add(”IJulia”)
```

Once the IJulia package is installed, you can launch the Jupyter Notebook interface that includes support for Julia by executing:

```
using IJulia
notebook()
```

This will open a new tab in your web browser with the Jupyter Notebook interface, where you can create and interact with Julia notebooks.

Having followed these steps, you now have Julia installed and your environment set up with tools to facilitate Julia programming. This environment will enhance your coding productivity and provide interactive capabilities suitable for both development and educational contexts.

1.3 First Steps: Running Your First Julia Program

This section covers the initial steps to write, execute, and understand your first Julia program. Here, we will write a simple "Hello, World!" program, which is a traditional starting point in learning any new programming language.

Firstly, ensure that you have Julia installed on your system. If not, refer to the previous section on setting up the Julia environment for detailed instructions.

Creating Your First Julia Script

To begin with, create a new file with a .jl extension. This extension is used for Julia scripts. Open your preferred text editor or Integrated Development Environment (IDE) and create a file named first_program.jl.

Next, enter the following line of code into your file:

```
println("Hello, World!")
```

This is a simple command that prints the string "Hello, World!" to the console. The println function in Julia outputs text followed by a newline.

Running Your Julia Program

To execute your script, open your terminal or command prompt. Navigate to the directory containing your first_program.jl file using the cd (change directory) command. For example:

```
cd path/to/your/directory
```

Once you are in the correct directory, run the script by typing:

```
julia first_program.jl
```

You should see the following output:

```
Hello, World!
```

This confirms that your Julia installation is functioning correctly, and you have successfully executed your first Julia script.

Understanding the Code

In Julia, functions are defined and called in a straightforward manner. The println function writes a line of text to the standard output. The argument passed to println, in this case, "Hello, World!", is the string to be printed.

A string in Julia is a sequence of characters enclosed in double quotes. Julia supports various types of data and provides different functions to manipulate them. Here, a string is directly passed to the println function, illustrating a fundamental aspect of Julia's ability to manage text data efficiently.

Interactive Execution Using Julia REPL

In addition to running scripts, Julia provides an interactive REPL (Read-Eval-Print Loop) environment. This allows you to execute Julia commands in an interactive manner and is useful for quick testing and debugging.

To start the Julia REPL, open your terminal and type julia:

```
julia
```

This will start the Julia REPL, indicated by the prompt:

```
julia>
```

At the REPL prompt, you can type Julia commands. To print "Hello, World!" interactively, type:

```
julia> println("Hello, World!")
Hello, World!
```

The REPL instantly evaluates and executes the command, displaying the output directly. Exit the REPL by typing exit() or pressing Ctrl-D.

Writing More Complex Programs

Once you are comfortable with basic commands, try expanding your program with additional functionality. Below is an example demonstrating variable assignment and arithmetic operations:

```
# Assign values to variables
a = 10
b = 20

# Perform addition
sum = a + b

# Print the result
```

```
println("The sum of ", a, " and ", b, " is ", sum)
```

Save this code in a file named sum_program.jl and run it using the same steps described above. The output will be:

```
The sum of 10 and 20 is 30
```

This example introduces several key concepts:

- Assignment: The = operator assigns values to variables a and b.
- Arithmetic operations: The + operator performs addition.
- String concatenation: The println function can concatenate strings and variables to form the output.

Through these exercises, you will gain a solid foundation in writing and executing Julia programs.

1.4 Julia REPL and Jupyter Notebooks

Julia, like many modern programming languages, provides a highly interactive interface for developing and testing code through its REPL (Read-Eval-Print Loop), and additionally supports Jupyter Notebooks for an enhanced interactive computing environment.

REPL stands for *Read-Eval-Print Loop*, which is a simple, interactive computer programming environment. REPL allows you to enter expressions, evaluate them, and display the results. It is an invaluable tool for exploring the language, debugging, and running experimental code snippets.

To start the Julia REPL, open a terminal (or Command Prompt on Windows) and type julia, then press Enter. You will be greeted with the Julia REPL prompt, which looks like this:

```
               _
   _       _ _(_)_     |  Documentation: https://docs.julialang.org
  (_)     | (_) (_)    |
   _ _   _| |_  __ _   |  Type "?" for help, "]?" for Pkg help.
  | | | | | | |/ _` |  |
  | | |_| | | | (_| |  |  Version 1.8.0 (2021-07-07)
 _/ |\__'_|_|_|\__'_|  |  Official https://julialang.org/ release
|__/
```

At the prompt, you can enter any valid Julia expression, and it will be evaluated on the spot. For example:

```
julia> 2 + 3
5

julia> println("Hello, Julia!")
Hello, Julia!
```

The REPL supports various mode commands which are prefixed by special characters:

- ?: Entering the ? symbol followed by a function or variable name provides documentation about it.
- ;: The semicolon command switches to the shell mode where you can run shell commands.
-]; Typing the closing square bracket enters the Pkg mode, where you can manage Julia packages.

For instance, using the help mode:

```
julia> ?
help?> println
search: println printstyled print print_with_color sprint @printf printshort

  println(xs...)

  Print (using print) xs followed by a newline.
```

To use the shell mode:

```
shell> ls
```

And to manage packages in Pkg mode:

```
pkg> add DataFrames
```

Another significant tool for Julia development and data science is Jupyter Notebooks, which allow for an interactive computing environment where code, equations, and visualizations can be combined in a single document. To use Jupyter Notebooks with Julia, follow these steps:

1. Install Jupyter via Anaconda or directly using pip. 2. Add the IJulia package in Julia by using the Pkg mode:

```
pkg> add IJulia
```

3. Open a Jupyter Notebook by running the following in the Julia REPL:

```
using IJulia
```

```
notebook()
```

This command will start a Jupyter server and open the Jupyter Notebook interface in your browser.

Inside a Jupyter Notebook, you can create and run Julia code cells. For example, a simple cell execution would look like:

```
# Cell content
x = 10
y = 20
x + y
```

Upon running the cell, Jupyter will evaluate the code and display the output directly beneath the cell:

```
30
```

Jupyter Notebooks are quite advantageous for data science and academic work due to their ability to contain rich text, code, and visual output in one place. Visualization libraries like Plots.jl integrate seamlessly, making it easy to produce graphical representations of data.

For instance, to plot a simple sine wave:

```
using Plots

x = 0:0.1:10
y = sin.(x)
plot(x, y, title="Sine Wave", xlabel="x", ylabel="sin(x)")
```

Executing this code inside a notebook cell generates an interactive plot within the notebook:

```
<Plot object with Sine Wave visualization>
```

Mastering the Julia REPL and Jupyter Notebooks are crucial for developing, debugging, and presenting Julia programs effectively. These tools offer a robust environment for exploration and rapid prototyping, enhancing the overall productivity and experience of working with Julia.

1.5 Basic Julia Syntax and Conventions

Julia's syntax is designed to be intuitive and concise, resembling that of other high-level programming languages while retaining performance characteristics closer to lower-level languages. Grasping the basic syntax and conventions is crucial for efficient programming and collaboration within the Julia community. This section details variables, data types, functions, control flow, and other fundamental aspects of Julia syntax.

Variables and Data Types

In Julia, variables are created via assignment using the = operator. There is no need to declare a variable's type explicitly, as Julia infers it automatically. For example:

```
x = 42 # Integer
y = 3.14 # Floating-point number
name = "Julia" # String
```

To check a variable's type, use the typeof() function.

```
typeof(x) # Output: Int64
typeof(y) # Output: Float64
typeof(name) # Output: String
```

Julia supports several built-in types, including integers, floats, booleans, characters, and complex numbers.

Functions

Defining functions in Julia is straightforward. Use the function keyword followed by the function name, arguments in parentheses, the function body, and the end keyword to close the function. For example:

```
function add(a, b)
    return a + b
end
```

Alternatively, for concise functions, the begin and end keywords can be omitted, using a one-line definition:

```
add(a, b) = a + b
```

Functions can also have optional arguments with default values:

```
function greet(name, greeting="Hello")
    println("$greeting, $name!")
end
```

Control Flow

Julia provides a set of control flow constructs for conditionals and loops, similar to other programming languages.

If-Else Statements

```
x = 10
```

```
if x > 0
    println("x is positive")
elseif x < 0
    println("x is negative")
else
    println("x is zero")
end
```

For Loops

```
for i in 1:5
    println(i)
end
```

While Loops

```
i = 1
while i <= 5
    println(i)
    i += 1
end
```

Array and Dictionary Operations

Arrays are a fundamental data structure in Julia, supporting various operations.

```
arr = [1, 2, 3, 4, 5]

# Accessing elements
first_element = arr[1] # Note: Julia uses 1-based indexing
last_element = arr[end] # The end keyword refers to the last index

# Modifying elements
arr[3] = 10

# Array concatenation
new_arr = [arr; 6, 7, 8]
```

Dictionaries in Julia map keys to values.

```
dict = Dict("apple" => 3, "banana" => 5)

# Accessing values
num_apples = dict["apple"]

# Adding new key-value pairs
dict["orange"] = 7

# Iterating over dictionary keys and values
for (key, value) in dict
    println("$key: $value")
end
```

Comprehensions

Julia supports comprehensions for generating arrays in a succinct manner. For example, to create an array of squares from 1 to 10:

```
squares = [i^2 for i in 1:10]
```

Comprehensions can also include conditions:

```
evens = [i for i in 1:10 if i % 2 == 0]
```

Comments

In Julia, single-line comments begin with #.

```
# This is a single-line comment
```

For multi-line comments, use #= to start and =# to end.

```
#=
This is a
multi-line comment
=#
```

This shared understanding of Julia's basic syntax allows for writing clear and efficient code, while adhering to these conventions facilitates better code maintenance and collaboration.

1.6 Understanding Julia's Type System

Julia's type system is central to its performance and expressiveness. Julia employs a rich and dynamic type system that supports both static and dynamic typing. Understanding the type system allows for writing efficient code while maintaining readability and flexibility.

At the foundational level, everything in Julia is an object. Julia's type system is hierarchical, starting from the abstract type Any at the top, which encompasses all other types.

```
julia> supertype(Int)
Signed

julia> supertype(Signed)
Integer

julia> supertype(Integer)
Real

julia> supertype(Real)
Number

julia> supertype(Number)
Any
```

The supertype function reveals the hierarchy for any given type. Int is an instance of Signed, which is a subtype of Integer, and so forth, until Any.

Julia's types can be broadly classified into abstract types and concrete types. Abstract types, like Number, Integer, and Real, serve as nodes in the type hierarchy and cannot be instantiated. Concrete types are the actual types that can hold values, such as Int64, Float64, and ComplexFloat64.

```
abstract type AbstractNumber end

abstract type Number <: AbstractNumber end
abstract type Real <: Number end
abstract type Integer <: Real end
abstract type Signed <: Integer end
abstract type Unsigned <: Integer end

struct Int8 <: Signed
    value::Core.Int8
end
struct Uint8 <: Unsigned
    value::Core.UInt8
end
```

The <: operator signifies that a type is a subtype of another type. Here, Signed and Unsigned are subtypes of Integer, which in turn is a subtype of Real.

Concrete types can be parametric. This means that a type can be defined in terms of a parameter, allowing for more flexible and reusable code. For instance, arrays in Julia are parametric types. An Array can be an array of any type, and this type is specified with a parameter.

```
julia> typeof([1, 2, 3])
Vector{Int64} (alias for Array{Int64, 1})

julia> typeof([1.0, 2.0, 3.0])
Vector{Float64} (alias for Array{Float64, 1})

julia> typeof([1 2; 3 4])
Matrix{Int64} (alias for Array{Int64, 2})
```

In each case, the type of array is specified by its element type (e.g., Int64 or Float64) and its dimensionality (e.g., 1D for vectors, 2D for matrices).

Julia also supports user-defined types, using the struct keyword. Structures by default are immutable, meaning that once an instance is created, its fields cannot be changed. Immutable types have performance benefits because they can be more easily optimized by the compiler.

```
struct Point
    x::Float64
    y::Float64
end

p = Point(1.0, 2.0)
p.x # Output: 1.0
p.y # Output: 2.0
```

If mutability is required, the mutable struct keyword allows for defining types whose fields can be modified after creation.

```
mutable struct PointMutable
    x::Float64
    y::Float64
end

p = PointMutable(1.0, 2.0)
p.x = 3.0
p.y = 4.0
@show p # Output: PointMutable(3.0, 4.0)
```

Julia's type system also includes union types, which enable variable values to be instances of more than one type. The Union keyword allows for this flexibility.

```
julia> typeof(Union{Int64, Float64})
Union{Int64, Float64}

julia> foo(x::Union{Int64, Float64}) = x + 1
foo (generic function with 1 method)

julia> foo(10)
11

julia> foo(10.5)
11.5
```

Union types can lead to more generic code that maintains type safety.

Finally, Julia uses type declarations to specialize functions for performance improvements. Function dispatch in Julia is type-driven, enabling multiple dispatch that selects the specific method depending on the types of the input arguments.

```
function add(x::Int, y::Int)::Int
    return x + y
end

function add(x::Float64, y::Float64)::Float64
    return x + y
end
```

Here, two methods of the function add are defined, one for Int inputs and another for Float64 inputs. Julia's compiler selects the appropriate method based on the input types, leading to optimized performance without needing explicit type checking in the function body.

Julia's type system, characterized by its hierarchies, parametric types, user-defined types, union types, and type-driven dispatch, provides both flexibility and optimization possibilities, empowering developers to write efficient and expressive code.

1.7 Getting Help and Using Documentation

In Julia, accessing help and using documentation is pivotal to mastering the language and navigating its extensive libraries. Julia provides a robust set of tools and resources for obtaining help on built-in functions, user-defined functions, and external packages. This section will elucidate various methods to seek assistance and leverage documentation effectively.

One of the primary ways to get quick help within the Julia environment is through the built-in help mode in the Julia REPL. By prefixing a query with a question mark, users can access the documentation for any function or macro.

```
?println
```

Executing the above command in the REPL will display the documentation for the println function, including its usage and examples.

Additionally, the help function can also be invoked programmatically to obtain similar information.

```
help("println")
```

For more detailed introspection, one may find the @which macro very useful. This macro returns the exact location where a method is defined.

```
@which println("Hello, World!")
```

The output will indicate the file and line number of the println method definition.

An illustrative technique for exploring the types and methods within Julia is the methods function. This function provides a list of all methods associated with a particular function.

```
methods(println)
```

The results will enumerate every method signature for println, helpful for understanding how the function behaves with different argument types.

For user-defined functions, it is possible to create custom documentation strings. These docstrings are written as multi-line comments immediately preceding the function definition using triple double quotes """.

```
"""
    greet(name::String)

Greet the person with the given name.
"""
function greet(name::String)
    println("Hello, $name!")
end
```

Requesting help for this function with ?greet or help("greet") will display the custom docstring provided.

Julia also integrates well with Jupyter Notebooks, offering interactive documentation capabilities. In a Jupyter Notebook cell, prefixing any function with a question mark or executing a cell with help() will present the same documentation available in the REPL.

Julia Packages often come with extensive documentation hosted online, usually accessible through a central documentation repository such as readthedocs. To find documentation for a package, one can typically visit the package's GitHub repository, which has links to its detailed documentation. For installed packages, the same REPL commands can be used to get immediate help:

```
?Pkg.add
```

Additionally, the Julia ecosystem includes comprehensive official documentation available at https://docs.julialang.org/. This resource covers a range of topics from language basics to advanced metaprogramming techniques.

Learning to utilize the Integrated Development Environment (IDE) features can further enhance productivity. IDEs such as Visual Studio Code with the Julia extension provide inline documentation access and auto-suggestions, enabling an efficient development experience.

Lastly, the Julia community is an invaluable resource. Forums like Julia Discourse (https://discourse.julialang.org/) and chat platforms such as Julia's Slack and Zulip channels offer spaces to ask questions and exchange knowledge with other Julia users and developers.

Utilizing these myriad avenues for help and documentation ensures that users can swiftly resolve issues and continue their progression toward expert-level proficiency.

1.8 Introduction to Julia's Ecosystem

The Julia programming language is not just defined by its syntax and performance capabilities but also by its rich ecosystem, which encompasses libraries, tools, and community resources. Understanding Julia's ecosystem is crucial for leveraging the language effectively for scientific computing, data analysis, machine learning, and other domains.

The ecosystem can be broadly categorized into packages, development tools, and community resources. Packages form the core of Julia's functionality, providing reusable code for various tasks. Development tools enhance the coding experience, offering facilities for debugging, profiling, and package management. Lastly, the community resources offer support, tutorials, and forums for knowledge sharing and problem-solving.

Packages Julia's package ecosystem is one of its standout features, enabling users to extend the language's capabilities without sacrificing performance. The primary hub for Julia packages is the Julia package registry, accessible via the built-in package manager known as Pkg. Packages are managed using Pkg, and virtually every scientific or general-purpose requirement can be met through these community-maintained packages.

To use a package in Julia, one must first install it using the \add command within the Pkg mode of Julia's REPL, or by using the Pkg API directly in a script or program.

```
using Pkg
Pkg.add("Plots")
```

After installing a package, it can be loaded into the current namespace using the using or import statements.

```
using Plots
```

Development Tools Development tools are essential for ensuring efficient and effective coding practices. Julia offers several tools catered to various aspects of development.

Integrated Development Environments (IDEs): Julia is supported by multiple IDEs, including Visual Studio Code (VSCode) with the Julia extension, Juno integrated with Atom, and more traditional text editors with Julia support. VSCode is highly recommended due to its robust support for debugging, linting, and inline plotting.

- VSCode: With the Julia extension, it supports features like variable exploration, integrated plotting, and more.
- Juno: Integrated within the Atom editor, it offers tools like execution overlays, inline results, and a Julia-specific server.

Profiling and Debugging: Julia's profiling tools help optimize performance by identifying bottlenecks in code using the @profile macro. For debugging, the VSCode extension offers an integrated debugger, while the Debugger.jl package provides an interactive command-line interface for stepping through code.

```
using Profile

@profile begin
    # Code block to profile
end
```

Package Management: Julia's package manager, Pkg, handles installing, updating, resolving dependencies, and even environments. It uses a project file (Project.toml) to manage dependencies and a manifest file (Manifest.toml) to record exact versions installed.

```
using Pkg
Pkg.status() # To check status of packages in current environment
Pkg.update() # To update all packages to their latest compatible versions
```

Community Resources Julia has a vibrant and active community that contributes to its growth through forums, user groups, conferences, and online courses. These community resources are crucial for continuous learning and support.

The JuliaLang Discourse: The official discourse forum (https://discourse.julialang.org/) is the primary platform for asking questions, sharing news, and discussing development. It is an invaluable resource for troubleshooting and learning best practices.

GitHub Repositories: Julia's source code, along with many packages, is hosted on GitHub. Contributing to or reporting issues on these repositories helps in the collaborative development of Julia.

Conferences and Workshops: Events like JuliaCon (the annual Julia Conference) offer opportunities to learn from and interact with experts. Workshops and meetups provide hands-on learning experiences.

Online Courses and Tutorials: Several online platforms offer courses on Julia, ranging from beginner to advanced levels. The official Julia documentation itself is comprehensive, covering detailed descriptions and examples of language features.

Julia's ecosystem, with its extensive packages, robust development tools, and supportive community resources, fosters an environment where scientific computing and data analysis tasks can be conducted efficiently and effectively, paving the way for innovative solutions across various fields.

1.9 Comparison with Other Programming Languages

To appreciate Julia's strengths and understand its potential applications, it is essential to compare it with other prevalent programming languages. This section delineates the characteristics that distinguish Julia, examining its performance, syntax ease, metaprogramming capabilities, and facilitating comparisons with Python, MATLAB, C/C++, and R.

Performance: One of Julia's hallmark features is its high performance, often comparable to that of statically compiled languages such as C and Fortran. This performance is attributed to several factors:

- Just-In-Time (JIT) Compilation: Julia utilizes the LLVM compiler framework for JIT compilation, allowing dynamic generation of optimized machine code.
- Type Declarations: While Julia supports dynamic typing, developers can optionally specify types, enabling the compiler to optimize code execution.
- Multiple Dispatch: Julia's multiple dispatch allows function behavior based on the combination of argument types, oftentimes

leading to more efficient and specialized code.

```
function add(x::Int, y::Int)::Int
    return x + y
end
```

Syntax Ease: Julia's syntax is intentionally simple and similar to other high-level languages, making it accessible for new learners and those transitioning from other languages. For example:

- Python: Like Python, Julia avoids boilerplate code, emphasizing readability and reducing the cognitive load on programmers.
- MATLAB: Julia borrows much of its array syntax from MATLAB, making it familiar to scientists and engineers.

```
# Python example
a = [1, 2, 3, 4]

# Julia equivalent
a = [1, 2, 3, 4]
```

Metaprogramming Capabilities: Julia excels in metaprogramming, a feature that allows the language to modify its own code at runtime. This is facilitated via macros, which are distinctive to Julia compared to many other languages. Macros in Julia are defined using the @ symbol followed by the macro name.

```
macro sayhello()
    return :( println("Hello, World!") )
end

@sayhello()
```

Comparison with Specific Languages:

Python: Despite their syntactic similarities, Julia and Python diverge significantly regarding performance.

- Python's interpreted nature often leads to slower execution times requiring optimizations through libraries like NumPy or Cython.
- Julia's JIT compilation ensures performance closer to statically compiled languages.

However, Python boasts an extensive ecosystem and a massive community, which provides a vast array of libraries and frameworks. Julia has been gaining traction; its ecosystem, although smaller, is rapidly growing, particularly in scientific and numerical computing.

MATLAB: Julia's direct competitor in the domain of numerical computing is MATLAB. Both languages offer similar functionalities, but:

- Julia is open-source, while MATLAB is a proprietary software.
- Julia's performance is generally superior due to its compilation mechanism.

```
MATLAB:
a = [1, 2, 3, 4];
b = sum(a);

Julia:
a = [1, 2, 3, 4]
b = sum(a)
```

C/C++: C and C++ are often the go-to languages for performance-critical applications. However, the trade-off includes longer development times and more verbose code.

- Julia approaches the performance of C/C++ while offering higher-level abstractions, reducing development time.
- Multithreading and parallel computing in Julia are more straightforward compared to the complexity in C/C++.

R: R is another prominent language, particularly in statistics and data analysis. While R provides an extensive range of packages and is deeply entrenched in the data science community:

- Julia often outperforms R in terms of execution speed.
- Julia's syntax for statistical computations is similar but more efficient due to its type system and compilation model.

```
R:
x <- c(1, 2, 3, 4)
mean(x)

Julia:
x = [1, 2, 3, 4]
mean(x)
```

Julia's rapid rise is a testament to its blend of performance, simplicity, and advanced programming features. By strategically combining the strengths of various languages while mitigating their drawbacks, Julia presents a versatile and powerful tool for developers across different domains.

1.10 Community and Resources

Julia has a vibrant and supportive community that plays a crucial role in the evolution of the language and its ecosystem. Engaging with this community can provide invaluable insights, support, and opportunities for collaboration. It is essential to know where to find resources and how to effectively participate in the community to make the most of what Julia has to offer.

- **Official Julia Documentation and Guides**:

  The primary resource for Julia is its official documentation, which is extensive and well-maintained. The documentation is available at https://docs.julialang.org/. It covers everything from installation guides, and core language features, to in-depth explanations of standard libraries and tools. There is also a section dedicated to performance tips, which is particularly useful given Julia's focus on high performance.

- **Julia Discourse Forum**:

  The Julia Discourse Forum (https://discourse.julialang.org/) is a popular platform where users can ask questions, share projects, and discuss various topics related to Julia. it is an excellent place to seek help from both beginners and experts. The forum is organized into various categories such as "Usage", "Development", and "Announcements", making it easy to navigate and find relevant discussions.

- **GitHub Repositories**:

  Much of Julia's development happens on GitHub (https://github.com/JuliaLang/julia), and it is open to contributions from the community. Users can browse through the issues, contribute to discussions, and even submit pull requests. Additionally, many Julia packages are hosted on GitHub, making it a central hub for finding and contributing to Julia projects.

- **Julia Slack Channel**:

  The Julia Slack workspace is another real-time communication tool where users can interact with the community. It covers numerous channels dedicated to various topics, such as "newbies", "random", "internals", and "data". By joining this workspace (https://julialang.org/slack/), users can get quick support and stay updated on the latest developments within the Julia community.

- **JuliaLang on Reddit**:

  There is an active Julia subreddit (https://www.reddit.com/r/Julia/), where users can find discussions, questions, and announcements related to Julia. The subreddit is community-moderated and often features interesting projects, tutorials, and news articles about Julia.

- **Julia YouTube Channel**:

  The official Julia YouTube channel (https://www.youtube.com/user/JuliaLanguage) hosts a wide range of content, including conference talks, tutorials, and webinars. This is an excellent visual learning resource for users who prefer video content. The channel includes playlists on introductory topics, as well as advanced features and applications of Julia.

- **Community Meetups and Conferences**:

  JuliaCon is the annual conference for the Julia community, featuring talks, workshops, and discussions on various aspects of the language and its ecosystem. In addition to JuliaCon, there are local Julia meetups and regional events around the world. Information on these can usually be found on the JuliaLang website and through community announcements.

- **Educational Resources and Online Courses**:

  Many educational resources are available for learning Julia, ranging from online courses to comprehensive textbooks. Platforms such as Coursera, edX, and Udemy offer courses on Julia, some of which are created by experts and academics in the field. Additionally, there are several free resources, including lecture notes and tutorials, that are accessible through the Julia community forums and GitHub repositories.

- **Blogs and Newsletters**:

  Numerous blogs and newsletters provide updates, tutorials, and insights related to Julia. Notable examples include the JuliaLang blog (https://julialang.org/blog/), which features official announcements and deep dives into new features, and JuliaObserver (https://juliaobserver.com/), a community-driven site that aggregates packages, statistics, and blog posts.

- **Social Media Presence**:

  The Julia community is active on various social media platforms, including Twitter (@JuliaLanguage), where they share updates, engage in discussions, and promote events. Following these accounts can help users stay informed about the latest developments in the Julia ecosystem.

Engaging with the Julia community through these resources can significantly enhance the learning experience. It allows users to receive feedback, find collaborators, discover new tools and packages, and keep up to date with the latest advancements in the language.

Chapter 2

Basic Syntax and Built-in Types

This chapter delves into the core syntax and built-in types of Julia, starting with variable assignments and basic data types such as integers, floats, booleans, and strings. It explores numeric operations, string manipulation, and formatting. The chapter progresses through tuples, named tuples, arrays, ranges, iterators, dictionaries, and symbols, and concludes with type inference and conversion, providing a robust foundation for understanding Julia's type system and data handling capabilities.

2.1 Variables and Assignment

Understanding how to declare variables and assign values is fundamental in grasping Julia's syntax and semantics. Variables in Julia are created by assigning values using the $=$ operator. The variables can store different types of data, such as integers, floating-point numbers, strings, arrays, functions, and even more complex structures.

$\mathrm{variable\_name}$ holds a reference to the data stored in memory. Here is a simple example of assigning values to variables:

```
a = 10 # Assigns an integer value to variable 'a'
b = 20.5 # Assigns a floating-point value to variable 'b'
c = "Hello, Julia" # Assigns a string to variable 'c'
```

Multiple variables can be assigned values simultaneously by separating each pair with a comma. This feature is particularly useful for swapping values or initializing multiple variables at once without intermediate steps.

```
x, y, z = 1, 2.5, "abc" # Assigns 1 to `x`, 2.5 to `y`, and "abc" to `z`
x, y = y, x # Swaps the values of `x` and `y`
```

Julia uses dynamic typing, allowing the type of a variable to change during execution. However, variable names must start with a letter and can be followed by letters, digits, or underscores. Julia is case-sensitive, so var and VAR would be treated as distinct variables.

```
mynum = 100 # valid variable name
MyNum = 150 # different from `mynum`
```

Variables in Julia can also be assigned with the results of expressions or function calls:

```
result = 2 + 3 * 4 # result will be 14
length = length("Julia") # length function returns the length of the string "Julia",
    which is 5
```

Julia supports Unicode characters in variable names, which allows the use of characters beyond the standard ASCII set. This can make mathematical formulas and other domain-specific uses more readable:

```
 = 1.5
 = + 2
```

Scopes in Julia define where a variable is accessible. Variables defined at the top level (global scope) are accessible throughout the program, while variables defined within a function or a block (local scope) are only accessible within that scope. When working with functions, variables passed as arguments, as well as those defined within the function, are locally scoped.

```
global_var = "I am global"

function scope_demo()
    local_var = "I am local"
    println(global_var) # Accesses global variable
    println(local_var) # Accesses local variable
end

scope_demo()

# This will result in an error as `local_var` is not accessible outside the function
#println(local_var)
```

It is essential to understand the distinction between mutable and immutable types in Julia when working with variables. Immutable types, such as numbers and tuples, cannot be changed once created. Mutability of types affects how variables point to data in memory:

```
# Immutable example
a = 5
a = a + 1 # 'a' now refers to a new integer object with value 6

# Mutable example
arr = [1, 2, 3]
push!(arr, 4) # 'arr' is modified, now arr = [1, 2, 3, 4]
```

Mutability allows in-place modifications of data structures, which can offer performance benefits by reducing the need to create new objects in memory for changes.

Julia also supports constants, which are variables that should not be changed after initialization. Constants are declared using the const keyword. Any attempt to modify a constant after its initial assignment will result in an error, aiding in ensuring program correctness:

```
const pi = 3.14159
# Trying to reassign 'pi' will result in an error
# pi = 3.14 # Uncommenting this line will cause an error
```

Variables' naming conventions and the disciplined use of constants and mutability considerations facilitate robust and maintainable code, providing a foundation needed for more advanced Julia programming concepts. This understanding is essential when transitioning to the next topics in the chapter.

2.2 Basic Data Types: Integers, Floats, Booleans, and Strings

In Julia, understanding basic data types is crucial for effective programming, as these types form the building blocks for more complex structures and operations. This section explores the fundamental data types available in Julia, including integers, floats, booleans, and strings.

Integers

Julia supports a variety of integer types, which are classified based on their size and whether they are signed or unsigned. The most common types include Int8, Int16, Int32, Int64, as well as their unsigned counterparts UInt8, UInt16, UInt32, and UInt64. These types are used to store whole numbers. Julia's default integer type is platform-dependent: on 64-bit systems, it is typically Int64. Here's an example of how to use different integer types:

```
x::Int8 = 127
y::UInt8 = 255
```

Assigning a value larger than the type's maximal value will cause an overflow. For example, Int8 has a range of -128 to 127, as illustrated in the following code:

```
z::Int8 = 128 # This will cause an overflow error
```

x and y indicate explicitly declared integer variables using type annotations, which can help with type checking and performance optimization.

Floats

Floating-point numbers represent real numbers and are particularly useful for scientific computations requiring a high degree of precision. Julia's primary floating-point types are Float16, Float32, and Float64, with the default being Float64. The double-precision floating-point type (Float64) provides about 15 to 17 decimal digits of accuracy, as shown below:

```
a::Float64 = 3.141592653589793
b::Float32 = 3.1415927
```

Here, a is assigned a double-precision value, whereas b is assigned a single-precision value, illustrating the difference in precision.

Booleans

Booleans are the simplest type, representing truth values. Julia's boolean type is denoted by Bool, which can hold true or false values. Boolean values are fundamental for control flow, logical operations, and comparisons. Example:

```
is_valid::Bool = true
is_greater = 5 > 3 # This evaluates to true
```

is_valid explicitly declares a boolean variable, while is_greater demonstrates a boolean resulting from a comparison.

Strings

Strings in Julia are sequences of characters and are denoted by the String type. Strings can be created using double quotes, and they support interpolation and multi-line formatting. Here's a sample demonstrating basic string operations:

```
greeting = "Hello, world!"
name = "Alice"
message = "Welcome, $name!" # String interpolation
multi_line_string = """This is a
multi-line string example."""
```

In the above code:

- greeting is a simple string.
- message uses string interpolation to insert the value of name into the string.
- multi_line_string spans multiple lines, allowing for more readable and formatted text blocks.

Operations on strings include concatenation, length measurement, and substrings:

```
full_message = greeting * " " * message # Concatenation using the * operator
length_of_greeting = length(greeting) # Getting the length of the string
substring = greeting[1:5] # Extracting a substring
```

This segment depicts the assembly of strings using concatenation, measurement using the length function, and extraction of a substring via indexing.

These basic data types are pivotal as they constitute the fundamental units upon which more complex data structures and algorithms are built. Understanding how to effectively utilize integers, floats, booleans, and strings will significantly enhance your ability to develop efficient and robust Julia programs.

2.3 Working with Numeric Types

Julia provides robust support for numeric types, which include integers, floating-point numbers, rational numbers, and complex numbers. This section will elucidate the operations and properties of these numeric types, enabling efficient computation and mathematical manipulation.

Integers in Julia can be represented by two primary types: Int and UInt. The Int type represents signed integers, whereas the UInt type denotes unsigned integers.

```
a = 10 # Signed integer
b = UInt(10) # Unsigned integer
```

Floating-point numbers are represented using the Float32 and Float64 types. They provide a way to denote non-integer numbers, typically used in scientific computing.

```
x = 3.14 # Float64 by default
y = Float32(3.14) # Explicitly specifying Float32
```

Julia's support for rational numbers is facilitated through the Rational type. Rational numbers are represented as the division of two integers, enabling exact arithmetic without floating-point precision issues.

```
r = 3//4 # Represents the rational number 3/4
```

Complex numbers, essential for many fields such as engineering and physics, are represented using the Complex type. You can define a complex number with a real and an imaginary component.

```
c = 1 + 2im # Represents the complex number 1 + 2i
```

Julia provides a plethora of arithmetic operations for numeric types, such as addition, subtraction, multiplication, division, exponentiation, and modulus.

```
sum_int = a + 5 # Addition
diff_float = x - 1.14 # Subtraction
prod_rational = r * (2//3) # Multiplication
quotient_complex = c / (1 + 1im) # Division
power_int = a ^ 2 # Exponentiation
modulo_int = a % 3 # Modulus
```

Numeric functions are essential for mathematical operations and transformations. Julia offers a rich library of such functions, including abs, sqrt, exp, log, sin, cos, among others. These functions facilitate computations and enhance numerical accuracy.

```
absolute_value = abs(-5) # Absolute value
square_root = sqrt(16) # Square root
exponential = exp(2) # Exponential function
logarithm = log(10) # Natural logarithm
sine_value = sin(pi/2) # Sine of /2
cosine_value = cos(0) # Cosine of 0
```

Handling numeric precision and types is crucial in computational tasks. Julia allows conversions between numeric types using type conversion functions.

```
float_conversion = Float64(a) # Converting integer to float
```

```
int_conversion = Int(x) # Converting float to integer (truncation)
rational_conversion = Rational(x) # Converting float to rational
```

Julia's promote function can be utilized to convert multiple numbers to a common numeric type, facilitating operations between mixed types.

```
a_float, x_promoted = promote(a, x) # Promotes 'a' and 'x' to Float64
```

When dealing with large numbers or high precision requirements, Julia offers the BigInt and BigFloat types. These types support arbitrary precision arithmetic, ensuring that large computations are handled accurately.

```
big_int = BigInt("12345678901234567890")
big_float = BigFloat("2.718281828459045")
```

BigInt and BigFloat can be crucial for algorithms requiring very high precision or when dealing with very large integers beyond the range of typical 64-bit integers.

Julia also integrates seamlessly with other numerical libraries and packages such as LinearAlgebra, SpecialFunctions, and ArbNumerics for advanced numerical operations.

In addition to these functionalities, Julia supports numeric literals with scientific notation, enhancing readability and precision specification.

```
scientific_notation = 1.23e4 # Represents 1.23 * 10^4
```

It is imperative to note that numeric operations in Julia are subject to the principles of IEEE 754 floating-point arithmetic. This standard governs floating-point computation rounding errors, overflow, underflow, and special values like NaN (Not a Number) and Infinity.

```
result = 1.0 / 0.0 # Infinity
undefined = 0.0 / 0.0 # NaN
```

Understanding and appropriately handling these special cases ensures accurate and reliable numerical computing in Julia. By leveraging Julia's comprehensive numerical capabilities, one can perform efficient and precise mathematical computations indispensable for various scientific and engineering applications.

2.4 String Manipulation and Formatting

Strings in Julia are sequences of characters, and they are represented by the String type. String manipulation is a fundamental aspect of programming, as it allows one to handle and process textual data efficiently. This section covers various string operations, including concatenation, interpolation, indexing, slicing, and formatting, enabling a clear comprehension of how to manage text data in Julia.

To define a string in Julia, one encloses the text within double quotes:

```
greeting = "Hello, World!"
```

String objects are immutable; once created, their content cannot be changed. However, one can create new strings based on existing ones through various operations.

Concatenation: Joining two or more strings together is a common operation known as concatenation. In Julia, the * operator is used for this purpose:

```
first_name = "Jane"
last_name = "Doe"
full_name = first_name * " " * last_name
println(full_name) # Output: Jane Doe
```

Interpolation: Julia supports string interpolation, which embeds variables or expressions inside a string using the $ symbol:

```
name = "John"
age = 30
info = "Name: $name, Age: $age"
println(info) # Output: Name: John, Age: 30
```

To include a literal $ in an interpolated string, one can escape it using a backslash:

```
price = 49.99
message = "The price is \$${price}"
println(message) # Output: The price is $49.99
```

Indexing and Slicing: Characters within a string can be accessed using indexing, with indices starting from 1:

```
text = "Julia"
first_char = text[1]
println(first_char) # Output: J
```

Negative indices are not supported, unlike some other languages. Slicing is done using the range notation:

```
substring = text[2:4]
println(substring) # Output: uli
```

Length: To obtain the length of a string, use the length function:

```
sentence = "Hello, World!"
len = length(sentence)
println(len) # Output: 13
```

String Functions: Julia provides several built-in functions for common string operations, such as uppercase, lowercase, startswith, endswith, contains, and replace:

```
str = "Julia Programming Language"

upper_case = uppercase(str)
println(upper_case) # Output: JULIA PROGRAMMING LANGUAGE

lower_case = lowercase(str)
println(lower_case) # Output: julia programming language

starts = startswith(str, "Julia")
println(starts) # Output: true

ends = endswith(str, "Language")
println(ends) # Output: true

has_programming = contains(str, "Programming")
println(has_programming) # Output: true

replaced_str = replace(str, "Language" => "System")
println(replaced_str) # Output: Julia Programming System
```

Splitting and Joining: For breaking a string into parts based on a delimiter, split is employed; conversely, join combines an array of strings into one:

```
csv = "red,green,blue"
colors = split(csv, ",")
println(colors) # Output: ["red", "green", "blue"]

joined_colors = join(colors, "|")
println(joined_colors) # Output: red|green|blue
```

Regular Expressions: Advanced string matching and manipulation leverage regular expressions (Regex). Using match and replace functions with regular expressions enhances flexibility:

```
text = "The quick brown fox jumps over the lazy dog."

pattern = r"quick\s(\w+)\sfox"
m = match(pattern, text)
println(m.match) # Output: quick brown fox
println(m.captures) # Output: ["brown"]
```

```
new_text = replace(text, r"\sfox" => " wolf")
println(new_text) # Output: The quick brown wolf jumps over the lazy dog.
```

Formatting: The Printf standard library offers formatted output similar to C's printf:

```
using Printf

name = "Alice"
order = 10
cost = 49.99

formatted_str = @sprintf("Customer: %s\nOrder Number: %d\nTotal Cost: \$%.2f",
        name, order, cost)
println(formatted_str)
# Output:
# Customer: Alice
# Order Number: 10
# Total Cost: $49.99
```

Expert handling of strings in Julia enhances data manipulation efficacy, providing tools for both basic operations and intricate text processing tasks.

2.5 Tuples and Named Tuples

In Julia, tuples are immutable, ordered collections of elements. Each element in a tuple can be of a different type, which makes tuples a versatile data structure for grouping disparate types together. They are particularly useful for functions that return multiple values. Tuples are defined using parentheses () and can contain any number of elements.

```
tup1 = (1, 2.5, "Hello", true)
println(tup1)
```

```
(1, 2.5, "Hello", true)
```

Elements within a tuple can be accessed using indexing, which starts at 1 in Julia. To access elements, use the syntax tuple[index]:

```
first_element = tup1[1]
println(first_element)
```

```
1
```

The immutability of tuples means that once a tuple is created, its values cannot be modified. Attempting to change a value in a tuple will result in an error:

```
# This will raise an error
tup1[2] = 3.5
```

Tuples can also be nested, and slicing is possible to obtain sub-tuples:

```
nested_tup = (1, (2.5, "world"), false)
sub_tup = nested_tup[2]
println(sub_tup)
```

```
(2.5, "world")
```

For operations on tuples, the most common functions include length, first, and last:

```
# Get the length of the tuple
len = length(tup1)
println(len)

# Get the first element
first_elem = first(tup1)
println(first_elem)

# Get the last element
last_elem = last(tup1)
println(last_elem)
```

```
4
1
true
```

Named tuples provide an extension to tuples by allowing each element to be accessed by a name, in addition to index-based access. This feature is useful for enhancing readability and maintainability of code involving complex data structures. Named tuples are defined using semicolons ; between key-value pairs:

```
ntup = (a=1, b=2.5, c="Hello", d=true)
println(ntup)
```

```
(a = 1, b = 2.5, c = "Hello", d = true)
```

Elements of named tuples can be accessed by their names:

```
a_value = ntup.a
println(a_value)

c_value = ntup.c
println(c_value)
```

```
1
"Hello"
```

Additionally, named tuples maintain all the properties of regular tuples, including immutability and ability to be used in multiple dispatch.

Named tuples can be indexed similarly to regular tuples:

```
# Indexing named tuple just like regular tuple
second_value = ntup[2]
println(second_value)
```

2.5

Named tuples are advantageous when the structure of data is known and access by name provides clearer code semantics, for instance, when returning multiple values from a function:

```
function rectangle_properties(width::Float64, height::Float64)
    area = width * height
    perimeter = 2 * (width + height)
    return (area=area, perimeter=perimeter)
end

props = rectangle_properties(3.0, 4.0)
println("Area: $(props.area), Perimeter: $(props.perimeter)")
```

Area: 12.0, Perimeter: 14.0

In constructing larger programs or algorithms, tuples and named tuples can serve as lightweight, immutable collections that enhance data integrity and code readability. This is achieved by combining their immutability with the efficiency of value-type elements in Julia. Such characteristics make tuples suitable for high-performance scenarios where data mutation is unnecessary or undesirable.

The ergonomic balance between tuples and named tuples allows developers to select the most appropriate data structure depending on the context and nature of the operations involved, whether it is simple grouping of different types or providing clear, named associations for complex data items.

2.6 Arrays and Their Operations

Arrays in Julia are versatile data structures that can store collections of elements. Arrays can be one-dimensional (vectors), two-dimensional (matrices), or even multi-dimensional. They can store elements of any type and can be dynamically resized. This section will provide an exhaustive overview of array creation, manipulation, and various operations that can be performed on arrays.

Array Creation

Arrays can be created using square brackets and separated by commas. For instance, a one-dimensional array (vector) can be created as follows:

```
a = [1, 2, 3, 4, 5]
```

To create a two-dimensional array (matrix), use a semicolon to separate the rows:

```
b = [1 2 3; 4 5 6; 7 8 9]
```

Alternatively, you can use the reshape function to convert a one-dimensional array into a two-dimensional array:

```
c = reshape([1, 2, 3, 4, 5, 6], 2, 3)
```

Accessing and Modifying Elements

Elements in an array can be accessed using square brackets with indices starting from 1. To access the first element of array a:

```
first_element = a[1]
```

To modify an element, simply assign a new value to the indexed position:

```
a[2] = 10
```

For multi-dimensional arrays, indices are separated by commas:

```
element = b[2, 3] # Access element in second row, third column
b[3, 2] = 20 # Modify element in third row, second column
```

Array Operations

Julia provides a wide array of operations to manipulate arrays efficiently. Here are a few fundamental operations:

Concatenation

Arrays can be concatenated vertically or horizontally using the vcat and hcat functions:

```
d1 = [1, 2]
d2 = [3, 4]
vertical = vcat(d1, d2) # Vertical concatenation
horizontal = hcat(d1, d2) # Horizontal concatenation
```

Arithmetic Operations

Arithmetic operations between arrays and scalars are element-wise:

```
e = [2, 4, 6] * 2 # Multiplies each element by 2
```

```
f = [10, 20, 30] - 5 # Subtracts 5 from each element
```

Operations between arrays of the same dimensions are also element-wise:

```
g = [1, 2, 3] + [4, 5, 6] # Adds corresponding elements
h = [10, 20, 30] ./ [2, 4, 5] # Element-wise division
```

Broadcasting

Julia supports broadcasting, where a function is applied element-wise to an array. This is indicated by placing a dot (.) before the operator:

```
i = [1, 2, 3]
j = i .^ 2 # Squares each element
```

Broadcasting can also be used with functions:

```
k = sqrt.(i) # Takes the square root of each element
```

Higher-Dimensional Arrays

Julia supports higher-dimensional arrays, and operations extend naturally to these structures. For example, creating a three-dimensional array:

```
l = reshape(1:27, 3, 3, 3)
m = l .* 2 # Element-wise multiplication with scalar
```

Aggregation Functions

Julia provides a host of functions to aggregate array elements:

```
n = [1, 2, 3, 4, 5]
sum_n = sum(n) # Sum of all elements
max_n = maximum(n) # Maximum element
min_n = minimum(n) # Minimum element
```

Array Transformations

Common transformations include transposition and reshaping:

```
o = [1 2 3; 4 5 6; 7 8 9]
transpose_o = transpose(o) # Transposes the matrix
reshape_o = reshape(o, 1, 9) # Converts to a 1x9 matrix
```

Advanced Operations

Boolean Indexing

Arrays can be indexed by boolean arrays, extracting elements where the condition is true:

```
p = [1, 2, 3, 4, 5]
boolean_index = p .> 3 # Creates a boolean array: [false false false true true]
selection = p[boolean_index] # Extracts elements satisfying the condition
```

Sorting and Searching

The sort function orders elements, while findall returns the indices meeting a condition:

```
q = [5, 3, 8, 1, 2]
sorted_q = sort(q) # Sorts the array
indices = findall(x -> x > 3, q) # Finds indices of elements greater than 3
```

Linear Algebra Operations

Julia supports extensive linear algebra functionalities. For instance, matrix multiplication and inversion can be performed using the * operator and inv function respectively:

```
r = [1 2; 3 4]
s = [5 6; 7 8]
product = r * s # Matrix multiplication
inverse_r = inv(r) # Matrix inversion
```

Arrays in Julia are powerful and flexible, providing a foundation for more complex data manipulations and computational tasks. Understanding these operations equips you with the essential tools to handle a vast range of numerical and analytical problems efficiently.

2.7 Ranges and Iterators

In Julia, ranges and iterators are crucial constructs that allow efficient iteration over sequences of numbers or other values. Ranges are compact representations of arithmetic sequences, while iterators generalize the concept to accommodate various data structures. Understanding these constructs is essential for writing concise and high-performance Julia code.

Range objects in Julia represent sequences with a defined start, stop, and an optional step size. For example, 1:10 generates a sequence from 1 through 10 inclusive, while 1:2:9 generates a sequence from 1 to 9 with a step size of 2. Ranges are memory-efficient as they store only the start, stop, and step values instead of storing each element.

Creating and using ranges can be demonstrated with the following example:

```
# Create a simple range from 1 to 10
simple_range = 1:10

# Create a range with a step size of 2
stepped_range = 1:2:9

# Print the ranges
println("Simple range: ", simple_range)
println("Stepped range: ", stepped_range)
```

Execution of the above code yields:

```
Simple range: 1:10
Stepped range: 1:2:9
```

Indexing into a Range is straightforward and similar to array indexing. Given r = 1:5, r[3] returns the third element, which is 3. Ranges are immutable; all operations that appear to modify them actually create new ranges.

Iterating over a range is highly efficient:

```
# Iterating over a range with a for loop
for i in 1:5
    println(i)
end
```

Execution yields:

```
1
2
3
4
5
```

Ranges can be combined with array comprehensions to generate arrays. For instance:

```
# Generating an array using a range and comprehension
array_from_range = [2*i for i in 1:5]
println(array_from_range)
```

The output is:

```
[2, 4, 6, 8, 10]
```

Iterators extend beyond numerical ranges to include more complex data structures. The IterTools library in Julia offers a variety of standard iterators such as product, permutations, and combinations. Here is an example using product, which iterates over the Cartesian product of input iterables:

```
using IterTools

# Cartesian product of two ranges
```

```
for item in product(1:2, 3:4)
    println(item)
end
```

Execution will result in:

```
(1, 3)
(1, 4)
(2, 3)
(2, 4)
```

Custom iterators can be created by defining the required methods from the Iteration interface. A custom iterator must implement start, done, and next methods:

```
struct MyIterator
    current::Int
    stop::Int
end

# Define start, done, and next methods
Base.start(it::MyIterator) = it.current
Base.done(it::MyIterator, state) = state > it.stop
Base.next(it::MyIterator, state) = (state, state + 1)

# Using the custom iterator
it = MyIterator(1, 5)
for i in it
    println(i)
end
```

The output is:

```
1
2
3
4
5
```

Iterators and ranges offer an optimized and expressive way to handle sequential data and looping constructs in Julia. Their application spans from simple numeric sequences to complex combinations of data types. Through efficient memory usage and intuitive syntax, they play a vital role in high-performance Julia programming. Understanding and leveraging these concepts enables developers to write code that is both concise and efficient.

2.8 Introduction to Dictionaries

Dictionaries in Julia, also known as associative arrays or hash maps in other programming languages, provide a flexible mechanism for storing key-value pairs. They are ideal for situations where quick lookup and retrieval of data associated with unique keys are necessary. In Julia, dictionaries are defined using the Dict type.

To construct a simple dictionary, you can use the Dict constructor, specifying keys and their corresponding values. For example, a dictionary mapping names to ages can be created as follows:

```
ages = Dict("Alice" => 30, "Bob" => 25, "Charlie" => 35)
```

Keys and values in a dictionary do not need to be of the same type. Julia will infer the types based on the entries provided. It is possible to explicitly declare the types for a dictionary using the following syntax:

```
ages = Dict{String, Int}("Alice" => 30, "Bob" => 25, "Charlie" => 35)
```

Here, String is the type of the keys, and Int is the type of the values.

A critical feature of dictionaries in Julia is their ability to handle various types of keys and values. For example, you might create a dictionary with integer keys and float values:

```
measurements = Dict{Int, Float64}(1 => 3.14, 2 => 2.71, 3 => 1.41)
```

Dictionaries support several essential operations:

- **Insertion and Updating**: You can add new key-value pairs or update existing keys with a simple assignment operation.

  ```
  ages["David"] = 40 # Adding a new key-value pair
  ages["Alice"] = 31 # Updating an existing key-value pair
  ```

- **Accessing Values**: Values can be accessed using their corresponding keys. If the key does not exist, an error is thrown.

  ```
  age_of_bob = ages["Bob"]
  ```

  To handle missing keys gracefully, the get function can be used, providing a default value:

  ```
  age_of_eve = get(ages, "Eve", "Not found")
  ```

- **Deleting Entries**: The delete! function removes a key-value pair from the dictionary.

  ```
  delete!(ages, "Charlie")
  ```

- **Key Checking**: The haskey function checks if a particular key exists in the dictionary.

```
haskey(ages, "Alice") # Returns true
haskey(ages, "Eve") # Returns false
```

Iterating over the keys and values of a dictionary is straightforward. Julia provides a convenient syntax for this purpose:

```
for (name, age) in ages
    println("Name: $name, Age: $age")
end
```

Additionally, dictionaries offer built-in functions to work with their keys and values:

- keys(dict): Returns an iterable of the dictionary's keys.
- values(dict): Returns an iterable of the dictionary's values.

For example:

```
all_keys = keys(ages)
all_values = values(ages)
```

Combining these elements, one might encounter sophisticated operations. For instance, merging two dictionaries can be accomplished as follows:

```
additional_ages = Dict("Eve" => 28, "Frank" => 33)
merged_ages = merge(ages, additional_ages)
```

The merge function combines ages and additional_ages, with values from additional_ages taking precedence if keys overlap.

Dictionaries in Julia are mutable, meaning that their contents can be changed without creating a new dictionary. This property is particularly useful for scenarios requiring dynamic data manipulation. Here is an example demonstrating dictionary mutability:

```
function update_age!(dict, name, increment)
    if haskey(dict, name)
        dict[name] += increment
    else
        println("Name not found")
    end
end

update_age!(ages, "Alice", 1) # Alice's age is incremented by 1
```

In contexts where dictionary performance is critical, Julia's implementation ensures efficient lookups and data manipulations. The underlying mechanism relies on hash tables, providing average-case constant time complexity, $O(1)$, for insertion, deletion, and lookup operations. This efficiency makes dictionaries highly suitable for a wide array of applications, from simple data retrieval tasks to complex algorithmic problem-solving scenarios.

Understanding and leveraging dictionaries in Julia can significantly enhance one's ability to manage and manipulate associative data structures, contributing to more efficient and effective programming practices.

2.9 Symbols and Their Uses

In Julia, Symbol is a built-in type that plays a critical role in metaprogramming and various other advanced features. A Symbol in Julia is an interned string, which means that it is stored uniquely in memory and can be compared quickly. Symbols are often used as identifiers or keys due to their immutability and efficient comparison operations.

To create a Symbol, you can use the colon : followed by an identifier.

```
x = :example_symbol
```

In the example above, x is assigned the Symbol :example_symbol. You can verify the type of x using the typeof function:

```
typeof(x)
```

```
Symbol
```

Symbols are particularly useful when used as keys in dictionaries, ensuring a constant-time complexity for lookups and consistent behavior in terms of memory usage. Below is an example demonstrating the use of symbols as keys in a dictionary:

```
dict = Dict(:name => "Julia", :type => "Programming Language", :version => 1.6)
```

In this dictionary, each key is a Symbol, making accessing values efficient:

```
dict[:name]
```

```
"Julia"
```

One of the key benefits of using Symbols over strings in such contexts is immutability. Since Symbols are immutable, they are hash-consed, meaning each Symbol with the same name points to the same memory location. This property guarantees that comparisons between Symbols are always fast and memory-efficient, as shown below:

```
a = :example_symbol
b = :example_symbol
a === b
```

```
true
```

While a == b would also return true, using === (the strict equality operator) confirms that both a and b are indeed pointing to the same memory location.

Symbols are often used in Julia's metaprogramming features. For instance, one common scenario is manipulating expressions. An expression in Julia can be created using the Expr type. Here, Symbols play an essential role in forming expressions:

```
expr = Expr(:call, :+, 1, 2)
```

This creates an expression that represents the operation $1 + 2$. You can evaluate this expression using the eval function:

```
result = eval(expr)
```

```
3
```

Metaprogramming leverages Symbols heavily due to their ability to efficiently represent variable names, function names, and other identifiers within code that manipulates other code. The above example demonstrates how Symbols can embody operations or functions symbolically within Julia's AST (Abstract Syntax Tree).

Moreover, Symbols can be dynamically generated, providing flexibility for automated code generation tasks. Consider the following code snippet, where a Symbol is created from a string:

```
sym = Symbol("dynamic_symbol")
```

This command creates a Symbol :dynamic_symbol. You can verify its type and effectively use it in various contexts.

When handling Symbols, it is crucial to recognize their efficiency and immutability, which make them ideal for use cases requiring fast comparisons and consistent identifiers. For instance, when dealing with a large amount of metadata or utilizing Symbols in Domain-Specific Languages (DSLs), their benefits are evident.

The following example demonstrates a more complex usage, incorporating symbols within a Named Tuple:

```
nt = (name = :julia, type = :language, version = 1.6)
```

Accessing elements in a named tuple by their Symbol keys ensures both readability and performance:

```
nt.name
```

```
:julia
```

Lastly, when considering performance, remember that operations involving Symbols generally do not generate garbage collection overhead, as every Symbol is globally unique and not subject to deallocation. This characteristic significantly boosts the performance of symbol-heavy applications, making Symbols a powerful feature in the Julia programming language.

2.10 Type Inference and Conversion

Julia's type system is dynamic and powerful, allowing for both flexibility and performance. Understanding how Julia infers types and how you can convert between types is crucial for effective programming. This section will delve into the mechanisms of type inference, the rules that govern it, and the various methods to explicitly convert between types.

Julia uses a combination of dynamic and static typing to infer types efficiently. The *type inference* process allows Julia to determine the types of expressions during compilation, enabling it to generate optimized machine code. This process is crucial for performance, particularly in computationally intensive tasks.

To examine basic type inference, consider the following example where we assign a value to a variable:

```
a = 10
```

In this case, Julia infers the type of a to be Int, specifically Int64 on a 64-bit system. You can query the type of any variable using the typeof function:

```
typeof(a)
```

The output will be:

```
Int64
```

Julia's ability to infer the type can be extended to more complex expressions involving arithmetic operations or functions. For instance:

```
b = 3.0 + 4
```

Here, b is inferred as Float64, since Julia promotes the integer 4 to a float to match the type of 3.0, following its type promotion rules.

Another critical element of Julia's type system is *type stability*. A function is considered type-stable if the return type can be inferred from the types of the inputs. Type stability enhances performance by reducing the need for dynamic type checks. Consider the following function:

```
function square(x)
    return x * x
end
```

The square function is type-stable because the return type is the same as the input type. To verify type stability, the @code_warntype macro can be employed:

```
@code_warntype square(5)
```

This will output type inference details, aiding in performance tuning and debugging.

Conversely, type instability can lead to significant performance degradation. For example:

```
function unstable(x)
    if x > 0
        return x
    else
        return "negative"
    end
end
```

This function is type-unstable because depending on the input, it might return either an integer or a string, prompting unnecessary runtime type checks.

Type Conversion

Julia offers explicit mechanisms for converting between types. This is especially important when interfacing with external libraries or performing specific arithmetic operations. The convert function is a generic interface for type conversion:

```
x = 42
y = convert(Float64, x)
```

Here, x is explicitly converted from Int64 to Float64. Another approach is to use T(x), where T is the target type:

```
z = Float64(x)
```

In both instances, the result is 42.0. Julia also supports numeric type promotion where smaller numeric types are promoted to larger types during arithmetic operations:

```
a = 3 # Int64
b = 4.5 # Float64
c = a + b
```

The variable c is inferred as Float64 due to type promotion.

Common Type Conversion Functions

- float: Converts an integer or a rational number to a floating-point number.

```
float(10) # converts Int to Float64
```

- round, floor, and ceil: Convert floating-point numbers to integers by rounding, flooring, or ceiling.

```
round(3.14) # 3
floor(3.14) # 3
ceil(3.14) # 4
```

- parse: Converts a string representing a number into its numeric type.

```
string_number = "12345"
parsed_number = parse(Int, string_number)
```

The result of parse will be an integer 12345. This is useful when parsing numeric user input or reading data from text files.

Custom Type Conversions

Julia also allows for defining custom type conversions for user-defined types. This is done by overloading the convert function for the custom type:

```
struct MyType
    value::Int
```

```
end

Base.convert(::Type{MyType}, x::Int) = MyType(x)
```

With this definition, $\mathrm{MyType}(10)$ is a valid expression, converting 10 into an instance of MyType.

Understanding and properly utilizing type inference and conversion in Julia leads to code that is both efficient and flexible. The capabilities of Julia's type system and its performance characteristics are integral to developing efficient programs and solving complex computational problems.

Chapter 3

Control Flow in Julia

This chapter covers the essential elements of control flow in Julia, including conditional statements with 'if', 'else', and 'elseif', and logical operators and comparisons. It details looping constructs such as 'for' and 'while' loops, and introduces comprehensions for concise iteration. The chapter also addresses exception handling with 'try', 'catch', and 'finally', short-circuit evaluation, 'break' and 'continue' statements, using iterators and generators, and best practices for managing variable scope and visibility in control structures.

3.1 Conditional Statements: if, else, elseif

Conditional statements in Julia are foundational constructs that enable the control of the flow of execution within a program. These constructs determine which code blocks are executed based on the evaluation of Boolean expressions. Julia provides the if, else, and elseif keywords to facilitate conditional execution.

The if statement evaluates a condition and executes a block of code if the condition is true. If the condition is false, the else block is executed if it is provided. For handling multiple conditions, the elseif keyword is used, allowing the chaining of several conditions in a sequential manner.

Here is the basic structure of an if-else construct in Julia:

```
if condition_1
    # Code to execute if condition_1 is true
elseif condition_2
    # Code to execute if condition_2 is true
else
    # Code to execute if none of the above conditions are true
end
```

Consider an example where we want to determine the state of water based on its temperature:

```
temperature = 25

if temperature <= 0
    println("The water is solid (ice).")
elseif temperature >= 100
    println("The water is gas (vapor).")
else
    println("The water is liquid.")
end
```

In this example, the program evaluates the condition temperature <= 0. If this condition is true, it prints "The water is solid (ice).". If the condition is false, it evaluates the elseif condition temperature >= 100. If this second condition is true, it prints "The water is gas (vapor).". If neither condition is satisfied, the else block is executed, printing "The water is liquid.".

Julia allows Boolean expressions involving comparison operators such as ==, !=, <, <=, >, and >=, which are used within conditional statements. Logical operators like && (logical AND), || (logical OR), and ! (logical NOT) can also be used to form complex conditions.

Here is an example that combines multiple conditions using logical operators:

```
x = 7
y = 10

if x > 5 && y < 15
    println("Both conditions are true.")
else
    println("At least one condition is false.")
end
```

In this example, the condition x > 5 && y < 15 must be true for the println("Both conditions are true.") statement to execute. If either condition is false, the program executes the else block.

Nested if-else statements can also be used when multiple levels of condition checks are required. Each if or else block can contain another if-else construct, allowing complex decision trees to be implemented.

However, excessive nesting can make code difficult to read and maintain, so it is generally advisable to keep nesting to manageable levels or refactor the logic into functions.

Here is an example demonstrating nested if-else statements:

```
number = 50

if number > 0
    if number % 2 == 0
        println("The number is positive and even.")
    else
        println("The number is positive and odd.")
    end
else
    println("The number is non-positive.")
end
```

In this example, the outer if statement checks if number is greater than 0. If true, the inner if-else statement evaluates whether number is even or odd. If number is not greater than 0, the else block executes, indicating the number is non-positive.

It is important to note that Julia's if, else, and elseif keywords are strictly conditional constructs. They must evaluate to expressions that return Bool values, and non-Boolean return values will result in a runtime error.

To enhance reliability and readability, it is a best practice to use parentheses around complex conditions, although not strictly required by Julia's syntax:

```
if (x > 5) && (y < 15)
    println("Both conditions are true.")
else
    println("At least one condition is false.")
end
```

This ensures that the condition's intent is clear and unambiguous, minimizing the risk of logical errors.

By understanding and effectively utilizing if, else, and elseif statements in Julia, one can implement versatile control flow within their programs, enabling sophisticated decision-making capabilities based on dynamic conditions.

3.2 Logical Operators and Comparisons

Logical operators and comparison operators play crucial roles in controlling the flow of execution within a program. In Julia, such operators are used to form logical expressions that evaluate to true or false. These expressions are commonly used in conditional statements and loops to determine the course of the program based on specific conditions.

Comparison Operators

Julia provides several fundamental comparison operators to compare values. These are similar to those found in many other programming languages and are used to compare numeric, string, and other comparable types. The primary comparison operators in Julia include:

- $==$: Returns true if both operands are equal.
- $!=$ or $\neq$: Returns true if the operands are not equal.
- $<$: Returns true if the left operand is less than the right operand.
- $<=$ or $\leq$: Returns true if the left operand is less than or equal to the right operand.
- $>$: Returns true if the left operand is greater than the right operand.
- $>=$ or $\geq$: Returns true if the left operand is greater than or equal to the right operand.

For instance:

```
x = 10
y = 20

println(x == y) # Prints false
println(x != y) # Prints true
println(x < y) # Prints true
println(x <= y) # Prints true
println(x > y) # Prints false
println(x >= y) # Prints false
```

The values of x and y are compared using the above operators, and the results are displayed accordingly.

Logical Operators

Logical operators allow us to combine multiple comparison expressions. The primary logical operators in Julia include:

- && : Logical AND operator. It returns true if both operands are true.
- || : Logical OR operator. It returns true if at least one of the operands is true.
- ! : Logical NOT operator. It returns true if the operand is false, and vice versa.

The following example demonstrates the use of logical operators:

```
a = true
b = false

println(a && b) # Prints false
println(a || b) # Prints true
println(!a) # Prints false
println(!b) # Prints true
```

Combining Comparison and Logical Operators

Logical operators can be used to create complex conditional expressions by combining multiple comparison operations. Consider the following example:

```
x = 15
y = 10
z = 20

println((x > y) && (x < z)) # Prints true
println((x > y) || (x > z)) # Prints true
```

Here, two comparison expressions are combined using the logical AND operator (&&) and the logical OR operator (||), and the combined result of these expressions is evaluated.

Short-Circuit Evaluation

Julia employs short-circuit evaluation for the && and || operators. This means that the evaluation of expressions stops as soon as the overall truth value is determined. Consider the following scenarios:

```
a = false
b = (println("This will not print") || true)

println(a && b) # Prints false; second operand (b) is not evaluated
println(a || b) # Prints true; second operand (b) is evaluated
```

Here, when evaluating a && b, Julia does not evaluate b because a is false and the result of the AND operation cannot be true if one operand is false. Conversely, when evaluating a || b, b is evaluated because a is false and the result of the OR operation could still be true if b is true.

Logical operators and comparison operators are essential tools in Julia for constructing precise and efficient control flow structures. Their proper utilization ensures that specific conditions and scenarios in the program are handled accurately.

3.3 Looping Constructs: for and while Loops

Looping constructs are fundamental to control flows in any programming language, allowing for the repeated execution of a block of code. In Julia, the primary constructs used for iteration are the for and while loops. This section explores these constructs in great detail, demonstrating their syntax, usage, and best practices.

For Loops

The for loop in Julia is used to iterate over a range of values, arrays, or any iterable collection. The basic syntax of a for loop is as follows:

```
for i in 1:10
    println(i)
end
```

Here, the variable i takes on values from 1 through 10, and the println function outputs each value on a new line.

Iterating Over Arrays

```
myArray = “[”apple, “”banana, “”cherry]

for fruit in myArray
    println(fruit)
end
```

In this example, the for loop iterates over the elements of myArray. The variable fruit takes on each element of the array, and println outputs the element.

Nested For Loops

Julia supports the nesting of loops, allowing for the iteration over multi-dimensional structures. The inner loop runs completely during each iteration of the outer loop.

```
for i in 1:3
    for j in 1:2
        println“(i = ”, i, “, j = ”, j)
    end
```

```
end
```

The output for this loop is:

```
i = 1, j = 1
i = 1, j = 2
i = 2, j = 1
i = 2, j = 2
i = 3, j = 1
i = 3, j = 2
```

While Loops

The while loop in Julia is another looping construct that continues to execute a block of code as long as a specified condition remains true. The syntax of a while loop is:

```
i = 1
while i <= 10
    println(i)
    i += 1
end
```

In this snippet, the variable i starts at 1 and increments by 1 during each iteration of the loop until i is greater than 10, at which point the loop terminates.

Breaking out of Loops

Both for and while loops can be prematurely terminated using the break statement. This control statement exits the loop immediately.

```
for i in 1:10
    if i == 5
        break
    end
    println(i)
end
```

The output only goes up to 4, as the loop breaks upon reaching 5.

```
1
2
3
4
```

while loops can also utilize the break statement:

```
i = 1
while true
    println(i)
    i += 1
    if i > 5
        break
    end
end
```

Skip Iterations

To skip the remaining code in the current iteration and move to the next iteration, the continue statement is used. This is applicable in both for and while loops.

```
for i in 1:10
    if i % 2 == 0
        continue
    end
    println(i)
end
```

Here, only odd numbers are printed, as continue skips the even numbers.

```
1
3
5
7
9
```

Best Practices in Looping Constructs

1. *Initialization*: Always ensure the loop variables are properly initialized outside the loop. 2. *Condition Check*: Ensure that the loop condition will eventually become false to avoid infinite loops. 3. *Mutating Loop Variable*: Ensure the loop variable is correctly updated within the body of the loop. 4. *Readability*: Maintain readable and manageable code within the loops; avoid overly nested loops unless necessary.

Performance Considerations

In Julia, loops are designed to be efficient. However, it is still valuable to adhere to best practices for writing performant loops: - Pre-allocate storage outside the loop if the size is known. - Favor for loops and array comprehensions over while loops when the number of iterations is known beforehand. - Utilize built-in functions that are optimized for performance when applicable, such as map and filter.

Through thoughtful application of these looping constructs, you can control and manage the flow of your Julia programs effectively, ensuring both readability and performance efficiency.

3.4 Comprehensions

Comprehensions in Julia provide a concise and expressive means to construct collections such as arrays, dictionaries, and more. They are reminiscent of the list comprehensions found in other programming languages like Python, and they offer a powerful syntactic shorthand for iterating through sequences and applying transformations or filters.

A comprehension typically consists of an expression followed by one or more for or if clauses encapsulated within brackets []. The syntax for list comprehensions to construct arrays is as follows:

```
[expression for variable in collection if condition]
```

For example, consider a scenario where we need to generate a list of squares for even numbers in a given range:

```
squares = [x^2 for x in 1:10 if x % 2 == 0]
```

The above comprehension is equivalent to:

```
squares = []
for x in 1:10
    if x % 2 == 0
        push!(squares, x^2)
    end
end
```

To illustrate the output:

```
[4, 16, 36, 64, 100]
```

Comprehensions can also handle nested iteration, and this capability extends their utility significantly. Consider generating a Cartesian product of two lists:

```
cartesian_product = [(x, y) for x in 1:3, y in 4:6]
```

This nested comprehension evaluates to:

```
[(1, 4), (1, 5), (1, 6), (2, 4), (2, 5), (2, 6), (3, 4), (3, 5), (3, 6)]
```

Comprehensions can likewise be utilized with multiple if conditions. For example, creating a list of pairs where both elements are even numbers:

```
even_pairs = [(x, y) for x in 1:4, y in 1:4 if x % 2 == 0 if y % 2 == 0]
```

Resulting output:

```
[(2, 2), (2, 4), (4, 2), (4, 4)]
```

Furthermore, comprehensions can generate dictionaries where the syntax involves curly brackets {}:

```
dict_comprehension = {x => x^2 for x in 1:5}
```

To depict this with output:

```
Dict(1 => 1, 2 => 4, 3 => 9, 4 => 16, 5 => 25)
```

Julia extends this powerful tool of comprehensions to generators as well. A generator comprehension uses parentheses () instead of brackets or braces. It allows for generating elements on-the-fly, which can be more memory efficient when dealing with large datasets.

Consider a generator example:

```
gen = (x^2 for x in 1:10 if x % 2 != 0)
```

This comprehension effectively describes an iterable collection without immediately creating and storing all items in memory.

To iterate over the generator:

```
for val in gen
    println(val)
end
```

The output produced will be:

```
1
9
25
49
81
```

Comprehensions are highly versatile and can be applied to various collection types or structures. They serve an essential role in writing clean, efficient, and readable Julia code. When utilized judiciously, comprehensions enhance both the developer experience and the performance of the resultant programs.

3.5 Exception Handling: try, catch, finally

Exception handling in Julia is a crucial aspect of creating robust and error-resilient programs. It allows developers to gracefully manage errors that might occur during program execution, ensuring that the software can handle unexpected situations without crashing. Julia provides a structured way to handle exceptions using the try, catch, and finally blocks.

The try block is where you place the code that might throw an exception. If an exception occurs within this block, Julia suspends normal execution and transfers control to the corresponding catch block, if present.

The finally block contains code that is always executed after the try and catch blocks, regardless of whether an exception was thrown or not. This structure allows for cleanup activities such as closing files or releasing resources.

```
try
    # Code that may throw an exception
    result = 10 / 0
catch e
    println("An error occurred: ", e)
finally
    println("This block always executes.")
end
```

In this example, the division by zero will raise a DivideError. When this happens, the control flow jumps to the catch block, which prints the error message. Regardless of the outcome, the finally block is executed, ensuring that the cleanup message is printed.

To handle specific types of exceptions, you can check the type or properties of the exception within the catch block. This allows for more granular error handling and customized responses depending on the error type.

```
try
    open("non_existent_file.txt")
catch e
    if isa(e, SystemError)
        println("File system error: ", e)
    elseif isa(e, ArgumentError)
        println("Argument error: ", e)
    else
        println("Some other error occurred: ", e)
    end
finally
    println("Cleanup actions go here.")
end
```

In this refined example, the catch block checks the type of the exception using the isa function and handles different types of errors accordingly. This approach provides precise control over how various exceptions are addressed.

Exception handling can also involve rethrowing exceptions to allow higher-level control flows to manage certain unusual conditions. This is accomplished using the rethrow() function within a catch block.

```
try
    # Code that may throw an exception
    x = 1 / 0
catch e
    println("Caught an error: ", e)
    rethrow()
finally
```

```
    println("Finalizing no matter what.")
end
```

Here, the catch block catches the DivideError and prints a message, but the rethrow() function rethrows the exception so that it can be potentially handled at a higher level in the program's call stack.

In practice, the finally block is often used to ensure that resources are properly released, like closing files, even if an error occurs. This ensures that your program does not leak resources, which is especially important in long-running applications or those with limited resources.

```
file = open("example.txt", "w")

try
    # Maybe some risky operations with the file
    write(file, "Hello, world!")
catch e
    println("An error occurred while writing to the file: ", e)
finally
    close(file)
    println("File closed successfully.")
end
```

In this final example, the file is opened for writing at the beginning. Regardless of whether writing to the file succeeds or an error is encountered, the finally block ensures that the file is closed, preventing potential resource leaks.

Using try, catch, and finally blocks properly helps to create stable programs that can manage unexpected situations gracefully. This error-handling approach not only prevents complete program failures but also offers efficient ways to manage and clean up resources, maintaining overall system stability and reliability.

3.6 Short-Circuit Evaluation

Short-circuit evaluation is a critical concept in conditional statements and logical operations. In Julia, as in many programming languages, short-circuit evaluation is employed to increase efficiency and prevent unnecessary operations.

The two logical operators that utilize short-circuit evaluation are the && (logical AND) and the || (logical OR) operators. These operators determine the result of a compound logical expression without necessarily evaluating all its components, which can lead to performance improvements and can be crucial in avoiding runtime errors.

&& (logical AND) evaluates the second operand only if the first operand is true. If the first operand is false, the overall expression is false regardless of the second operand, thereby short-circuiting the evaluation.

```
a = false
b = (10 / 0 == 0)

# Short-circuit evaluation ensures that 'b' is not evaluated, as 'a' is false.
result = a && b
println(result) # Output: false
```

In this example, the division by zero operation in b would normally result in an error. However, due to short-circuit evaluation, the second operand b is not evaluated because the first operand a is false.

Similarly, the || (logical OR) operator evaluates the second operand only if the first operand is false. If the first operand is true, the overall expression is true, and the second operand is not evaluated.

```
a = true
b = (10 / 0 == 0)

# Short-circuit evaluation prevents the evaluation of 'b', as 'a' is true.
result = a || b
println(result) # Output: true
```

Understanding short-circuit behavior can help developers write more efficient and error-resistant code. Consider the following practical example:

```
function check_divisible(x, y)
    return y != 0 && (x % y == 0)
end
```

In the check_divisible function, y != 0 is evaluated first. If y is zero, then x % y == 0 is not evaluated, preventing a division by zero error. Short-circuit evaluation thus provides a convenient mechanism for ensuring safe conditional checks.

Moreover, short-circuit evaluation can be leveraged in functions and flow control. Consider the following scenario:

```
function read_file(filename)
    return isfile(filename) && open(filename, "r") do file
        return read(file, String)
    end
end
```

In the read_file function, the isfile(filename) function checks if the file exists. If the file does not exist, the open function is not called, and the evaluation is halted, returning false. This behavior safeguards against attempting to open non-existent files.

Short-circuit evaluation is particularly useful when combined with early returns within functions. For instance, consider a function that processes user input:

```
function process_input(input)
    input == nothing && return "No input provided"
    # Additional processing here
    return "Input processed: $input"
end
```

If input is nothing, the function terminates early with the message "No input provided," leveraging the short-circuit evaluation of the && operator to avoid unnecessary processing.

Short-circuit evaluation is integral to writing concise, readable, and efficient Julia code, enabling developers to streamline their conditional logic and safeguard against unsafe operations. Understanding and employing this technique is essential for effective control flow management in Julia programs.

3.7 Break and Continue Statements

In Julia, the break and continue statements are control flow mechanisms primarily used within loops to manipulate the flow of iteration. These statements provide more control over the execution of code blocks, contributing to cleaner and more readable programs. Understanding their functionality and appropriate usage is essential for developing sophisticated algorithms.

The break statement terminates the innermost loop that encloses it. When a break statement is encountered, Julia immediately exits the loop, skipping any remaining iterations or statements inside the loop body. This can be particularly useful when a certain condition is met, and further looping would be redundant or wasteful.

Consider the following example, where we search for the first multiple of 5 within a given range:

```
for i in 1:10
    if i % 5 == 0
        println("Found multiple of 5: ", i)
        break
    end
end
```

The output of this code will be:

```
Found multiple of 5: 5
```

Here, the loop iterates from 1 to 10, and when i equals 5, $i \% 5 == 0$ evaluates to true. Consequently, the println statement is executed, followed by the break statement, which terminates the loop.

On the other hand, the continue statement is used to skip the current iteration of the loop and proceed to the next iteration, bypassing any code that follows it within the loop body. This is beneficial when a particular condition invalidates the current iteration, making further processing unnecessary.

Illustrate this concept with the following example, where we print all numbers from 1 to 10 except for multiples of 3:

```
for i in 1:10
    if i % 3 == 0
        continue
    end
    println(i)
end
```

The output of this code will be:

```
1
2
4
5
7
8
10
```

In this example, when i equals 3, 6, or 9, the expression $i \% 3 == 0$ evaluates to true, causing the continue statement to execute. This skips the println(i) call for those values, thus they are not printed.

Both break and continue can be combined with other control flow statements such as if conditions and within nested loops for more complex operations.

Consider another example where nested loops are utilized, and we want to exit the inner loop upon finding a specific element:

```
for i in 1:3
    println("Outer loop iteration: ", i)
    for j in 1:3
        if j == 2
            println(" Found within inner loop at j: ", j)
            break
        end
        println(" Inner loop iteration: ", j)
    end
end
```

The output of this code will be:

```
Outer loop iteration: 1
  Inner loop iteration: 1
  Found within inner loop at j: 2
Outer loop iteration: 2
  Inner loop iteration: 1
  Found within inner loop at j: 2
Outer loop iteration: 3
  Inner loop iteration: 1
  Found within inner loop at j: 2
```

In this case, break is used to exit the inner loop when j equals 2. As a result, after finding $j == 2$, the inner loop terminates and control returns to the outer loop.

It's essential to note that the break statement only affects the nearest enclosing loop. In scenarios requiring termination of outer loops, one would need to implement additional logic, such as flags or condition checks in the outer loop upon exiting the inner.

Now, let's look at a more advanced usage scenario where both break and continue statements are employed to filter data within nested loops:

```
for i in 1:5
    if i % 2 == 0
        println("Skip even number: ", i)
        continue
    end

    for j in 1:5
        if i * j > 10
            println("Product too large, breaking inner loop at i=", i, ", j=", j)
            break
        end
        println("Product: ", i * j)
    end
end
```

The output of this code will be:

```
Product: 1
Product: 2
Product: 3
Product: 4
Product: 5
Skip even number: 2
Product: 3
Product: 6
Product: 9
Product too large, breaking inner loop at i=3, j=4
Product: 4
Product: 8
Product too large, breaking inner loop at i=4, j=3
Product: 5
Product: 10
Product too large, breaking inner loop at i=5, j=3
```

In this example, the outer loop skips even numbers using continue. The inner loop multiplies i by j and prints the product unless it exceeds 10, in which case it breaks the inner loop.

Overall, the break and continue statements significantly enhance control over loop operations by providing mechanisms to exit loops early or skip iterations. This control, when leveraged appropriately, leads to more efficient and readable code implementations.

3.8 Using Iterators and Generators

Iterators and generators provide a powerful way to traverse through elements of collections and generate sequences on the fly without precomputing the entire sequence in memory. Julia supports both built-in iterables and user-defined iterators and generators to enhance efficiency and readability in handling sequences.

Iterators in Julia are objects that allow the programmer to iterate over collections like arrays, dictionaries, or ranges. The iteration protocol in Julia consists of three core functions: iterate, start, and done. However, most iterators only require the iterate function, which returns a tuple of the form (item, state) or nothing if the iteration is complete. Let's examine an example:

```
struct Counter
    start::Int
    stop::Int
end

function Base.iterate(counter::Counter, state=counter.start)
    state > counter.stop ? nothing : (state, state + 1)
end
```

Here, we define a simple custom iterator Counter, which counts from start to stop. We implement the iterate function to handle the iteration logic.

```
julia> for i in Counter(1, 5)
           println(i)
       end
1
2
3
4
5
```

Generators are expressions that allow the creation of iterables in a straightforward manner. In Julia, generator expressions resemble comprehensions and provide a lazy way to generate iterables. Unlike list comprehensions, they do not immediately compute the elements. Generators are defined using a similar syntax to comprehensions but in parentheses.

```
gen = (2*i for i in 1:5)
```

This generator will lazily generate multiples of 2 for the range 1 to 5. To retrieve elements, you can use methods like collect to materialize the generator into an array or iterate through it.

```
julia> collect(gen)
5-element Vector{Int64}:
  2
  4
  6
  8
 10
```

Chaining Iterators and Generators can be achieved through the Base.Iterators module. This allows combining multiple iterators to create complex iteration patterns. Consider the product of two ranges:

```
using Base.Iterators
prod = Iterators.product(1:2, 3:4)
```

```
julia> for (i, j) in prod
           println((i, j))
       end
(1, 3)
(1, 4)
(2, 3)
(2, 4)
```

Julia's IterTools package extends the functionalities of iterators with additional methods for more sophisticated iteration patterns such as IterTools.flatten, IterTools.groupby, etc.

Example Algorithm: Generating Primes

Next, we illustrate the implementation of an iterator that generates prime numbers up to a given number using the Sieve of Eratosthenes algorithm:

Algorithm 1: Prime Number Generator using the Sieve of Eratosthenes

Input: An integer n
Output: Primes up to n

```
is_prime ← trues(n+1);
for i ← 2 to √n do
    if is_prime[i] then
        for j ← i*i to $n$ by i do
            is_prime[j] ← false;
for k in 2:$n$ do
    if is_prime[k] then
        yield(k)
```

The iterator version of this algorithm in Julia:

```
struct Primes
    n::Int
end

function Base.iterate(primes::Primes, state=2)
    sieve = trues(primes.n)
    for i in 2:floor(Int, sqrt(primes.n))
        if sieve[i]
            for j in i*i:primes.n:i
                sieve[j] = false
            end
        end
    end
    while state <= primes.n
        sieve[state] && return (state, state + 1)
        state += 1
    end
    return nothing
end
```

This custom iterator leverages the Sieve of Eratosthenes to efficiently generate prime numbers up to a given integer n.

```
julia> for prime in Primes(20)
           println(prime)
       end
2
3
5
7
11
13
17
19
```

Iterators and generators in Julia enable efficient, memory-optimized sequence handling, crucial for developing algorithms and manipulating large datasets. Understanding and implementing these constructs can significantly enhance the efficiency and readability of Julia programs, especially when dealing with iterative and repetitive tasks.

3.9 Controlling Scope and Variable Visibility

In Julia, the scope of a variable determines its visibility and lifetime within the code. Understanding variable scope is fundamental for writing robust and error-free programs. Julia has several types of scopes, including global, local, and module scope. This section delves into the rules and best practices for managing variable scope and visibility in Julia.

Global Scope refers to the top level of a Julia session or module. Variables declared at this level are accessible throughout the entire session or module. However, a variable within a function does not, by default, modify a global variable with the same name unless explicitly instructed using the global keyword. Consider the following example:

```
x = 10 # Global variable

function modify_global()
    global x # Indicating that x refers to the global variable
    x = 20
end

modify_global()
println(x) # This will print 20
```

Without the global keyword, Julia treats variables within a function as local by default, meaning the changes wouldn't affect the global variable:

```
x = 10 # Global variable

function modify_local()
    x = 20 # Local to the function
end

modify_local()
println(x) # This will print 10
```

Local Scope is typically introduced within functions or by using certain control constructs such as loops or comprehensions. Variables declared in a local scope are not accessible outside of that scope. For example:

```
function calculate()
    local_var = 30
    println(local_var) # Accessible within the function
end

calculate()
# println(local_var) # This would throw an error because local_var is not defined in
      this scope
```

In addition to functions, Julia uses local scopes in constructs like loops and comprehensions:

```
for i in 1:5
    local_var = i
    println(local_var) # Accessible within this loop iteration
end
# println(local_var) # This would throw an error because local_var is not defined in
      this scope
```

Nested local scopes arise when scopes are further divided, such as within a nested function or nested loop. The innermost local scope can access variables from its enclosing scopes:

```
function outer_function()
    outer_var = 100
    function inner_function()
        inner_var = 200
        return outer_var + inner_var # Can access outer_var from the enclosing scope
    end
    return inner_function()
end

println(outer_function()) # This will print 300
```

Module Scope encompasses variables and functions defined within a module. By encapsulating code in modules, you can manage and control the scope of variables more systematically. To access variables from another module, you may need to import the module or use its qualifying name:

```
module SampleModule
export var_a, get_var

var_a = 42

function get_var()
    return var_a
end
end

using .SampleModule
println(SampleModule.get_var()) # This will print 42
```

`let` Block also introduces a new scope, useful for creating temporary variables without affecting the outer scope:

```
x = 50

let
    x = 88 # Local to the let block
    println(x) # This will print 88
end

println(x) # This will print 50, as the outer scope's x is unaffected
```

Soft Scope primarily pertains to REPL (Read, Eval, Print Loop) and is employed to make interactive sessions more user-friendly. Soft scope permits certain naming and reassignment flexibility that diverges slightly from strict local and global rules. For example:

```
x = 1
for i in 1:3
    x = i # In REPL, this modifies the global x due to soft scope
end

println(x) # Prints 3 in the REPL environment
```

Best Practices for managing scope and variable visibility in Julia include:

- Minimize the use of global variables for better performance and clear code structure.
- Use local variables where possible to avoid unintended side effects.
- Encapsulate related functions and variables within modules to manage scope efficiently.
- Clearly indicate when a function modifies a global variable using the global keyword.

Understanding and controlling scope and variable visibility effectively ensures that your programs are not only efficient but also maintainable and free of unintended side effects.

3.10 Best Practices for Control Flow

To ensure the efficiency, readability, and maintainability of your Julia programs, it is essential to adhere to a set of best practices when dealing with control flow. These practices optimize both performance and clarity, while mitigating potential pitfalls that could arise from improper usage.

1. Simplify Conditions: Strive to write conditions that are easy to read and understand. Use meaningful variable names, and break complex conditions into simpler ones. Consider the following example:

```
# Complex condition
if (age > 18 && age < 30) && (income > 50000 || education == "Master")

# Simplified conditions
isAgeAppropriate = (age > 18) && (age < 30)
isIncomeSufficient = income > 50000
isEducationSufficient = education == "Master"
if isAgeAppropriate && (isIncomeSufficient || isEducationSufficient)
```

2. Leverage Short-Circuit Evaluation: Julia's logical operators && and || use short-circuit evaluation. This means that evaluation stops as soon as the result is determined. Utilize this feature to prevent unnecessary computations or potential errors:

```
# Avoid unnecessary computation
if (denominator != 0) && (numerator / denominator > threshold)
    # Safe division
end

# Prevent error by checking if the element exists before accessing
if (index <= length(array)) && (array[index] == value)
    # Safe access
end
```

3. Embrace Comprehensions Where Appropriate: List comprehensions in Julia offer a more concise and readable way to create collections as compared to traditional loops. Use comprehensions when they make your code clearer:

```
# Using 'for' loops
squares = []
for i in 1:10
    push!(squares, i^2)
end

# Using comprehensions
squares = [i^2 for i in 1:10]
```

4. Use Explicit else and elseif: Explicitly specifying else and elseif branches can make the control flow more comprehensive and easier to understand:

```
# Use 'else' to handle all other cases
if x > 0
    println("positive")
elseif x < 0
    println("negative")
```

```
else
    println("zero")
end
```

5. Handle Exceptions Appropriately: Exception handling is crucial in ensuring robust programs. Use try, catch, and finally constructs to manage exceptions effectively and clean up resources:

```
try
    # Code that might throw an exception
    result = risky_computation()
catch e
    # Handle the error
    println("An error occurred: ", e)
finally
    # Cleanup code
    close(resource)
end
```

6. Avoid Deep Nesting: Deeply nested control structures can significantly reduce the readability of your code. Refactor nested conditions by separating logic into functions or using early returns:

```
# Deep nesting
function complex_function(x)
    if x > 0
        if x < 10
            println("x is positive and less than 10")
        end
    end
end

# Refactor with early return
function complex_function(x)
    if x <= 0
        return
    end

    if x < 10
        println("x is positive and less than 10")
    end
end
```

7. Comment Wisely: While comments are helpful, they should not state the obvious. Instead, use comments to explain the rationale behind non-trivial decisions or intricate details:

```
# Correct
# Check if x is within a specific range
if 1 <= x <= 10
    println("x is in the range of 1 to 10")
end

# Incorrect
# Check if x is greater than or equal to 1 and less than or equal to 10
if 1 <= x <= 10
    println("x is in the range of 1 to 10")
```

```
end
```

8. Consistent Indentation and Naming Conventions: Maintain consistent indentation and use a naming convention that enhances readability. Follow Julia's style guide whenever possible:

```
# Consistent indentation and naming
function process_data(input_data)
    if isempty(input_data)
        return "No data to process"
    end

    processed_data = [x^2 for x in input_data if x > 0]
    return processed_data
end
```

By implementing these best practices, you can enhance both the performance and legibility of your Julia code, leading to programs that are easier to understand, maintain, and extend.

Chapter 4

Functions and Methods

This chapter introduces the concepts of defining and using functions in Julia, covering simple function definitions, function arguments and parameters, and multiple dispatch and method overloading. It includes discussions on anonymous and nested functions, higher-order functions, and variable scope within functions. The chapter also explores recursive functions, built-in functions and utilities, performance considerations, and best practices for writing efficient and maintainable functions in Julia.

4.1 Defining Simple Functions

In Julia, functions are fundamental building blocks that encapsulate a series of instructions to perform specific tasks. Understanding how to define and use functions effectively is pivotal for writing efficient and maintainable code.

To define a simple function in Julia, the function keyword is utilized, followed by the function name, its parameters in parentheses, and the function body enclosed in a {}. The function concludes with the end keyword. Let's consider a basic example of a function that takes two numbers as parameters and returns their sum:

```
function add_numbers(a, b)
    return a + b
end
```

The add_numbers function is now defined and can be called using:

```
result = add_numbers(5, 3)
println(result) # Outputs: 8
```

The return statement is used to output a value from the function. If return is omitted, Julia automatically returns the value of the last evaluated expression. For instance:

```
function multiply_numbers(a, b)
    a * b
end
```

Calling this function as multiply_numbers(4, 2) will return 8, because the result of a * b is implicitly returned.

Julia supports flexible function definitions. Functions can accept an arbitrary number of parameters, including optional and keyword parameters:

Optional Parameters: Optional parameters are specified with default values. For example:

```
function greet(name, greeting="Hello")
    println("$greeting, $name!")
end

greet("Alice") # Outputs: Hello, Alice!
greet("Bob", "Hi") # Outputs: Hi, Bob!
```

Here, "Hello" is the default value for the greeting parameter. If no second argument is passed when calling the function, "Hello" is used. Otherwise, the provided argument is utilized.

Keyword Parameters: Keyword parameters are specified with a semicolon before the list of parameters:

```
function describe_person(name; age=nothing, occupation=nothing)
    description = "Name: $name"
    if age != nothing
        description *= ", Age: $age"
    end
    if occupation != nothing
        description *= ", Occupation: $occupation"
    end
    println(description)
end

describe_person("Charlie", age=25, occupation="Engineer")
# Outputs: Name: Charlie, Age: 25, Occupation: Engineer
```

In this example, age and occupation are keyword parameters with default values of nothing. They can be optionally specified when calling the function.

Multiple Return Values: Julia functions can return multiple values using the unrestricted tuple data structure. This is particularly useful for functions that need to return several pieces of related information:

```
function divide_and_remainder(a, b)
    quotient = div(a, b)
    remainder = rem(a, b)
    return quotient, remainder
end

q, r = divide_and_remainder(10, 3)
println("Quotient: $q, Remainder: $r")
# Outputs: Quotient: 3, Remainder: 1
```

Here, divide_and_remainder returns both the quotient and remainder of the division, which can be unpacked into q and r respectively.

Passing Functions as Arguments

Julia allows functions to be passed as arguments to other functions. This capability enables higher-order functions and promotes code reusability and functional programming paradigms.

```
function apply_operation(f, x, y)
    return f(x, y)
end

result = apply_operation(add_numbers, 10, 15)
println(result) # Outputs: 25
```

In this instance, the function apply_operation takes another function f as an argument and applies it to the parameters x and y.

Anonymous Functions

Functions do not need to be named explicitly. Anonymous functions can be defined inline using the -> operator:

```
square = x -> x^2
println(square(4)) # Outputs: 16
```

The anonymous function x -> x2 takes x and computes its square.

Function Documentation

Documenting functions is a good practice for maintaining clarity and usability. Julia provides a convenient way to add documentation strings using triple double quotes:

```
"""
    add_numbers(a, b)

Add two numbers and return their sum.
"""
function add_numbers(a, b)
    return a + b
end
```

The documentation string precedes the function definition, and tools like Julia's REPL can display this information using the ? operator:

```
?add_numbers
# Displays:
# add_numbers(a, b)
#
# Add two numbers and return their sum.
```

Properly defining functions in Julia allows for the creation of reusable, modular, and maintainable code. Function definitions are not limited to the examples provided here, as Julia's flexible syntax accommodates various advanced function features, encouraging the development of sophisticated software solutions.

4.2 Function Arguments and Parameters

Julia provides versatile mechanisms for defining function arguments and parameters, facilitating the creation of flexible and reusable code. Understanding these mechanisms is crucial to leveraging the full power of the language. The key aspects to cover include positional arguments, keyword arguments, optional and variadic arguments, as well as handling variable scope within functions.

Positional Arguments

Positional arguments are the most straightforward to use. These arguments are passed to the function in the order in which they are defined. Consider the following example:

```
function add(a, b)
    return a + b
end
```

In this example, a and b are positional arguments. When calling add(3, 5), the function will return 8.

Positional arguments are useful when the number of arguments is fixed and order-dependent.

Keyword Arguments

Keyword arguments provide more flexibility, allowing the caller to specify arguments by name. These are defined using a semicolon in the function definition. For example:

```
function greet(name; greeting="Hello")
    println("$(greeting), $(name)!")
end
```

Here, greeting is a keyword argument with a default value of "Hello". The caller can override this value by passing a different value for greeting. When calling greet("Alice"), the output will be:

```
Hello, Alice!
```

If called with greet("Alice", greeting="Hi"), the output will be:

```
Hi, Alice!
```

Optional Arguments

Julia allows for optional arguments by providing default values in the function definition. Optional arguments enable functions to handle different numbers of inputs without overloading. Define an optional argument by assigning it a default value within the function's parameter list. For example:

```
function divide(x, y=1)
    return x / y
end
```

In this case, y is an optional argument with a default value of 1. Calling divide(10) will return 10, whereas calling divide(10, 2) will return 5.

Variadic Arguments

Variadic functions can accept a variable number of arguments. These are indicated by three dots ... in the function definition. The arguments are then collected into a tuple. For instance:

```
function sum_all(args...)
    total = 0
    for num in args
```

```
        total += num
    end
    return total
end
```

Calling sum_all(1, 2, 3, 4) will return 10. Variadic arguments allow for flexible function interfaces without requiring explicit overloading for every possible number of arguments.

Combining Different Types of Arguments

Julia supports combining positional, keyword, optional, and variadic arguments within the same function. Take the following example:

```
function complex_function(a, b; c=3, d=4, args...)
    println("Positional arguments: a=$(a), b=$(b)")
    println("Keyword arguments: c=$(c), d=$(d)")
    println("Variadic arguments: args=$(args)")
end
```

Calling complex_function(1, 2, e=5, f=6, 7, 8) will result in an error because keyword arguments must be named correctly and variadic arguments must follow all positional and keyword arguments.

To properly call the function, ensure all arguments respect their types:

```
complex_function(1, 2, c=5, d=6, 7, 8)
```

This call will output:

```
Positional arguments: a=1, b=2
Keyword arguments: c=5, d=6
Variadic arguments: args=(7, 8)
```

Handling Variable Scope in Functions

Variable scope determines the accessibility of variables within functions. Julia distinguishes between local scope, where variables are accessible only within the block in which they are defined, and global scope, where variables are accessible throughout the module.

Variables in function definitions are locally scoped by default. Local variables are not affected by variables in the global scope, ensuring function encapsulation and reducing side effects. Consider:

```
x = 10

function test_scope()
    x = 5
    println("Inside function: x=$(x)")
end
```

```
test_scope()
println("Outside function: x=$(x)")
```

This will produce:

```
Inside function: x=5
Outside function: x=10
```

This illustrates that the variable x inside test_scope is local and does not affect the global variable x.

Using the global keyword inside a function can alter global variables. For example:

```
function modify_global()
    global x = 20
end

modify_global()
println("Modified global: x=$(x)")
```

This will change the value of x in the global scope, producing:

```
Modified global: x=20
```

Care should be taken when using global variables, as it can lead to unintended side-effects, complicating the debugging process.

Understanding the various types of function arguments and parameters empowers the programmer to write more flexible and robust Julia code. By mastering these concepts, one can efficiently handle a variety of invocation patterns, creating clear, maintainable, and reusable functions.

4.3 Multiple Dispatch and Method Overloading

One of the most powerful features of Julia is its support for multiple dispatch, which allows the selection of a method to be based on the types of all its arguments, not just the first one. This is a significant departure from single dispatch systems, where the method to be executed is determined by the type of one (usually the first) argument or by the object's class or interface. Multiple dispatch makes Julia particularly adept at mathematical programming and other domains requiring complex polymorphic behavior.

Defining Methods with Multiple Dispatch

In Julia, function definitions can be overloaded, meaning you can define multiple methods for the same function name but with different argument types. The appropriate method to call is dispatched based on the types of all arguments. Consider the following set of function definitions:

```
function area(shape::Circle)
    return * shape.radius^2
end

function area(shape::Rectangle)
    return shape.length * shape.width
end

function area(shape::Triangle)
    return 0.5 * shape.base * shape.height
end
```

Each of these methods calculates the area of a different geometric shape. Julia will automatically choose the correct method to call based on the type of the shape provided. This mechanism simplifies code maintenance and extension, as new methods can be added without modifying existing ones.

Method Dispatch Rules

Julia follows a specific set of rules to determine which method to execute:

- Methods with more specific type annotations take precedence over those with more general ones.
- If there is a tie (i.e., multiple methods match equally well), Julia will raise an ambiguity error, prompting you to define a more specific method to resolve the ambiguity.
- Type parameters can be used within function signatures to further refine method dispatch criteria.

To illustrate, consider the following example that highlights dispatch based on type specificity:

```
function describe(x::Int)
    return "This is an integer."
end

function describe(x::Number)
    return "This is a number."
end
```

```
function describe(x::AbstractString)
    return "This is a string."
end
```

For an input of type Int, Julia will invoke describe(x::Int). If an argument of type Float64 (a subtype of Number) is provided, describe(x::Number) is called. Similarly, for a String argument, describe(x::AbstractString) is selected. This hierarchical organization simplifies reasoning about code behavior and allows sophisticated method specialization.

Method Overloading

In Julia, method overloading refers to defining multiple methods for the same function name but with differing argument types. Method overloading paired with multiple dispatch enables concise and expressive function definitions. Let us define a function promote_and_add to add numbers while promoting them to a common type:

```
function promote_and_add(x::Int, y::Int)
    return x + y
end

function promote_and_add(x::Int, y::Float64)
    return x + y
end

function promote_and_add(x::Float64, y::Float64)
    return x + y
end
```

Here, promote_and_add is overloaded to handle various combinations of integer and floating-point arguments. Julia's type promotion rules implicitly convert values to a common type when necessary to maximize compatibility and minimize data loss.

Performance Implications of Multiple Dispatch

While multiple dispatch enhances flexibility and capability, it also has performance implications. Julia's Just-In-Time (JIT) compiler utilizes type information available at runtime to generate specialized, efficient code for each method. As a result, method dispatch incurs minimal overhead compared to traditional interpreted languages or virtual machines. However, frequent type checks or complex dispatch hierarchies can introduce overhead, somewhat offsetting the benefits of JIT optimization.

Profiling tools, such as @time and @profiles, facilitate performance tuning by providing insights into time spent in method dispatch versus actual execution:

```
@time result = area(Circle(5.0))
@profile describe(42)
```

Analyzing such profiles helps identify bottlenecks attributable to dispatch and allows judicious use of type annotations and simpler dispatch paths.

Effective use of multiple dispatch and method overloading involves balancing flexibility with performance. Leveraging Julia's dispatch mechanism judiciously can lead to clean, maintainable, and highly performant code, especially in domains requiring rich polymorphism and complex type behavior.

4.4 Anonymous and Nested Functions

Anonymous functions, also known as lambda functions, and nested functions are powerful features in Julia that allow for more flexible code structuring and functional programming. Anonymous functions are particularly useful for short-lived operations, while nested functions aid in encapsulating functionality and maintaining cleaner scope.

Anonymous functions in Julia are defined using the syntax (parameters) -> expression. For instance, an anonymous function that calculates the square of a number can be written as follows:

```
square = x -> x^2
```

You can then call this function like any other function:

```
result = square(5)
```

25

Alternatively, if the function needs multiple parameters, they can be specified inside parentheses:

```
add = (x, y) -> x + y
```

This function can be called with two arguments to compute their sum:

```
sum_result = add(3, 7)
```

10

Anonymous functions are highly practical when used in higher-order functions. A common scenario is passing a lambda function to functions like map and filter. For example:

```
squared_list = map(x -> x^2, [1, 2, 3, 4])
```

The above code will apply the squaring operation to each element in the list:

```
[1, 4, 9, 16]
```

Regarding nested functions, they are defined within other functions and are locally scoped to their containing function. Consider the following example:

```
function outer_function(x)
    function inner_function(y)
        return x + y
    end
    return inner_function
end
```

In this case, inner_function is defined within outer_function and has access to the variables of outer_function. You can assign the returned inner_function to another variable and invoke it:

```
nested = outer_function(10)
result = nested(5)
```

Nested functions have the advantage of lexical scoping, meaning the inner function can access variables from its enclosing function. This behavior allows for the creation of closures, where the inner function captures variables from its environment:

```
function make_multiplier(factor)
    return x -> x * factor
end

quadruple = make_multiplier(4)
result = quadruple(5)
```

In this example, the anonymous function x -> x * factor captures the factor variable from make_multiplier, creating a closure that multiplies its input by 4.

Using nested functions can improve code organization by dividing complex functions into smaller, self-contained sub-functions. For instance:

```
function complex_calculation(a, b)
    function intermediate_step1(x, y)
        return x + y
```

```
    end
    function intermediate_step2(z)
        return z * 2
    end
    step1_result = intermediate_step1(a, b)
    final_result = intermediate_step2(step1_result)
    return final_result
end
```

Calling complex_calculation with two arguments will proceed through the nested functions:

```
complex_result = complex_calculation(3, 7)
```

20

By structuring the code this way, each intermediate step is encapsulated, making the complex_calculation function easier to understand and maintain.

When combining anonymous and nested functions, you can dynamically create functions within other functions. For instance:

```
function combined_example(x)
    return (y -> x + y) # Returns an anonymous function
end

combined_func = combined_example(10)
result = combined_func(7)
```

17

This example demonstrates defining an anonymous function inside another function while utilizing the outer function's variable.

Anonymous and nested functions are crucial elements for creating efficient, readable, and maintainable Julia programs. Leveraging these features allows developers to write more modular and expressive code. As you advance in your understanding of Julia, integrating these functions seamlessly into your programming toolkit will enhance both the functionality and clarity of your projects.

4.5 Higher-Order Functions

A higher-order function is one that takes other functions as arguments or returns a function as its result. This concept is central in functional programming paradigms and is supported robustly by the Julia language. Higher-order functions provide a powerful way to compose behaviors and abstract common patterns of computation.

Function as Argument

In Julia, you can pass a function as an argument to another function. Here is a simple example:

```
# Define a function that applies a given function to all elements of an array
function apply_function(arr::Vector{T}, func::Function) where T
    return [func(x) for x in arr]
end

# Define a specific function to be passed as an argument
square(x) = x^2

# Use the apply_function with the square function
result = apply_function([1, 2, 3, 4], square)
```

Executing the code above will produce the following output:

```
4-element Vector{Int64}:
  1
  4
  9
 16
```

In this example, apply_function is a higher-order function that takes an array and another function as arguments, applies the function to each element of the array, and returns a new array containing the results.

Returning Functions

A function in Julia can also return another function. This is typically used to create customized functions.

```
# Define a function that returns another function
function multiplier(factor::Number)
    return x -> x * factor
end

# Obtain a new function that multiplies by 3
times_three = multiplier(3)

# Use the new function
result = times_three(10)
```

On execution, the output will be:

```
30
```

Here, the multiplier function generates a new function that multiplies its input by the specified factor. The returned function is then applied to the number 10, yielding 30.

Common Higher-Order Functions

Julia has many built-in higher-order functions. Some of the most commonly used ones include map, filter, and reduce.

Map

The map function takes a function and a collection and applies the function to each item in the collection.

```
# Use the map function to square all elements in the array
map(square, [1, 2, 3, 4])
```

This will produce:

```
4-element Vector{Int64}:
 1
 4
 9
 16
```

Filter

The filter function selects elements from a collection that satisfy a condition defined by a function.

```
# Filter even numbers in the array
filter(x -> x % 2 == 0, [1, 2, 3, 4, 5, 6])
```

This will result in:

```
3-element Vector{Int64}:
 2
 4
 6
```

Reduce

The reduce function applies a binary function to reduce a collection to a single value.

```
# Reduce array by summing all elements
reduce(+, [1, 2, 3, 4])
```

The output will be:

```
10
```

Combining Higher-Order Functions

Higher-order functions can be combined to perform more complex operations in a concise manner. Consider the task of first filtering out even numbers and then squaring the remaining numbers.

```
# Combine filter and map functions
result = map(square, filter(x -> x % 2 != 0, [1, 2, 3, 4, 5, 6]))
```

Executing this will yield:

```
3-element Vector{Int64}:
 1
 9
 25
```

filter selects the odd numbers, and map squares them.

Anonymous Functions

Anonymous functions, also known as lambda functions, are often used as arguments in higher-order functions for their brevity and clarity.

```
# Use an anonymous function in map
result = map(x -> x^2, [1, 2, 3, 4])
```

This produces:

```
4-element Vector{Int64}:
 1
 4
 9
 16
```

By using an anonymous function, you avoid the need to define a separate function like square explicitly.

Performance Considerations

When working with higher-order functions, it's crucial to be mindful of performance, especially in a high-performance language like Julia. Function barriers and type stability are key considerations. Using concrete types and avoiding excessive allocations can help maintain performance.

```
# Ensure type stability by specifying types for higher-order functions
function apply_function(arr::Vector{Int64}, func::Function)::Vector{Int64}
    return [func(x) for x in arr]
end

# Example usage
result = apply_function([1, 2, 3, 4], x -> x^2)
```

Type annotations can help the Julia compiler optimize the code and detect type instabilities, leading to more efficient execution.

By understanding and effectively using higher-order functions, you can write more abstract, reusable, and expressive code, harnessing the full power of Julia's functional programming capabilities.

4.6 Variable Scope in Functions

Understanding variable scope within functions is crucial for avoiding unexpected behavior and ensuring the correctness of your code. In Julia, variables have different scopes depending on where they are declared and used. These scopes mainly include global scope, local scope, and non-local or nested scopes, which can influence how variables are accessed and modified within functions.

At the core, Julia distinguishes between global and local scopes.

Global scope refers to the scope that exists throughout the entire program or interactive session. Variables declared in the global scope are accessible from anywhere within the program.

Local scope refers to the scope within blocks of code such as function bodies, loops, conditionals, etc. Variables declared in local scope are only accessible within the block where they are declared.

```
x = 10 # global scope

function sampleFunction()
    y = 5 # local scope
    println("Inside function, y = $y")
end

sampleFunction()
println("Outside function, x = $x")
```

```
Inside function, y = 5
Outside function, x = 10
```

In the example above, x is defined in the global scope and y is defined in the local scope of the function sampleFunction(). The variable y is not accessible outside the function, which illustrates the isolation provided by local scope.

Local Scope in Functions

When a variable is declared within a function, it's generally only accessible within that function. This local scope allows you to reuse variable names without worrying about conflicts with variables defined outside the function.

```
z = 20

function anotherFunction()
    z = 30 # this z is local to anotherFunction
    println("Inside anotherFunction, z = $z")
end

anotherFunction()
```

```
println("Outside anotherFunction, z = $z")
```

Inside anotherFunction, z = 30
Outside anotherFunction, z = 20

Here, z inside anotherFunction is local to that function and does not affect the global variable z.

Modifying Global Variables

To modify a global variable within a function, Julia requires explicit declaration using the global keyword. By default, reassigning a global variable within a function creates a local variable instead.

```
a = 100

function modifyGlobal()
    global a = 200
    println("Inside modifyGlobal, a = $a")
end

modifyGlobal()
println("Outside modifyGlobal, a = $a")
```

Inside modifyGlobal, a = 200
Outside modifyGlobal, a = 200

Without the global keyword, the modification to a would only affect a local copy of a within the function.

Nested and Non-local Scopes

Julia also supports nested local scopes, where inner functions or blocks can access variables from their enclosing scopes, referred to as non-local scopes. This enables the creation of closures and higher-order functions with access to variables outside of their immediate local scope.

```
function outerFunction()
    outerVar = 10

    function innerFunction()
        println("Inner function can access outerVar = $outerVar")
    end

    innerFunction()
end

outerFunction()
```

Inner function can access outerVar = 10

In this example, innerFunction is able to access outerVar from outerFunction's scope, demonstrating the concept of non-local scope.

Scope in Loops and Conditional Blocks

Loops and conditional blocks define their own local scopes as well. Variables declared in for-loops, while-loops, and if-statements are local to those blocks.

```
for i = 1:3
    blockVar = i
    println("blockVar inside loop = $blockVar")
end

# blockVar is not accessible here
```

```
blockVar inside loop = 1
blockVar inside loop = 2
blockVar inside loop = 3
```

Trying to access blockVar outside the loop would result in an error since it's local to the loop block.

Performance Considerations

Understanding variable scope is not only important for correctness but also for performance. Inappropriate use of global variables in perfomance-critical code sections can lead to significant slowdowns because global variables are subject to type instability. Local variables, on the other hand, are more optimized in compiled code due to their predictable scope.

The following is an example illustrating poor performance due to the use of a global variable:

```
global b = 0

function sumGlobal(n)
    for i = 1:n
        global b += i
    end
    return b
end

@time sumGlobal(10^6)
```

To mitigate this, avoiding global variables or making use of local variables within functions is recommended. Alternate approach can be:

```
function sumLocal(n)
    local sum = 0
    for i = 1:n
        sum += i
    end
    return sum
end

@time sumLocal(10^6)
```

Appropriate use of variable scopes ensures efficient, maintainable, and correct coding practices in Julia.

4.7 Recursive Functions

A recursive function is a function that calls itself in order to solve a problem. In Julia, recursion can be a powerful tool for solving problems that can be broken down into smaller, identical problems. Recursive functions often provide elegant and straightforward solutions, particularly for problems related to sequences, such as the computation of factorials and Fibonacci numbers.

The definition of a recursive function typically involves two parts:

- **Base Case:** The condition under which the function stops calling itself. This prevents infinite recursion and provides the simplest, smallest instance of the problem that can be solved directly.
- **Recursive Case:** The part of the function where the function calls itself with a modified argument, moving towards the base case.

Consider the classic example of computing the factorial of a non-negative integer n. The mathematical definition of factorial $n!$ is:

$$n! = \begin{cases} 1 & \text{if } n = 0 \\ n \times (n-1)! & \text{if } n > 0 \end{cases}$$

In Julia, the recursive definition of the factorial function can be written as follows:

```
function factorial(n::Int)
    if n == 0
        return 1
    else
        return n * factorial(n - 1)
    end
end
```

When $\text{factorial}(5)$ is called, the computation proceeds as:

$$\begin{aligned} &5 \times factorial(4) \rightarrow 5 \times (4 \times factorial(3)) \\ &\rightarrow 5 \times (4 \times (3 \times factorial(2))) \\ &\rightarrow 5 \times (4 \times (3 \times (2 \times factorial(1)))) \\ &\rightarrow 5 \times (4 \times (3 \times (2 \times (1 \times factorial(0))))) \end{aligned}$$

Finally, $\text{factorial}(0)$ returns 1, and the entire computation resolves to $5 \times 4 \times 3 \times 2 \times 1 = 120$. The complete call stack unwinds, providing the final result of 120.

Another common example of recursion is calculating Fibonacci numbers. The Fibonacci sequence is defined as:

$$F(n) = \begin{cases} 0 & \text{if } n = 0 \\ 1 & \text{if } n = 1 \\ F(n-1) + F(n-2) & \text{if } n > 1 \end{cases}$$

The corresponding recursive function in Julia is:

```
function fibonacci(n::Int)
    if n == 0
        return 0
    elseif n == 1
        return 1
    else
        return fibonacci(n-1) + fibonacci(n-2)
    end
end
```

Despite its clarity, the above implementation is inefficient due to repeated calculations. For example, $\text{fibonacci}(5)$ requires the computation of $\text{fibonacci}(4)$ and $\text{fibonacci}(3)$, but $\text{fibonacci}(4)$ also requires $\text{fibonacci}(3)$ and $\text{fibonacci}(2)$, leading to redundant calculations of $\text{fibonacci}(3)$ and smaller values multiple times.

To optimize this, we can use memoization, a technique where we store previously computed values to avoid redundant computations. In Julia, this can be done using a dictionary:

```
function fibonacci(n::Int, memo=Dict{Int, Int}())
    if haskey(memo, n)
        return memo[n]
    elseif n == 0
        result = 0
    elseif n == 1
        result = 1
    else
        result = fibonacci(n-1, memo) + fibonacci(n-2, memo)
    end
    memo[n] = result
    return result
end
```

With memoization, the function only computes each Fibonacci number once, significantly improving performance.

It is essential to recognize scenarios where recursive solutions can lead to performance bottlenecks, especially with deep recursion that might lead to stack overflow errors or excessive memory use. When dealing with such scenarios, iterative solutions or other optimization techniques like tail recursion can be considered.

Tail recursion is a specific form of recursion where the recursive call is the last operation in the function. Julia can optimize tail-recursive functions to prevent excessive stack growth. Rewriting the factorial function using tail recursion ensures better performance for large inputs:

```
function factorial_tail(n::Int, acc::Int=1)
    if n == 0
        return acc
    else
        return factorial_tail(n-1, n*acc)
    end
end
```

In this tail-recursive version of the factorial function, the accumulator acc carries the result through recursive calls, and the recursion is the final operation within the function. This enables Julia's compiler to optimize tail calls, maintaining a constant stack size.

Recursive functions are powerful and expressive for various computational problems, allowing elegant and concise implementations when used appropriately.

4.8 Built-in Functions and Function Utilities

Julia comes equipped with a comprehensive suite of built-in functions and utilities that streamline the development process. These built-in functions encompass a wide range of operations, from mathematical computations to data manipulation, enhancing both the functionality and readability of your code.

```
# Example of basic built-in mathematical functions
x = abs(-5) # Absolute value: x equals 5
y = sqrt(16) # Square root: y equals 4.0
z = log(2.71828) # Natural logarithm: z approximately equals 1.0
```

The abs function returns the absolute value of its argument. The sqrt function computes the square root, while the log function computes the natural logarithm. These basic mathematical functions are highly optimized for performance.

Julia also includes functions for number-theoretic operations, as shown below.

```
# Example of number-theoretic functions
a = gcd(24, 36) # Greatest common divisor: a equals 12
b = lcm(24, 36) # Least common multiple: b equals 72
c = lcm([24, 36, 48]) # LCM of an array: c equals 144
```

Here, gcd computes the greatest common divisor, and lcm computes the least common multiple. These functions are useful in various mathematical and engineering applications.

Beyond mathematical functions, Julia's built-in functions also support robust data manipulation. Consider the following examples:

```
# Example of data manipulation functions
data = [1, 3, 2, 4]
sorted_data = sort(data) # Sorting: sorted_data equals [1, 2, 3, 4]
reversed_data = reverse(data) # Reversing: reversed_data equals [4, 2, 3, 1]
```

The sort function arranges the elements of an array in ascending order, while the reverse function reverses the order of the array. These operations are fundamental in data pre-processing and manipulation tasks.

Function utilities in Julia often provide enhanced flexibility for handling various data types. An example is the map function, which applies a given function to all elements of a collection:

```
# Applying a function to each element of an array
squared_data = map(x -> x^2, data) # squared_data equals [1, 9, 4, 16]
```

Here, map applies the lambda function x -> x^2 to each element in data. This concise expression showcases how higher-order functions can be leveraged for efficient data transformation.

Utilities such as filter and reduce also play a crucial role in functional programming paradigms within Julia:

```
# Filtering based on a condition
filtered_data = filter(x -> x % 2 == 0, data) # filtered_data equals [2, 4]

# Reducing to a single value
sum_data = reduce(+, data) # sum_data equals 10
```

The filter function selects elements of an array that satisfy a given predicate, whereas reduce combines elements using a specified binary operation, such as addition. These utilities support expressive and concise code.

Additional built-in functions contribute to string manipulation and parsing:

```
# Example of string manipulation functions
```

```
s = "Hello, World!"
uppercase_s = uppercase(s) # Uppercasing: uppercase_s equals "HELLO, WORLD!"
lowercase_s = lowercase(s) # Lowercasing: lowercase_s equals "hello, world!"
substring_s = s[1:5] # Substring: substring_s equals "Hello"
```

Here, the uppercase and lowercase functions convert strings to uppercase and lowercase, respectively. The substring operation efficiently extracts a portion of a string based on specified indices.

File I/O operations are also streamlined by Julia's built-in functions:

```
# Example of file I/O operations
open("example.txt", "w") do file
    write(file, "This is a test file.")
end

content = read("example.txt", String) # Reading the content of the file
```

The open function, used with a do-block, simplifies file writing operations while ensuring that the file is properly closed after the block executes. The read function reads the content of a file, here casting it to a String.

Julia's array comprehension capabilities allow for succinct and expressive creation and transformation of arrays:

```
# Example of array comprehensions
squared_data_comp = [x^2 for x in data] # squared_data_comp equals [1, 9, 4, 16]
filtered_data_comp = [x for x in data if x % 2 == 0] # filtered_data_comp equals [2,
     4]
```

Array comprehensions enable the construction of arrays in a concise manner, integrating transformations and filters directly into their syntax.

Random number generation is another area where Julia offers built-in functions, useful for simulations and algorithm development:

```
# Example of random number generation
using Random

rand_num = rand() # Random number in [0,1): rand_num could be 0.5
rand_int = rand(1:10) # Random integer in 1 through 10: rand_int equals 7
rand_array = rand(1:100, 5) # Array of 5 random integers in 1 through 100:
     rand_array could be [37, 73, 90, 29, 89]
```

The rand function generates random numbers or arrays, crucial for Monte Carlo methods and other probabilistic algorithms.

Several built-in utilities aid in the debugging and optimization of functions:

```
@time fib(10) # Benchmarking the execution time of the function fib
@profile fib(10) # Profiling to collect detailed performance data
```

```
@code_warntype fib(10) # Type checking the compiled code for the function
```

Here, @time measures the execution time, @profile collects performance profiles, and @code_warntype examines type stability, which are invaluable when optimizing functions.

Leveraging Julia's rich set of built-in functions and utilities can greatly enhance productivity and code performance, making them indispensable tools in any developer's toolkit.

4.9 Performance Considerations for Functions

Performance is a critical aspect of programming, especially in high-level languages like Julia that are often used for computationally intensive tasks. Understanding how to write functions that perform efficiently can greatly enhance the overall performance of your program. This section delves into practical techniques to consider when aiming for performance optimization in Julia functions.

Type Declarations and Stability:

A primary method to enhance function performance is the correct use of type declarations. Julia is a dynamically typed language, but specifying types can lead to faster code by enabling the compiler to produce more optimized machine code. Type declarations inform the compiler about the expected types of variables and function arguments, reducing runtime type checks and dispatch overhead.

```
function add(x::Int, y::Int)::Int
    return x + y
end
```

Ensuring type stability—where the type of a function's return value is predictable based on the types of input arguments—is crucial for performance. Type instability can lead to performance losses due to dynamic dispatch and type inference overhead. The @code_warntype macro is useful for diagnosing type stability issues.

```
@code_warntype add(2, 3)
```

```
Variables
  #self#::Core.Const(add)
  x::Int64
  y::Int64

Body::Int64
1  %1 = (x + y)::Int64
        return %1
```

Avoiding Global Variables:

Global variables can significantly slow down Julia code. This is because their types can change at any time, making it difficult for the compiler to optimize. It is advisable to pass variables as function arguments and to avoid modifying global states.

```
# Avoid this
global_sum = 0
function add_to_global_sum(x)
    global global_sum
    global_sum += x
end

# Prefer this
function add_to_sum(sum, x)
    sum += x
    return sum
end
```

In-place Operations:

Memory allocation and garbage collection can be major performance bottlenecks. Using in-place operations, which modify existing arrays or objects rather than creating new ones, can reduce memory overhead and improve speed. In Julia, many built-in functions have in-place variants denoted by a ! at the end of their names.

```
# Regular operation (not in-place)
function add_arrays(arr1, arr2)
    return arr1 + arr2
end

# In-place operation
function add_arrays!(arr1, arr2)
    for i in eachindex(arr1, arr2)
        arr1[i] += arr2[i]
    end
end
```

Loop Optimizations:

Efficiently written loops can significantly enhance performance. Julia's loop structures are highly optimized, but there are a few techniques to maximize their efficiency. Use @inbounds to eliminate bounds checking within loops, and @simd to enable Single Instruction Multiple Data

(SIMD) optimization where possible.

```
function sum_array(arr)
    s = 0
    @inbounds @simd for i in 1:length(arr)
        s += arr[i]
    end
    return s
end
```

Avoiding Unnecessary Allocations:

Preallocating memory for arrays and other data structures can prevent unnecessary memory allocations, thereby speeding up computations. Use techniques like array comprehension and the zeros, ones, or similar functions to create arrays of the desired size beforehand.

```
# Avoid
function compute_sum(arr)
    result = []
    for x in arr
        push!(result, sum(x))
    end
    return result
end

# Prefer
function compute_sum(arr)
    result = Vector{Int}(undef, length(arr))
    for i in 1:length(arr)
        result[i] = sum(arr[i])
    end
    return result
end
```

Profiling and Benchmarking:

To concretely measure the performance impact of your optimizations, use Julia's profiling and benchmarking tools. The @time macro provides a quick measure of execution time and memory allocation. For more detailed performance analysis, the Profile and BenchmarkTools packages are indispensable.

```
using BenchmarkTools

function fibonacci(n)
    if n <= 2
        return 1
    else
        return fibonacci(n-1) + fibonacci(n-2)
    end
end

@benchmark fibonacci(20)
```

```
BenchmarkTools.Trial: 10000 samples with 999 evaluations.
 Range (min … max):   1.932  s … 76.285  s
 Time  (median):      1.980  s
 Time  (mean ± ):     2.015  s ± 0.634  s
 Memory estimate:  208 bytes, allocs estimate: 4
```

These techniques, when judiciously applied, can significantly enhance the performance of functions in Julia, leading to faster and more efficient programs.

4.10 Best Practices for Writing Functions

Effective function development goes beyond writing code that works; it involves creating maintainable, efficient, and robust functions that stand the test of time. This section will delve into the best practices for writing functions in Julia, ensuring that your code is not only correct but also high-quality and professional.

1. Use Descriptive Names: Choosing clear, descriptive names for functions and parameters enhances code readability and maintainability. Avoid abbreviations or single-letter variable names unless they are universally understood. For instance, calculate_mean is better than calcMn.

2. Keep Functions Short and Focused: A function should do one thing and do it well. Functions that are too long or perform multiple tasks can be harder to debug, understand, and maintain. Aim to keep functions focused on a single responsibility. Break down complex tasks into simpler, smaller functions.

3. Leverage Multiple Dispatch: Julia's multiple dispatch is a powerful feature that allows you to define function behaviors for different combinations of argument types. Use type annotations judiciously to leverage this feature. This not only improves performance but also makes the code more explicit and easier to understand. For example:

```
function area(shape::Circle)
    return  * shape.radius^2
end

function area(shape::Rectangle)
    return shape.length * shape.width
end
```

4. Avoid Global Variables: Functions should rely on their inputs rather than external variables to produce outputs. Using global variables can lead to unpredictable behaviors and makes the function harder to test in isolation. Always pass necessary data as function parameters.

5. Handle Errors Gracefully: Proper error handling ensures that functions fail gracefully and provide useful error messages. Use Julia's built-in try/catch blocks to manage exceptions. For example:

```
function safe_divide(a, b)
    try
        return a / b
    catch e
        println("Error: Division by zero is not allowed.")
        return nothing
    end
end
```

6. Document Functions Thoroughly: Good documentation is crucial. Use docstrings to describe the purpose of the function, its parameters, and return values. This aids other developers (or your future self) in understanding and using the function correctly. For example:

```
"""
    max_value(a::Array)

Returns the maximum value in the array `a`.

# Arguments
- `a::Array`: An array of numeric values.

# Returns
- The maximum value in `a`.
"""
function max_value(a::Array)
    return maximum(a)
end
```

7. Write Testable Functions: Design functions to be easily testable. This can be achieved by ensuring functions have well-defined inputs and outputs and by avoiding side-effects. Utilize Julia's Test standard library to create unit tests that verify the correctness of your functions.

```
using Test

@testset "Testing max_value function" begin
    @test max_value([1, 2, 3, 4, 5]) == 5
    @test max_value([-1, -2, -3, -4, -5]) == -1
end
```

8. Optimize for Performance: Performance tuning can significantly affect the efficiency of your functions. Use the @benchmark macro from the BenchmarkTools package to measure performance and identify bottlenecks. Consider type stability and minimizing memory allocations. For example:

```
using BenchmarkTools
```

```
function sum_elements(a::Vector{Int})
    s = 0
    for x in a
        s += x
    end
    return s
end

@benchmark sum_elements([1, 2, 3, 4, 5])
```

9. Follow Consistent Coding Standards: Adopt consistent coding styles and conventions across your codebase. This includes indentation, spacing, and naming conventions. Following good style practices enhances readability and maintainability.

10. Modularize Code: Break down large programs into smaller, reusable modules. Group related functions together logically, and utilize Julia's module system to encapsulate functionality. This encourages code reuse and better organization.

11. Utilize Built-in Functions: Before writing new functions, check if Julia's standard library already provides the functionality. Reusing tested and optimized built-in functions can save time and reduce errors.

By applying these best practices, your functions in Julia will be robust, efficient, and manageable, contributing to high-quality software development.

Chapter 5

Collections and Data Structures

This chapter provides an in-depth look at Julia's collections and data structures, starting with arrays, tuples, and dictionaries. It explores sets and their operations, introduces DataFrames for tabular data, and discusses custom data structures. The chapter also covers multidimensional arrays and matrices, memory management, and iteration over collections. Advanced data structures and best practices for using collections in Julia are also examined, offering a comprehensive guide to efficient data handling.

5.1 Introduction to Collections

In Julia, collections are fundamental data structures that allow for the organization, storage, and manipulation of data. A collection, in its simplest form, is a container that holds multiple elements, which can be of various types. Understanding how to work with collections is crucial for efficient data handling and performance optimization in any computational task. This section introduces the primary types of collections in Julia, including arrays, tuples, dictionaries, and sets. These foundational concepts will be elaborated upon in subsequent sections of this chapter.

An array is one of the most commonly used collection types in Julia, renowned for its flexibility and ease of use. Arrays allow elements of uniform data type to be stored sequentially in memory, facilitating efficient access and manipulation. Arrays can be one-dimensional, two-dimensional, or multi-dimensional, supporting a wide range of applications from simple lists to complex data representations.

```
# Creating a one-dimensional array
array_1d = [1, 2, 3, 4, 5]

# Creating a two-dimensional array (matrix)
array_2d = [1 2 3; 4 5 6; 7 8 9]
```

Tuples are another fundamental collection type, distinguished from arrays by their immutability; once a tuple is created, its elements cannot be altered. This characteristic makes tuples suitable for storing fixed collections of heterogeneously typed elements, such as coordinates, RGB color values, or constant configurations.

```
# Creating a tuple
coordinate = (10.0, 20.0)

# Accessing elements of a tuple
x = coordinate[1] # 10.0
y = coordinate[2] # 20.0
```

Dictionaries in Julia are collections of key-value pairs, enabling efficient data retrieval based on unique keys. Unlike arrays and tuples, dictionaries do not retain the order of their elements but provide rapid access to values associated with specific keys, which is especially useful in applications such as associative arrays or maps.

```
# Creating a dictionary
student_scores = Dict("Alice" => 95, "Bob" => 87, "Charlie" => 92)

# Accessing dictionary elements
alice_score = student_scores["Alice"]
```

Sets represent collections of distinct elements, efficiently supporting membership tests and basic set operations like union, intersection, and difference. Sets are particularly useful in tasks requiring unique element collections and operations on aggregate datasets.

```
# Creating a set
unique_numbers = Set([1, 2, 3, 2, 1])

# Set operations
another_set = Set([3, 4, 5])
union_set = union(unique_numbers, another_set) # {1, 2, 3, 4, 5}
```

The breadth of Julia's collections provides flexible and powerful tools to model and manipulate data effectively. In the following sections, we delve deeper into each of these collection types, examining their characteristics, use cases, and performance implications. Understanding how these collections work and when to use them is critical for writing efficient and maintainable Julia code.

5.2 Working with Arrays

Arrays are fundamental data structures in Julia, offering an efficient means for managing collections of elements. An array in Julia can store elements of any type and is defined by its rank (number of dimensions) and size (number of elements along each dimension).

To create an array, use the Array constructor or array literal syntax. For instance, a one-dimensional array (vector) of integers can be created as follows:

```
a = [1, 2, 3, 4, 5]
```

To confirm the type and dimensions of a, we use the typeof and size functions:

```
println(typeof(a)) # Array{Int64, 1}
println(size(a)) # (5,)
```

```
Array{Int64, 1}
(5,)
```

Arrays can have more than one dimension. For a two-dimensional array (matrix), the syntax involves using semicolons or line breaks:

```
b = [1 2 3; 4 5 6; 7 8 9] # 3x3 matrix
```

Checking the type and size:

```
println(typeof(b)) # Array{Int64, 2}
println(size(b)) # (3, 3)
```

```
Array{Int64, 2}
(3, 3)
```

Julia supports a variety of operations on arrays, including indexing, slicing, and modifying elements. Indexing in Julia starts at 1, not 0. To access the third element of a:

```
println(a[3]) # 3
```

```
3
```

For slicing arrays, specify a range of indices using the colon operator:

```
sub_a = a[2:4]
println(sub_a) # [2, 3, 4]
```

```
[2, 3, 4]
```

Similarly, elements of a matrix can be accessed or modified using their row and column indices:

```
println(b[2, 3]) # 6
b[1, 1] = 10
println(b) # [10 2 3; 4 5 6; 7 8 9]
```

```
6
[10 2 3; 4 5 6; 7 8 9]
```

For more complex manipulations and built-in functionalities, Julia provides numerous functions such as push!, pop!, append!, and delete!. Consider the following example of appending elements:

```
push!(a, 6)
println(a) # [1, 2, 3, 4, 5, 6]
```

```
[1, 2, 3, 4, 5, 6]
```

To remove the last element:

```
pop!(a)
println(a) # [1, 2, 3, 4, 5]
```

```
[1, 2, 3, 4, 5]
```

The append! function concatenates another array to the end of the current array:

```
append!(a, [6, 7])
println(a) # [1, 2, 3, 4, 5, 6, 7]
```

```
[1, 2, 3, 4, 5, 6, 7]
```

To delete an element at a specific position:

```
deleteat!(a, 2)
println(a) # [1, 3, 4, 5, 6, 7]
```

```
[1, 3, 4, 5, 6, 7]
```

Arrays can be reshaped using the reshape function. For example, converting a one-dimensional array to a matrix:

```
c = reshape(a, 3, 2)
println(c) # [1 3; 4 5; 6 7]
```

[1 3; 4 5; 6 7]

Moreover, arrays support arithmetic operations element-wise. For instance:

```
d = b .+ 2
println(d) # [12 4 5; 6 7 8; 9 10 11]
```

[12 4 5; 6 7 8; 9 10 11]

The broadcasting mechanism in Julia, indicated by the dot operator before the addition sign, applies the operation to each element of the array.

Arrays in Julia can also be iterated over using loops. Consider the example of summing the elements:

```
sum = 0
for elem in a
    sum += elem
end
println(sum) # 26
```

26

Julia allows for multidimensional array manipulations using efficient built-in functions and external packages, optimizing performance for large-scale data operations. Functions such as map, filter, and comprehensions provide concise and expressive means to transform and manage arrays.

Understanding the intricacies of array operations in Julia is crucial for developing efficient code, particularly in data-intensive applications. Proficiency with arrays is foundational for leveraging Julia's capabilities in scientific computing, data analysis, and beyond.

5.3 Understanding and Using Tuples

Tuples in Julia serve as an immutable, ordered collection of elements. Unlike arrays, once a tuple is created, its elements cannot be modified. This immutability provides advantages in terms of performance because tuples can be stack-allocated, leading to faster access times and lower memory overhead.

A tuple is defined using parentheses, with elements separated by commas.

```
tuple1 = (1, 2, 3)
```

```
tuple2 = ("a", "b", "c")
```

The elements of a tuple can be accessed using indexing, which is one-based in Julia. Negative indices can also be used to access elements from the end of the tuple.

```
first_element = tuple1[1] # Accesses the first element
last_element = tuple1[end] # Accesses the last element
```

To demonstrate the immutability of tuples, attempting to modify an element of a tuple will result in an error.

```
tuple1[1] = 10 # This will result in an error
```

ERROR: MethodError: no method matching setindex!(::Tuple{Int64, Int64, Int64}, ::Int64, ::Int64)

Concatenation and Splitting

Tuples can be concatenated using the cat function. This function combines multiple tuples or other collections into a new tuple.

```
tuple1 = (1, 2, 3)
tuple2 = (4, 5, 6)
tuple3 = [7, 8, 9]

combined_tuple = cat(tuple1, tuple2, tuple3, dims=1)
```

(1, 2, 3, 4, 5, 6, 7, 8, 9)

Splitting a tuple into its components can be achieved using destructuring assignments.

```
a, b, c = (1, 2, 3)
```

If the number of variables does not match the tuple size, Julia will throw an error.

```
a, b = (1, 2, 3) # Error due to mismatch in number of elements
```

ERROR: DimensionMismatch("destination and source have different lengths")

Named Tuples

While standard tuples use positional indexing to access elements, named tuples use field names. Named tuples enhance code readability by allowing access via names.

```
named_tuple = (a=1, b=2, c=3)
```

Accessing elements via field names is straightforward.

```
a_value = named_tuple.a # This will return 1
```

Performance Considerations

Due to their immutability and stack allocation, tuples can often be more performant than arrays for small collections of elements. Consider the following benchmark comparison:

```
using BenchmarkTools

array = [1, 2, 3]
tuple = (1, 2, 3)

@benchmark sum(array)
@benchmark sum(tuple)
```

Performing such benchmarks typically reveals that the sum of a tuple executes faster than that of an array due to reduced overhead in accessing elements from a tuple.

Tuples in Functions

Tuples are often used in functions to return multiple values. Julia's ability to return multiple values conveniently without the need for creating a complex data structure is facilitated by tuples.

```
function divide(x, y)
    quotient = x ÷ y
    remainder = x % y
    return quotient, remainder
end

q, r = divide(10, 3)
```

The divide function returns a tuple containing both the quotient and the remainder, demonstrating the utility of tuples in function return values.

Gradient of Tuples in Mathematical Expressions

When working with mathematical expressions, tuples can be used to store gradient or partial derivatives which allows for structured return of multi-component derivative information.

```
function derivatives(x, y)
    df_dx = 2x + y
    df_dy = x + 2y
    return df_dx, df_dy
end

gradient_x, gradient_y = derivatives(1, 2)
```

In this example, the derivatives function computes the partial derivatives of a function with respect to its input variables and returns them as a tuple.

Understanding and utilizing tuples effectively can significantly optimize both performance and code clarity. The immutable nature of tuples helps ensure data integrity, making them a reliable choice for fixed-size collections.

5.4 Dictionaries: Key-Value Pairs

Dictionaries in Julia, also known as associative arrays, are versatile data structures that map unique keys to corresponding values. This section delves into the essential functions and operations associated with dictionaries, providing a robust understanding of their usage.

Dictionaries are defined using the Dict keyword, followed by curly braces. Each entry in the dictionary comprises a key-value pair separated by a => symbol. Keys can be of any data type that supports hashing and equality comparison, while values can be of any type.

```
# Example of creating a dictionary
my_dict = Dict("a" => 1, "b" => 2, "c" => 3)
```

To access a value associated with a specific key, use the indexing operation with square brackets.

```
# Accessing values
value_a = my_dict["a"]
println(value_a) # Output: 1
```

Adding or updating a key-value pair is a straightforward process. Simply assign a value to a key using the indexing syntax.

```
# Adding a new key-value pair
my_dict["d"] = 4

# Updating an existing key-value pair
my_dict["a"] = 10
```

To remove a key-value pair, employ the delete! function. It's worth noting that attempting to remove a non-existent key will raise an error.

```
# Removing a key-value pair
delete!(my_dict, "b")
```

Checking for key existence is commonly executed using the haskey function, which returns a Bool indicating whether the key is present in the dictionary.

```
# Checking for key existence
exists = haskey(my_dict, "c") # Output: true
not_exists = haskey(my_dict, "z") # Output: false
```

Iteration over a dictionary can be performed using a for loop. By default, Julia provides the ability to iterate over both keys and values simultaneously.

```
# Iterating over a dictionary
for (key, value) in my_dict
    println("Key: $key, Value: $value")
end
```

In certain scenarios, extracting only keys or values is beneficial. Julia facilitates this via the keys and values functions.

```
# Extracting keys and values
all_keys = keys(my_dict)
all_values = values(my_dict)

for key in all_keys
    println(key)
end

for value in all_values
    println(value)
end
```

Merging dictionaries is an essential operation, particularly for aggregating datasets. Use the merge function to combine dictionaries. The merge! function performs in place merging, modifying the original dictionary.

```
# Merging dictionaries
dict1 = Dict("x" => 1, "y" => 2)
dict2 = Dict("y" => 3, "z" => 4)

merged_dict = merge(dict1, dict2) # Non-mutating merge
merge!(dict1, dict2) # In-place merge
```

When dictionaries include nested collections or custom data structures, the concepts of deep-copying versus shallow-copying become relevant. The deepcopy function ensures a recursive copy of the dictionary, safeguarding against unintentional modifications.

```
# Deep copying a dictionary
nested_dict = Dict("one" => [1, 2], "two" => [3, 4])
copied_dict = deepcopy(nested_dict)

# Modifying the copied dictionary does not affect the original
push!(copied_dict["one"], 5)
```

Understanding the internal implementation of dictionaries in Julia can aid in optimizing performance. Julia's Dict utilizes hash tables, providing average-time complexity of $O(1)$ for insertion and lookup operations. However, users should be aware of potential hash collisions and the underlying amortized analysis that maintains these performance characteristics.

Handling default values in dictionaries is another frequent requirement. Julia's get function fetches a value for a key, but also allows specifying a default value in case the key does not exist.

```
# Accessing a value with a default
value = get(my_dict, "nonexistent_key", "default_value")
println(value) # Output: default_value
```

For more advanced key-value operations, dictionaries support parameterized types. Julia allows the explicit specification of types for keys and values, ensuring type stability and potential performance benefits.

```
# Parameterized dictionary
typed_dict = Dict{Int, String}()
typed_dict[1] = "one"
typed_dict[2] = "two"
```

To summarize the various functions and their protections, the table below encapsulates common dictionary operations and their intended usage scenarios:

Function	**Usage**
Dict	Create a dictionary
[]	Access value by key
[] (assignment)	Add or update key-value pair
delete!	Remove key-value pair
haskey	Check key existence
keys	Extract keys
values	Extract values
merge	Merge dictionaries
deepcopy	Deep copy dictionary
get	Access value with default

A comprehensive understanding of these operations equips users to utilize dictionaries effectively in Julia, facilitating efficient and dynamic data handling.

5.5 Sets and Their Operations

In Julia, Set is an essential data structure that stores unique elements, ensuring no duplicates are present. A Set is an unordered collection, meaning that the order of the elements is not guaranteed. Sets are particularly useful when the primary requirement is to test for membership or to eliminate duplicate elements from a collection. Here, we delve into the creation of sets, basic set operations, and more advanced uses.

Creating Sets

To create a Set in Julia, the Set constructor is used. It can accept any iterable, such as arrays or ranges.

```
# Create a set from an array
s1 = Set([1, 2, 3, 4, 5])

# Create a set from a range
s2 = Set(1:5)

# Create an empty set and add elements
s3 = Set{Int}()
push!(s3, 1)
push!(s3, 2)
```

The elements within the set are displayed as:

```
Set([1, 2, 3, 4, 5])
Set([1, 2, 3, 4, 5])
Set([1, 2])
```

Basic Set Operations

Several fundamental set operations exist in Julia, including union, intersection, and set difference:

```
# Define two sets
set_a = Set([1, 2, 3, 4])
set_b = Set([3, 4, 5, 6])

# Union of two sets
union_ab = union(set_a, set_b)

# Intersection of two sets
intersect_ab = intersect(set_a, set_b)

# Set difference
diff_ab = setdiff(set_a, set_b)

# Symmetric difference
symdiff_ab = symdiff(set_a, set_b)
```

The resulting sets are:

```
Set([1, 2, 3, 4, 5, 6])
Set([3, 4])
Set([1, 2])
Set([1, 2, 5, 6])
```

Testing Membership

Testing whether an element belongs to a set is a fundamental operation and is straightforward in Julia.

```
# Membership test
element_in_a = in(3, set_a)
element_in_b = 5 in set_a
```

The outputs will be:

```
true
false
```

Adding and Removing Elements

Adding and removing elements from a set can be done using the push! and delete! functions, respectively.

```
# Add element to a set
push!(set_a, 7)

# Remove element from a set
delete!(set_a, 2)

# Check the modified set
set_a
```

The modified set set_a is:

```
Set([3, 4, 7, 1])
```

Subset and Superset

Determining whether one set is a subset or superset of another is also supported in Julia.

```
# Define another set
set_c = Set([3, 4])

# Check if set_c is a subset of set_a
is_subset = issubset(set_c, set_a)

# Check if set_a is a superset of set_c
is_superset = issuperset(set_a, set_c)
```

The results will be:

```
true
true
```

Iterating Over Sets

Iteration over the elements of a set in Julia can be done using a for loop, just like with other iterable collections.

```
# Iterate over elements in a set
for element in set_a
    println(element)
end
```

This will print each element in the set. Since sets do not guarantee order, the elements may appear in any sequence.

Advanced Set Operations

Julia provides several higher-order functions to operate on sets, including map and filter.

```
# Map a function over a set
squared_set = map(x -> x^2, set_a)

# Filter elements of a set
filtered_set = filter(x -> x > 2, set_a)
```

The results are as follows:

```
Set([9, 16, 1, 49])
Set([3, 4, 7])
```

Sets in Julia are efficient and provide a robust set of operations that make them ideal for various scenarios where uniqueness and membership testing are required. By leveraging sets, one can ensure data integrity and simplify the manipulation of collections.

5.6 Introduction to DataFrames

In Julia, handling and manipulating tabular data can be efficiently achieved using the DataFrames.jl package. DataFrame is a powerful data structure for managing collections of heterogeneous data types, allowing easy exploration, manipulation, and analysis of data.

To utilize DataFrames in your Julia environment, you must initially install and import the package. Use the following commands:

```
using Pkg
Pkg.add("DataFrames")
using DataFrames
```

A DataFrame can be instantiated in multiple ways. One of the simplest methods is by using the DataFrame() constructor to create an empty DataFrame:

```
df = DataFrame()
```

More commonly, DataFrame objects are created from arrays, dictionaries, or other tabular data sources. Here is an example of creating a DataFrame from arrays:

```
df = DataFrame(A = 1:4, B = ["apple", "banana", "cherry", "date"], C = [true, false,
    true, false])
```

This code produces a DataFrame with three columns named A, B, and C, populated with integer, string, and boolean data types, respectively:

```
4×3 DataFrame
 Row  A     B        C

  1   1     apple    true
  2   2     banana   false
  3   3     cherry   true
  4   4     date     false
```

DataFrames also allow data to be constructed from dictionaries, where keys represent column names and the corresponding values are arrays of data:

```
data_dict = Dict("Name" => ["Alice", "Bob", "Charlie"], "Age" => [25, 30, 35], "
    Salary" => [50000, 60000, 70000])
df = DataFrame(data_dict)
```

This would create a DataFrame with columns for Name, Age, and Salary.

```
3×3 DataFrame
 Row  Name     Age   Salary

  1   Alice    25    50000
  2   Bob      30    60000
  3   Charlie  35    70000
```

Accessing and manipulating data within a DataFrame follows a coherent syntax akin to array indexing and dictionary access. To access a specific column, you can utilize the column name as an index:

```
ages = df[!, :Age]
```

This command retrieves the Age column as an Array. Alternatively, the df[:Age] or df[!, "Age"] syntax can be used, but the ! operator solidifies that the entire column is being accessed.

Moreover, individual elements of a DataFrame can be accessed via row and column indexing:

```
element = df[2, :Salary]
```

In this case, element would hold the value 60000 from the second row and the Salary column.

DataFrames support a wide range of operations, including but not limited to filtering, aggregation, and merging. One of the fundamental operations is filtering rows based on certain conditions. For instance, filtering rows where Age is greater than 28 can be achieved as follows:

```
filtered_df = df[df.Age .> 28, :]
```

This produces a DataFrame containing only rows satisfying the condition:

```
2×3 DataFrame
 Row   Name      Age    Salary

   1   Bob       30     60000
   2   Charlie   35     70000
```

For aggregation and summarization, the combine, groupby, and select functions are essential. To calculate the average Salary, first group the data by a relevant column (e.g., Age) and then aggregate:

```
grouped_df = groupby(df, :Name)
aggregated_df = combine(grouped_df, :Salary => mean => :MeanSalary)
```

The combine function here computes the mean salary for each unique Name group and assigns it to a new column, MeanSalary:

```
3×2 DataFrame
 Row   Name      MeanSalary

   1   Alice     50000.0
   2   Bob       60000.0
   3   Charlie   70000.0
```

DataFrames.jl integrates seamlessly with other Julia packages, enabling extensive data analysis capabilities. For example, direct plotting of DataFrame content can be performed using the Plots.jl package. Consider the following example to produce a bar plot of Name against Salary:

```
using Plots
bar(df.Name, df.Salary, title="Salaries of Individuals", xlabel="Name", ylabel="Salary
    ")
```

This creates a bar plot where the Name is plotted along the x-axis and the Salary along the y-axis, providing a visual representation of the data.

DataFrame manipulations are powerful in Julia due to their versatility and the number of built-in functions available for performing a variety of operations. As such, DataFrames.jl is an essential tool for any data scientist working within the Julia programming language, ensuring that data handling tasks are executed efficiently and effectively.

5.7 Working with Custom Data Structures

In Julia, defining custom data structures is essential for building complex applications tailored to specific needs. This section delves into the creation and utilization of custom data structures, exploring their implementation, benefits, and performance considerations to ensure efficient data handling.

Custom data structures in Julia are typically implemented using struct and mutable struct. The primary difference between these keywords is that struct defines immutable objects, while mutable struct allows for mutable objects. Immutable structures are advantageous for thread safety and can lead to optimized performance because the compiler has guarantees about the structure's immutability.

Consider the following example, which demonstrates the definition of a simple immutable struct to represent a point in a two-dimensional space:

```
struct Point
    x::Float64
    y::Float64
end
```

In this Point structure, x and y are initialized as Float64 types. Instances of this structure are created as follows:

```
p1 = Point(3.0, 4.0)
p2 = Point(5.5, -2.7)
```

Given that Point is immutable, any attempt to modify the fields of p1 or p2 directly will result in an error. If mutability is required—for instance, if the coordinates of the point need to be altered after creation—mutable struct is used instead.

```
mutable struct PointMutable
    x::Float64
    y::Float64
end
```

With PointMutable, it is possible to modify the coordinates after instantiation:

```
mp = PointMutable(1.0, 2.0)
mp.x = 2.5
mp.y = 3.5
```

Custom data structures can also include methods, which are functions that operate specifically on instances of the structure. This is done to encapsulate functionality and promote object-oriented design principles. Methods are defined as part of the module or, more commonly, as part of the type's implementation.

Here, we define a method to compute the Euclidean distance between two points:

```
function distance(p1::Point, p2::Point)
    return sqrt((p1.x - p2.x)^2 + (p1.y - p2.y)^2)
end
```

This method can be invoked as follows:

```
d = distance(p1, p2)
```

This computes the Euclidean distance between p1 and p2, storing the result in d.

Custom data structures are not limited to simple scalar fields—they can include other data structures, enabling the creation of complex, hierarchical entities. For example, one might define a structure to represent a geometric shape consisting of multiple points:

```
struct Shape
    points::Vector{Point}
end
```

This Shape structure contains a vector of Point objects. Instances of Shape can be created and manipulated as shown:

```
s = Shape([Point(0.0, 0.0), Point(1.0, 1.0), Point(2.0, 1.5)])
```

To ensure better encapsulation and data integrity, functions that operate on custom data structures can be defined to prevent external modification. For example, adding a point to a shape:

```
function add_point!(shape::Shape, point::Point)
    push!(shape.points, point)
end
```

The add_point! function appends a new point to the shape, maintaining encapsulation and preventing direct manipulation of the points vector from outside the object.

Performance considerations are critical when working with custom data structures, especially in high-performance computing applications. Immutable structures benefit from compiler optimizations and can be stack-allocated, reducing heap allocation overhead. Conversely, mutable structures offer flexibility but might incur additional costs associated with heap allocation and garbage collection.

Profiling and benchmarking are tools for ensuring that custom data structures do not become performance bottlenecks. Utilizing the BenchmarkTools package allows for accurate performance measurement:

```
using BenchmarkTools

@benchmark distance(p1, p2)
```

The output from executing the above code snippet provides insights into execution time and memory allocation, aiding in the identification of performance issues.

```
BenchmarkTools.Trial:
  memory estimate:  0 bytes
  allocs estimate:  0
  --------------
  minimum time:     2.235 ns (0.00% GC)
  median time:      2.721 ns (0.00% GC)
  mean time:        2.752 ns (0.00% GC)
  maximum time:     19.652 ns (0.00% GC)
  --------------
  samples:          10000
  evals/sample:     1000
```

The effective use of custom data structures in Julia hinges on balancing immutability for performance and thread safety with the need for mutability to accommodate application requirements. Proper encapsulation and method definitions contribute to maintainable and scalable code.

5.8 Multidimensional Arrays and Matrices

Multidimensional arrays and matrices are crucial components in scientific computing, machine learning, and numerical analysis. Julia provides robust support for these data structures, allowing for efficient and expressive manipulations. This section delves into the creation, manipulation, and utilization of these arrays in Julia.

A Matrix in Julia is essentially a two-dimensional array, while Array{T, N} represents an N-dimensional array of elements of type T. To define a multidimensional array, the Array constructor can be used or various other convenient methods provided by Julia.

```
# Creating a 2x3 matrix with elements from 1 to 6
matrix = [1 2 3; 4 5 6]
```

```
# Creating a 3D array (2x2x2) with elements from 1 to 8
array_3d = reshape(1:8, 2, 2, 2)
```

Individual elements in a multidimensional array can be accessed and assigned using indexing. Julia arrays use 1-based indexing, contrary to the 0-based indexing in many other languages like Python or C++.

```
# Accessing elements in a 2x3 matrix
element = matrix[2, 3] # Returns 6

# Assigning a new value
matrix[1, 2] = 10
```

For a three-dimensional array, indexing follows the same principle but with an additional dimension. For example, array_3d[1, 2, 1] accesses the element in the first row, second column, and first depth layer of the array.

To facilitate data manipulation, Julia provides several built-in functions for operations such as slicing, reshaping, and concatenation. Slicing allows the extraction of a subarray from a multidimensional array.

```
# Slicing the first row of the matrix
first_row = matrix[1, :]

# Slicing the second column
second_column = matrix[:, 2]
```

The reshape function mentioned earlier is useful for changing the dimensions of an array without altering the data. This is particularly useful in mathematical and scientific computations where the shape of the data must be transformed.

```
# Reshaping the 2x2x2 array into a 2x4 matrix
reshaped_matrix = reshape(array_3d, 2, 4)
```

Concatenation of arrays can be performed horizontally or vertically using the hcat and vcat functions, respectively.

```
# Horizontal concatenation of two matrices
matrix_A = [1 2; 3 4]
matrix_B = [5 6; 7 8]
matrix_C = hcat(matrix_A, matrix_B)

# Vertical concatenation
matrix_D = vcat(matrix_A, matrix_B)
```

Julia's support for linear algebra is both extensive and efficient, making it an ideal choice for numerical computing. The LinearAlgebra standard library module provides various functions for matrix factorizations, eigenvalue problems, and other linear algebra operations.

```
using LinearAlgebra

# Performing the matrix multiplication
result = matrix_A * matrix_B

# Transposing a matrix
transposed_matrix = transpose(matrix_A)

# Computing the determinant
det_A = det(matrix_A)
```

Efficient memory management is a critical consideration when working with large multidimensional arrays. Julia optimizes memory usage by employing techniques like in-place operations and array views. In-place operations modify the original array, reducing the need for additional memory allocation.

```
# In-place multiplication of a matrix by a scalar
matrix_A .*= 2

# Creating an in-place permutation of the matrix
L, U, p = lu(matrix_A)
```

Views offer a way to create a subarray without copying the data. This is particularly useful for large datasets where performance and memory usage are crucial.

```
# Creating a view of the original array
subset_view = @view matrix_A[1:2, 1]

# Modifying the view also modifies the original array
subset_view[1] = 10
```

Advanced users can leverage multidimensional arrays and matrices to implement complex algorithms and simulations. They are pivotal in applications ranging from image processing, where images are often represented as three-dimensional arrays (height, width, color channels), to solving partial differential equations on multidimensional grids.

Algorithmic operations such as matrix decompositions, solving linear systems, and performing fast Fourier transforms (FFTs) are also efficiently handled by Julia, offering optimized performance that competes with traditional languages used in scientific computing.

Algorithm 2: Gaussian Elimination with Partial Pivoting

Input: Matrix $\mathrm{A} \in \mathbb{R}^{n \times n}$, vector $\mathrm{b} \in \mathbb{R}^{n}$
Output: Solution vector $\mathrm{x} \in \mathbb{R}^{n}$

$n \leftarrow$ length(b);
for $k \leftarrow 1$ **to** $n-1$ **do**
  max $\leftarrow$ arg max$(|\mathrm{A}[k:n,k]|)+k-1$;
  A[[k, max], :] $\leftarrow$ A[[max, k], :];
  b[[k, max]] $\leftarrow$ b[[max, k]];
  for $i \leftarrow k+1$ **to** n **do**
    $f \leftarrow \mathrm{A}[i,k]/\mathrm{A}[k,k]$;
    A[i, k:n] $\leftarrow$ A[i, k:n] - $f \cdot \mathrm{A}[k,k:n]$;
    b[i] $\leftarrow$ b[i] - $f \cdot \mathrm{b}[k]$;

$\mathrm{x} \leftarrow$ Vector(undef, n);
For$i \leftarrow n$ **to** 1 $\mathrm{x}[i] \leftarrow (\mathrm{b}[i]-\mathrm{A}[i,(i+1):n]\cdot\mathrm{x}[(i+1):n])/\mathrm{A}[i,i]$;
return x;

Multidimensional arrays and matrices in Julia empower users to perform high-level data manipulations and mathematical operations with ease, laying a strong foundation for advanced computational tasks.

5.9 Collections and Memory Management

Memory management in Julia is a crucial topic for achieving high performance and efficiency when working with collections. Julia's memory model and garbage collection mechanisms provide robust tools for managing memory allocation and deallocation. To utilize these tools effectively, it is essential to understand how Julia handles memory for different collections and the implications of these mechanisms on performance.

Memory management involves two primary operations: allocation and deallocation. Allocation is the process of reserving a block of memory to store data, while deallocation releases that memory back to the system for future use. Julia, as a high-level language, abstracts these operations from the user, but understanding the underlying processes can lead to optimizations that improve code performance.

Julia employs a garbage collector (GC) that automatically manages memory allocation and deallocation. The garbage collector identifies and frees memory that is no longer needed by the program. This section elaborates on how different types of collections are managed in memory and explores techniques to optimize memory usage.

When dealing with arrays, memory is allocated in a contiguous block, allowing efficient access. Arrays in Julia are mutable, meaning their contents can be modified without creating a new array. However, the size of the array remains fixed once it is created. To illustrate, consider the following example:

```
array_example = [1, 2, 3, 4, 5]
array_example[2] = 10 # Modifies the second element
```

In the above example, the array array_example is allocated a contiguous block of memory to store five integers. Modifying the value at the second index does not change the array's memory footprint, as long as the data type remains consistent. However, appending elements beyond the preallocated size would require a new allocation.

Tuples, on the other hand, are immutable, meaning their contents cannot be changed once they are created. This immutability results in a different memory management approach compared to arrays. When a tuple is created, Julia allocates memory for it, and since its contents do not change, there is no need for additional allocations or deallocations during its lifetime. Here's an example of tuple usage:

```
tuple_example = (1, 2, 3, 4, 5)
# Any attempt to modify tuple elements will result in an error
```

In dictionaries, memory management is more complex due to the underlying hash table implementation. Dictionaries in Julia manage key-value pairs, and the memory allocated for a dictionary grows dynamically as new entries are added. The garbage collector ensures that unused entries are cleaned up, but allocating and deallocating memory for dictionaries can be more resource-intensive compared to arrays or tuples.

```
dict_example = Dict("a" => 1, "b" => 2, "c" => 3)
dict_example["d"] = 4 # Adds a new entry to the dictionary
```

When a new key-value pair (in this case, "d" => 4) is added, the dictionary may need to reallocate memory to accommodate the new entry. This reallocation can involve resizing the underlying hash table, which can be computationally costly.

Sets, similar to dictionaries, are implemented using hash tables. The memory for a set grows as new elements are introduced, and Julia's garbage collector handles unused memory. Here is an example of working with sets:

```
set_example = Set([1, 2, 3, 4, 5])
push!(set_example, 6) # Adds a new element to the set
```

As with dictionaries, the insertion of a new element (6) into the set may necessitate reallocation if the existing memory is insufficient.

An important aspect of memory management is understanding the role of the garbage collector. The garbage collector in Julia uses a mark-and-sweep algorithm, which involves identifying objects that are no longer in use (marking) and collecting them (sweeping) to free up memory. This process runs automatically but can also be triggered manually using the following command:

```
GC.gc()
```

Manual invocation of the garbage collector can be useful in scenarios where immediate memory cleanup is necessary, but frequent use can affect performance.

Optimizing memory usage often involves minimizing redundant allocations and leveraging the immutability of data structures when possible. For example, reusing preallocated arrays or making use of Julia's in-place modifying functions can lead to significant performance gains.

```
function modify_in_place!(array)
    for i in 1:length(array)
        array[i] = array[i] * 2
    end
end

array_example = [1, 2, 3, 4, 5]
modify_in_place!(array_example) # Modifies the array in place
```

In-place modification, as shown above, updates the original array rather than creating a new one, thus avoiding additional memory allocation and reducing garbage collection overhead.

Understanding memory management in the context of collections is fundamental to writing efficient Julia code. Leveraging Julia's memory model effectively can lead to significant improvements in computational performance, especially when working with large datasets or performing memory-intensive operations.

5.10 Iterating Over Collections

Julia provides robust mechanisms for iterating over collections, which is fundamental to efficiently process and manipulate data. Whether using arrays, tuples, dictionaries, sets, or more complex structures like DataFrames, understanding iteration patterns and best practices is crucial.

The simplest and most common form of iteration is the for loop. It allows traversal over each element of a collection in a straightforward and readable manner. Consider the following example with an array:

```
array = [1, 2, 3, 4, 5]
for element in array
    println(element)
end
```

```
1
2
3
4
5
```

In this example, the for loop iterates over each element of the array, executing the println function that outputs the element to the console. This pattern applies to all collections, including tuples, sets, and dictionaries.

To iterate over a dictionary, access both keys and values using pairs, keys, or values functions:

```
dict = Dict("a" => 1, "b" => 2, "c" => 3)
for (key, value) in dict
    println("Key: $key, Value: $value")
end
```

```
Key: a, Value: 1
Key: b, Value: 2
Key: c, Value: 3
```

Here, pairs(dict) function is implicitly called, providing tuple pairs of keys and values that can be unpacked in the for loop.

Understanding enumerate is also critical. This function packages an iterator into a series of index-element pairs, beneficial when both the index and value are needed:

```
for (index, value) in enumerate(array)
    println("Index: $index, Value: $value")
end
```

```
Index: 1, Value: 1
Index: 2, Value: 2
Index: 3, Value: 3
Index: 4, Value: 4
Index: 5, Value: 5
```

Iteration over multidimensional arrays extends the same principles but often requires the CartesianIndices function for handling complex indices. Here is an example with a 2D array:

```
matrix = [1 2 3; 4 5 6; 7 8 9]
for idx in CartesianIndices(matrix)
    println("Index: $idx, Value: $(matrix[idx])")
end
```

```
Index: CartesianIndex(1, 1), Value: 1
Index: CartesianIndex(1, 2), Value: 2
Index: CartesianIndex(1, 3), Value: 3
Index: CartesianIndex(2, 1), Value: 4
Index: CartesianIndex(2, 2), Value: 5
Index: CartesianIndex(2, 3), Value: 6
Index: CartesianIndex(3, 1), Value: 7
Index: CartesianIndex(3, 2), Value: 8
Index: CartesianIndex(3, 3), Value: 9
```

In cases where the performance and memory footprint are critical, Iterators module functions introduce lazy evaluation strategies. For instance, using Iterators.filter provides a way to iterate only over the elements of a collection satisfying a predicate condition without creating an intermediate array:

```
filtered_iterator = Iterators.filter(x -> x % 2 == 0, array)
for element in filtered_iterator
    println(element)
end
```

```
2
4
```

Moreover, Iterators.product allows iterating over all combinations of elements from multiple collections:

```
for (i, j) in Iterators.product(1:3, 1:2)
    println("($i, $j)")
end
```

```
(1, 1)
(1, 2)
(2, 1)
(2, 2)
(3, 1)
(3, 2)
```

Understanding these tools and their appropriate use cases ensures efficient and readable code. Julia's iteration functionalities provide both simplicity for common tasks and flexibility for complex requirements, minimizing computational overhead and maximizing performance.

5.11 Advanced Data Structures

In this section, we delve into the intricacies of advanced data structures available in Julia, enabling efficient data manipulation and storage for complex computational tasks. We will cover key data structures including the B-Tree, Red-Black Tree, and the Trie. These are typically used when handling large volumes of data or when specific performance characteristics are desired, such as balanced search times or efficient prefix searches.

B-Tree:

A B-Tree is a self-balancing tree data structure that maintains sorted data and allows searches, insertions, deletions, and sequential access in logarithmic time. It is particularly suitable for systems that read and write large blocks of data, such as databases and file systems.

To implement a B-Tree in Julia, one needs to understand the fundamental properties: - All leaf nodes must be at the same level. - Each node can contain multiple keys and children. - B-Tree nodes have a maximum and minimum number of keys, defined by the degree of the tree.

Below is an example of a simplified B-Tree implementation in Julia:

```
struct BTreeNode
    keys::Vector{Int}
    children::Vector{BTreeNode}
    is_leaf::Bool
end

function BTreeNode(t::Int, is_leaf::Bool)
    keys = Vector{Int}(undef, 2 * t - 1)
    children = Vector{BTreeNode}(undef, 2 * t)
    return BTreeNode(keys, children, is_leaf)
end

mutable struct BTree
    root::BTreeNode
    t::Int
end

function BTree(t::Int)
    root = BTreeNode(t, true)
    return BTree(root, t)
end

# Insertion and deletion functions would follow, ensuring the properties of B-Tree are
    maintained.
```

Red-Black Tree:

A Red-Black Tree is a balanced binary search tree with an additional color attribute for each node, which can be either red or black. The key properties that ensure balance are: - Each node is either red or black. - The root and leaves (NIL) are black. - Red nodes cannot have a red parent. - Every path from a node to its descendant NIL nodes has the same number of black nodes.

Below is an example outline for implementing a Red-Black Tree in Julia:

```
enum Color begin
    RED
    BLACK
end

mutable struct RBTreeNode
    key::Int
    color::Color
    left::RBTreeNode
    right::RBTreeNode
    parent::RBTreeNode
end

RBTreeNode(key::Int) = RBTreeNode(key, Color.RED, nothing, nothing, nothing)

mutable struct RBTree
    root::RBTreeNode
end

RBTree() = RBTree(nothing)

# Functions to insert a node, fix violations, and perform rotations would be required.
```

The insertion routine involves standard binary search tree insertion followed by fixing potential violations to maintain the Red-Black Tree properties.

Trie:

A Trie, or prefix tree, is a tree-like data structure that stores a dynamic set of strings. Tries are particularly useful for tasks such as autocomplete and spell-checking. Each node represents a common prefix of some strings in the set.

Here is an example implementation of a Trie in Julia:

```
mutable struct TrieNode
    children::Dict{Char,TrieNode}
    is_end_of_word::Bool
end

TrieNode() = TrieNode(Dict{Char,TrieNode}(), false)

mutable struct Trie
    root::TrieNode
```

```
end

Trie() = Trie(TrieNode())

function insert!(trie::Trie, word::String)
    current_node = trie.root
    for char in word
        if !haskey(current_node.children, char)
            current_node.children[char] = TrieNode()
        end
        current_node = current_node.children[char]
    end
    current_node.is_end_of_word = true
end

function search(trie::Trie, word::String)::Bool
    current_node = trie.root
    for char in word
        if !haskey(current_node.children, char)
            return false
        end
        current_node = current_node.children[char]
    end
    return current_node.is_end_of_word
end
```

Complex operations such as deletion and prefix searches can also be implemented, adhering to the properties of Tries to ensure optimal performance.

Understanding and implementing advanced data structures allows for efficient data access, manipulation, and storage, making them essential tools for any computational task requiring sophisticated data handling capabilities.

5.12 Best Practices for Using Collections

Efficient handling and utilization of collections in Julia is a cornerstone of optimized performance and readability in your code. This section delves into best practices to ensure that collections are employed in the most effective manner, considering both computational and memory efficiency, as well as code maintainability and readability.

Immutable vs. Mutable Types: Understanding the difference between immutable and mutable types is fundamental when working with collections. Immutable types, such as Tuple, do not change once they are created. This makes them ideal for use as keys in dictionaries or for storing fixed sequences of items. Mutable types, like Array and Dict, on the other hand, can be modified in place, making them suitable for scenarios where the collection's contents change over time.

Choosing the Right Collection Type: Selecting the appropriate collection type based on the operation and data characteristics is crucial. Arrays are preferred for numeric computations and when the size of the collection is known and static. Dictionaries are excellent for maintaining associations between unique keys and values, and provide average O(1) time complexity for lookups, insertions, and deletions. Sets ensure that each element is unique and also offer average O(1) complexity for common operations.

Avoiding Unnecessary Copies: When manipulating collections, avoid unnecessary copying of data. Using view to create a lightweight, non-owning reference to the original data instead of creating a full copy can save memory and computational resources. Consider the following example using an array slice:

```
using BenchmarkTools

arr = rand(1:100, 100000)

# Creating a copy (expensive)
@btime copy_arr = arr[1:50000]

# Creating a view (efficient)
@btime view_arr = @view arr[1:50000]
```

Preallocating Storage: For operations involving large amounts of data, preallocating storage can significantly improve performance. Julia's sizehint! function can help when the number of elements in a collection is known in advance, thereby minimizing reallocations:

```
# Allocating storage for 1,000,000 elements
arr = Vector{Int}(undef, 0)
sizehint!(arr, 1000000)

for i in 1:1000000
    push!(arr, i)
end
```

Avoiding Global Variables: Access to global variables in Julia is slower due to the lack of type stability. When working with collections inside functions, always pass them as arguments and avoid global scope where possible. This promotes better performance due to type inference by the Julia compiler.

```
global_arr = [1, 2, 3, 4, 5]

# Inefficient
function sum_global()
    sum = 0
    for x in global_arr
```

```
        sum += x
    end
    return sum
end

# More efficient
function sum_local(arr)
    sum = 0
    for x in arr
        sum += x
    end
    return sum
end

@btime sum_global()
@btime sum_local(global_arr)
```

Using Functional Programming Constructs: Leverage Julia's functional programming constructs such as map, filter, and reduce for cleaner and more expressive code. These functions work particularly well with immutable collections and can often lead to easier-to-read and maintainable code.

```
# Applying a function to each element (functional)
squared = map(x -> x^2, [1, 2, 3, 4])

# Filtering elements (functional)
evens = filter(x -> x % 2 == 0, [1, 2, 3, 4, 5])

# Reducing to a single value (functional)
sum_value = reduce(+, [1, 2, 3, 4, 5])
```

Vectorization: Whenever possible, utilize vectorized operations for arrays, as these are often internally optimized and can leverage Julia's performance capabilities:

```
arr = rand(1:100, 100000)

# Element-wise addition (vectorized)
arr2 = arr .+ 10

# Broadcasting (vectorized)
arr3 = @. arr * 2 + 5
```

Multithreading: With the advent of multi-core processors, taking advantage of multithreading can lead to significant performance gains. Julia allows for easy parallelism using the Threads module:

```
using Base.Threads

arr = rand(1:100, 100000)
output = zeros(Int, length(arr))

@threads for i in 1:length(arr)
    output[i] = arr[i] * 2
end
```

Profiling and Optimization: Finally, profiling and optimization are essential to identify bottlenecks in your code. Use tools like Julia's @time, @btime from the BenchmarkTools package, and the built-in Profile module to analyze and optimize the performance of your code.

```
using BenchmarkTools

function compute(arr)
    result = 0
    for x in arr
        result += x^2
    end
    return result
end

arr = rand(1:100, 100000)
@btime compute($arr)
```

Adopting these best practices will ensure that your use of collections is both effective and efficient, enabling you to write high-performance, maintainable Julia code.

Chapter 6

Julia Packages and Modules

This chapter explores the powerful package and module system in Julia, starting with managing packages using the Pkg package manager. It explains installing and updating packages, creating your own Julia package, and understanding modules and namespaces. The chapter also covers using external packages, project environments, writing modular and reusable code, and documentation and testing for packages. Additionally, it provides guidelines for publishing and sharing packages, along with best practices for package development.

6.1 Introduction to Packages and Modules

Julia's package and module system forms the backbone of how users organize, share, and utilize code. This section delves into understanding the foundations of packages and modules, which are crucial for efficient code management and reuse.

Packages in Julia are collections of Julia code, organized in a structured manner, and designed to be reusable across different projects. A package can contain modules, which encapsulate the code and provide namespaces to avoid name conflicts.

A **module** is a way to group related code, providing an isolated namespace to prevent naming collisions. Modules can contain functions, variables, and other definitions, allowing developers to write modular, maintainable code.

Pkg, Julia's package manager, simplifies the process of installing, updating, and managing packages. Users can easily add packages from public repositories, such as the Julia package registry, or from private sources.

Modules: Anatomy and Usage

To declare a module in Julia, use the module keyword, followed by the module name, and end with the end keyword. Here is a basic example:

```
module MyModule

export myFunction

function myFunction(x)
    return x^2
end

end
```

In the above snippet:

- module MyModule declares a new module named MyModule.
- export myFunction allows the function myFunction to be accessible when the module is used.
- myFunction is a function within MyModule.

To use the module in another part of a Julia program, the using or import keyword is employed:

```
using .MyModule

result = myFunction(4)
```

Here, the using .MyModule statement makes the functions and variables exported by MyModule available in the current scope. The dot (.) before the module name indicates a relative path, referencing the module defined in the current script or package.

Packages vs. Modules

While modules encapsulate code and provide namespaces, packages serve as distributable units. A package typically includes one or more modules, documentation, test scripts, and metadata files like

Project.toml and Manifest.toml, which define package dependencies and configurations.

Below is a minimal example of a package directory structure:

```
MyPackage/

  src/
     MyPackage.jl
  test/
     runtests.jl
  Project.toml
```

In this structure:

- MyPackage.jl contains the primary code for the package, typically including module definitions.
- runtests.jl includes tests to ensure the package functions correctly.
- Project.toml specifies dependencies and metadata.

To create a package, Julia offers the Pkg.generate function:

```
using Pkg

Pkg.generate("MyPackage")
```

This command generates the basic directory structure for a new package named MyPackage.

Public vs. Private Modules

Public modules are designed to be used by other packages and projects, making it crucial to maintain well-documented and stable APIs. In contrast, private modules are intended for internal use within a package, supporting the primary functionality without being exposed as part of the public API.

Public modules should be carefully exported and documented. For instance:

```
module PublicModule

export public_function

function public_function(x)
    return x + 1
end
```

```
function _private_helper(y)
    return y * 2
end

end
```

Here, public_function is exported and intended for public use, while _private_helper is a private function to support internal operations.

Loading and Precompilation

Julia optimizes package loading through precompilation. When a package is first loaded, Julia compiles the code into an intermediate form and caches it. Subsequent uses of the package load this precompiled code, significantly improving performance. To facilitate this, the __precompile__() macro can be placed at the top of the module file:

```
module MyModule

__precompile__()

export myFunction

function myFunction(x)
    return x^2
end

end
```

The __precompile__() macro instructs Julia to precompile the module, aiding in faster loading times for users.

By understanding these core concepts and mechanics, one can leverage Julia's package and module system to create clean, efficient, and reusable code structures. This robust framework supports the growth of an extensive ecosystem of Julia packages, facilitating seamless collaboration and innovation among developers.

6.2 Managing Packages with Pkg

The Julia language includes a built-in package manager called Pkg which is powerful and flexible. Utilizing Pkg, users can install, update, and remove packages, in addition to creating their own packages. This section explores the fundamentals of managing packages using Pkg, highlighting commands and their outputs, ensuring the concepts are clearly elucidated.

The primary interface for Pkg is through the Julia REPL. To enter the package manager mode, one simply needs to press the] key within the REPL. The prompt changes from julia> to pkg>, indicating that Pkg mode is active.

To illustrate package management, consider the following example where we navigate through key commands such as adding, updating, and removing packages. These examples will help in gaining a hands-on understanding of managing packages with Julia's Pkg.

```
julia> ]
pkg>
```

```
pkg> add Example
```

The add command allows users to install a specific package. In this case, Example is installed. During the installation process, Pkg resolves dependencies and ensures all required packages are installed.

To list all installed packages:

```
pkg> status
```

The status command displays the current state of the package environment, listing all installed packages and their versions.

To update all installed packages to their latest versions, utilize the update command:

```
pkg> update
```

The update command checks for newer versions of the installed packages and updates them. It ensures the environment is current and that packages are consistent with the latest compatible versions.

For instance, if specific packages need updates, specify the package names:

```
pkg> update Example
```

Let's consider upgrading or downgrading a package to a specific version. This can be performed using the add command with the specified version number:

```
pkg> add Example@0.3.0
```

This command will install version 0.3.0 of the Example package.

In some cases, packages may need removal due to redundancy or conflicts. The remove command will handle this:

```
pkg> remove Example
```

This operation removes the Example package from the current environment.

To explore available packages one can use the add command as follows:

```
pkg> add <TAB>
```

Pressing <TAB> after the add command lists available packages for installation.

Consider an advanced usage, such as working with a development version of a package. If a package resides in a local directory or a Git repository, use the dev command:

```
pkg> dev /path/to/local/package
```

or

```
pkg> dev https://github.com/user/repo
```

This links the local or remote repository for development purposes, allowing modifications and testing within the package environment.

Additionally, the resolve command is beneficial when dependency resolution needs explicit management. It re-evaluates the state of installed packages and applies necessary changes:

```
pkg> resolve
```

Finally, package environments ensure consistency and reproducibility of package states. The environment is stored in two primary files, Project.toml and Manifest.toml. The Project.toml file lists the top-level dependencies, and the Manifest.toml file records the exact versions of all packages and their dependencies. This dual-file structure aids in managing and sharing environments effectively.

Initializing a new environment can be achieved by activating or instantiating environments:

```
pkg> activate MyProject
```

This command creates and activates a new environment named MyProject.

To instantiate an environment with predefined dependencies listed in

Project.toml:

```
pkg> instantiate
```

Executing this command installs all packages specified in the Project.toml and Manifest.toml files, ensuring the working environment mirrors the defined state.

Understanding these commands provides a robust foundation for managing packages using Julia's Pkg system, enabling efficient and effective package management.

6.3 Installing and Updating Packages

Julia utilizes the Pkg package manager to manage package installation and updates efficiently. This section provides a detailed guide on installing and updating packages using Pkg. To install a package, you need to use the Pkg.add() function, while updating a package can be achieved with the Pkg.update() function.

First, ensure that you have imported the Pkg module:

```
using Pkg
```

To install a package, use Pkg.add() with the package name as a string. For example, to install the DataFrames package, you would execute:

```
Pkg.add("DataFrames")
```

The Pkg manager will resolve any dependencies and initiate the installation process. The output will indicate steps such as downloading, extracting, and compiling the package.

```
Resolving package versions...
Installed DataFrames  v1.2.2
Updating `~/.julia/environments/v1.6/Project.toml`
[a93c6f00] + DataFrames v1.2.2
Updating `~/.julia/environments/v1.6/Manifest.toml`
[a93c6f00] + DataFrames v1.2.2
```

Once installed, you can load the package using using or import:

```
using DataFrames
```

Updating packages ensures you have the latest features and security patches. To update a specific package, use Pkg.update() with the package name:

```
Pkg.update("DataFrames")
```

To update all installed packages to their latest versions, call Pkg.update() without any arguments:

```
Pkg.update()
```

The Pkg manager will check online repositories for newer versions and update the packages accordingly.

```
Updating registry at `~/.julia/registries/General`
Updating `~/.julia/environments/v1.6/Project.toml`
[a93c6f00] DataFrames v1.2.2  v1.3.0
Updating `~/.julia/environments/v1.6/Manifest.toml`
[a93c6f00] DataFrames v1.2.2  v1.3.0
```

If you need to uninstall a package, you can use Pkg.rm():

```
Pkg.rm("DataFrames")
```

This command will remove the specified package from your environment.

For package management, it is important to understand the concept of project environments. Each project can have its own environment with specific dependencies. You can create a new project environment by navigating to the project directory and running:

```
Pkg.activate(".")
Pkg.instantiate()
```

The Pkg.activate(".") command initiates the current directory as a new environment. Pkg.instantiate() will then install all dependencies listed in the Project.toml and Manifest.toml files, ensuring the environment matches the project's specification.

To review the status and installed packages within the current environment, use:

```
Pkg.status()
```

This will output the list of installed packages and their versions, helping you keep track of your environment's state.

```
Status `~/.julia/environments/v1.6/Project.toml`
[a93c6f00] DataFrames v1.3.0
```

Adhering to these practices ensures a consistent and reliable development process, leveraging Julia's package ecosystem effectively.

6.4 Creating Your First Julia Package

In this section, we will detail the steps to create a Julia package from scratch. This involves structuring your code in an organized manner, adding necessary files and configurations, and finally, testing and documenting your package. Julia's package manager, Pkg, simplifies many of these tasks, allowing you to focus more on writing effective code.

Begin by creating a new package using the built-in functionality of the Pkg module:

```
using Pkg
Pkg.generate("MyFirstPackage")
```

This creates a directory structure for your new package called MyFirstPackage, which includes several files such as Project.toml and src/MyFirstPackage.jl.

The Project.toml file contains metadata about your package including its name, version, dependencies, and authors. Here is an example of what it might look like:

```
name = "MyFirstPackage"
uuid = "12345678-abcd-efgh-ijkl-123456789abc"
authors = ["Your Name <your.email@example.com>"]
version = "0.1.0"
```

The src/MyFirstPackage.jl file is the main source file for your package. The initial content of this file looks like:

```
module MyFirstPackage

greet() = println("Hello, World!")

end # module
```

This is a simple module containing a function greet that prints "Hello, World!". You can test this package by activating the project environment and using the Pkg.instantiate() and Pkg.activate() commands:

```
pkg> activate .
pkg> instantiate
julia> using MyFirstPackage
julia> MyFirstPackage.greet()
```

The result should be:

```
Hello, World!
```

To expand your package, you can add more functionalities by editing the src/MyFirstPackage.jl file and creating additional source files as needed. For example, add a new file src/greeting.jl:

```
module MyFirstPackage

include("greeting.jl")

end # module
```

And then, within greeting.jl:

```
function greet(name::String)
    println("Hello, $name!")
end
```

After editing these files, loading and using the package will reflect the additions:

```
julia> using MyFirstPackage
julia> MyFirstPackage.greet("Alice")
```

With the output:

```
Hello, Alice!
```

Testing your package is crucial to ensure that all functions and features work as intended. Julia uses the Test module for writing and running tests. Create a new directory named test and within it, a file named runtests.jl:

```
using Pkg
Pkg.add("Test")
using Test
using MyFirstPackage

@testset "Greet Function" begin
    @test greet("Bob") == "Hello, Bob!"
end
```

You can run the tests using:

```
pkg> activate .
pkg> test MyFirstPackage
```

In documenting your package, it is important to provide both extensive comments within the code and separate documentation files. You can use Julia's built-in documentation system, which utilizes markdown-based docstrings. Here is how you might annotate your greet function:

```
"""
    greet(name::String)

Prints a greeting to the given `name`.

# Examples
```

```
julia> greet("Charlie")
Hello, Charlie!

"""
function greet(name::String)
    println("Hello, $name!")
end
```

To generate comprehensive documentation, you can use external tools like Documenter.jl. Create a new directory titled docs with subdirectories and configuration files as needed. The Documenter.jl documentation provides extensive details on setup and usage.

By structuring the package correctly, adding documentation, and consistently testing new features, you ensure that your package remains maintainable and user-friendly.

6.5 Modules and Namespaces

In Julia, a *module* is a code structuring and namespace management tool that encapsulates functions, types, and variables. Modules provide a means to separate and organize code into discrete, reusable components, and they help avoid naming conflicts by introducing namespaces.

To define a module in Julia, use the module keyword followed by the name of the module. Everything between the module and end keywords belongs to that module's namespace. Here is a basic example demonstrating the definition of a module:

```
module MyModule
    export say_hello

    say_hello() = println("Hello, World!")
end
```

In this snippet, MyModule is defined with a single function say_hello. The export keyword makes the say_hello function accessible when the module is imported elsewhere. To use say_hello in another part of your code, you would use the using or import statement:

```
using .MyModule

say_hello() # Calls the say_hello function from MyModule
```

The . before MyModule indicates that it's a relative path reference within the current file's scope. Alternatively, if you need a more granular control over what's imported, you can use the import statement:

```
import .MyModule.say_hello

say_hello()
```

Here's a more comprehensive illustration incorporating custom types and nested modules:

```
module OuterModule
    export MyType, inner_func

    struct MyType
        value::Int
    end

    function inner_func(x::MyType)
        return x.value * 2
    end

    module InnerModule
        export nested_func

        nested_func() = println("Nested function call")
    end
end

using .OuterModule
using .OuterModule.InnerModule

t = MyType(10)
println(inner_func(t)) # Output: 20
nested_func() # Output: "Nested function call"
```

This example showcases a module OuterModule containing a custom type MyType and a function inner_func. Additionally, OuterModule encapsulates another module, InnerModule, which introduces the function nested_func.

Namespaces are crucial for maintaining clear and conflict-free codebases, especially in large projects or when integrating multiple packages. By enclosing the relevant components in modules, Julia helps mitigate issues such as name collisions and allows for more readable and maintainable code.

You can also control the visibility of names with export and import. The export statement inside a module makes functions, types, or variables available when the module is loaded with using. However, if import is used, you must explicitly list each name you wish to bring into scope:

```
module VisibilityExample
    export visible_function

    visible_function() = println("I am visible!")
```

```
    hidden_function() = println("I stay within the module.")
end

using .VisibilityExample
visible_function() # Works because it's exported

# hidden_function() # Would result in an error because it's not exported
```

Modules are not just a means to keep the global scope clean; they also provide a way to create hierarchically organized and logically separated code. For example, modules can include other modules, and any identifier declared in the parent module is accessible in its child module unless explicitly overridden.

Lastly, modules can serve as a basis for code reusability by encapsulating functionalities that can be seamlessly imported and integrated into different projects. Delivering Julia code in the form of modules ensures encapsulation and modular design, promoting maintainability and scalability in software development.

6.6 Using External Packages

External packages are essential for leveraging shared functionality and libraries within the Julia ecosystem. This section elaborates on how to incorporate external packages into your Julia projects, harnessing their capabilities to enhance your code's efficiency and functionality. Julia's package management system, based on the Pkg module, streamlines the process of adding, using, and managing these packages.

To start using an external package, it must first be installed. For instance, installing the DataFrames package is accomplished with the Pkg.add() function:

```
using Pkg
Pkg.add("DataFrames")
```

Upon executing this command, Pkg fetches the package from the registry and installs it locally. The DataFrames package, a popular tool for handling tabular data, illustrates the process. After installation, the package can be loaded into the current namespace using the using keyword:

```
using DataFrames
```

This command makes the functionalities provided by DataFrames accessible within your script or interactive session. For example, constructing a DataFrame is straightforward:

```
df = DataFrame(Name = ["Alice", "Bob", "Charlie"], Age = [25, 30, 35])
```

To inspect the contents of df, simply print it:

```
println(df)
```

The output will be displayed in a tabular format as follows:

```
3×2 DataFrame
 Row  Name    Age

   1  Alice    25
   2  Bob      30
   3  Charlie  35
```

When using multiple packages, namespace conflicts might occur if different packages export functions or types with the same names. Julia addresses this issue through explicit imports and qualified names. For example, if the StatsBase package and another package define a conflicting function mean, one can disambiguate by using the module name:

```
using StatsBase
StatsBase.mean([1, 2, 3])
```

Alternatively, the import keyword can be used to import specific functions or types, reducing the potential for conflicts:

```
import StatsBase: mean
mean([1, 2, 3])
```

Another powerful feature of Julia's package system is precompilation, which enhances performance by precompiling the package code the first time it is imported. This behavior is automatic but can also be controlled via package configurations.

When collaborating on projects or distributing code, ensuring that all necessary packages and their correct versions are included is crucial. Julia's project environments facilitate this through Project.toml and Manifest.toml files, which detail the project's dependencies and their exact versions, respectively.

To create a new project environment, initiate a new folder and activate it:

```
using Pkg
Pkg.activate("my_project")
Pkg.status() # Verify the environment is active
```

Then, add the required packages within this environment:

```
Pkg.add("DataFrames")
Pkg.add("StatsBase")
```

These commands generate or update the Project.toml and Manifest.toml files accordingly, ensuring reproducibility.

When working with external packages, it is often necessary to reference package documentation and source code to understand their functionalities fully. Julia packages typically include comprehensive documentation accessible online or locally after installation via the ? help mode in the Julia REPL:

```
?DataFrame
```

To further ensure coherent and maintainable code, it is advisable to document dependencies explicitly in the project's main README file or documentation, detailing the purpose of each external package used.

Understanding these practices and tools for managing external packages will enable you to exploit Julia's ecosystem efficiently, resulting in more robust and maintainable code.

6.7 Understanding Project Environments

Project environments in Julia provide an isolated and organized way to manage dependencies for various projects. By providing a self-contained workspace, they help to ensure that different projects do not interfere with each other, which is particularly valuable when working on multiple projects that may require different versions of the same package. This section unveils the key concepts and methodologies involved in creating, managing, and utilizing project environments in Julia.

A project environment in Julia is essentially a directory containing two crucial files: Project.toml and Manifest.toml. The Project.toml file specifies the dependencies and their versions required for the project, while the Manifest.toml file records the detailed, exact state of the complete dependency graph, ensuring reproducibility.

To begin with, you can create a new project environment using the following command in Julia's REPL:

```
import Pkg
Pkg.activate("MyProject")
```

Here, "MyProject" refers to the directory that will serve as your project's root. If the directory does not exist, it will be created. Upon activation, Julia will look for the Project.toml and Manifest.toml files in the specified directory. If they do not exist, Julia will initialize a new project:

```
Pkg.activate("MyProject", shared=true)
Pkg.instantiate()
```

The shared=true argument allows the environment to be shared across various Julia sessions. The Pkg.instantiate() function installs all the packages listed in the Project.toml file, ensuring they match the versions specified in the Manifest.toml file if it exists.

Adding dependencies to a project environment is straightforward. For example, to add the Plots package to your environment, you can run:

```
Pkg.add("Plots")
```

This command modifies the Project.toml and Manifest.toml files to include Plots and its dependencies. To check the status of your current environment, use:

```
Pkg.status()
```

Outputs from running Pkg.status() might look like this:

```
    Status `~/MyProject/Project.toml`
  [91a5bcdd] Plots v1.14.1
```

It's possible to precompile all the packages for enhanced performance using the following command:

```
Pkg.precompile()
```

When you are done with a project, you can deactivate the current environment by calling:

```
Pkg.activate()
```

Running this command without a specific path reverts Julia to the default environment, typically located in $HOME/.julia/environments/v1.x, where x corresponds to your Julia version.

To manage a project environment more efficiently, especially when shared among multiple developers or systems, Manifest.toml plays a critical role. It ensures that every machine sets up the exact environment required by the project. You can share the directory with Project.toml and Manifest.toml files with collaborators, and they can use:

```
Pkg.activate("/path/to/shared/project")
Pkg.instantiate()
```

This ensures that they install the exact set of packages and versions specified in the manifest, resulting in a consistent development environment across all instances.

Another advanced topic in managing project environments in Julia involves the use of named environments and stacked environments. Named environments allow you to create and reference environments by name, while stacked environments allow multiple environments to coexist, sharing their namespaces.

To create a named environment, use:

```
Pkg.activate("@myenv")
Pkg.add("DataFrames")
```

Here, myenv indicates a named environment called myenv, which will be stored in the $HOME/.julia/environments directory. When switching between named environments, you can seamlessly use:

```
Pkg.activate("MyProject")
Pkg.activate("@myenv")
```

Stacked environments allow the layering of environments, such that the availability of packages can be extended without modifying the underlying environment. This can be achieved with:

```
Pkg.activate("MyProject")
Pkg.activate("@additionalEnv")
```

In this scenario, the packages in @additionalEnv are accessible within the MyProject environment but remain logically separated.

Understanding and managing these project environments effectively enables developers to maintain clean, consistent, and reproducible codebases throughout various stages of development as well as across different systems and team collaborations. The described strategies and commands allow for efficient handling of dependencies and environments, facilitating smoother and more robust project workflows.

6.8 Writing Modular and Reusable Code

Writing modular and reusable code is a fundamental practice for efficient software development in Julia. It enhances readability, maintainability, and testability of the code. This section delves into the principles and techniques that enable code to be modular and reusable in Julia, leveraging the language's powerful features such as multiple dispatch, parametric types, and modules.

One of the primary goals is to organize code into self-contained units that can be easily understood and reused across different projects. Here, we explore this practice in detail.

Organizing Code with Modules In Julia, a module is a named region of code that encapsulates variables, functions, types, and other modules, protecting them from the global namespace. To create a module, use the module keyword followed by the module name and the end keyword to close it.

```
module MyModule
export greet

function greet(name::String)
    println("Hello, $name!")
end

end
```

To use the code within a module, the module must be imported or included in another script or module. This can be done using the using or import statement.

```
using .MyModule

greet("World")
```

Encapsulation and Abstraction Modules in Julia allow you to encapsulate implementation details, exposing only the necessary interface through the export statement. This abstraction ensures that users of the module interact only with the intended functions and types.

```
module MyModule

export greet

function greet(name::String)
    println("Hello, $name!")
```

```
end

function internal_function()
    println("This is an internal function")
end

end
```

In the above example, the function internal_function is not exported and thus not available outside MyModule, serving as an internal implementation detail.

Writing Generic Functions Generic programming in Julia promotes writing functions that work with many data types. This is achieved through multiple dispatch and parametric types.

Multiple dispatch allows defining function behavior across different combinations of argument types. Here is an example of a generic function:

```
function add(a, b)
    return a + b
end
```

This same add function works for integers, floats, arrays, and other data types.

Parametric types allow the definition of types that work generically with various data types. For example:

```
struct MyContainer{T}
    value::T
end

function get_value(container::MyContainer{T}) where T
    return container.value
end

container = MyContainer(1.5)
println(get_value(container)) # Output: 1.5
```

Leveraging Standard Libraries and Packages Julia's standard libraries and external packages provide a robust ecosystem for building modular and reusable code. Leveraging these resources reduces duplication of effort and promotes code reuse.

```
using Statistics

values = [1.0, 2.0, 3.0, 4.0]
mean_value = mean(values)
```

```
println("Mean: ", mean_value)
```

The Statistics package is a part of Julia's standard library and offers a range of statistical functions, demonstrating how integrated packages can enhance code modularity and reusability.

Modular File Structure Organizing code into multiple files within the same module is a practice that improves readability and manageability. Julia's include function is used to incorporate files into a module. For example:

```
# File: MyModule.jl
module MyModule

include("greet.jl")
include("farewell.jl")

end

# File: greet.jl
function greet(name::String)
    println("Hello, $name!")
end

# File: farewell.jl
function farewell(name::String)
    println("Goodbye, $name!")
end
```

Both greet and farewell functions reside in separate files, included in MyModule for a modular file structure.

Documentation and Comments Including comprehensive documentation and comments is vital for maintaining modular and reusable code. Documenting modules, functions, and types clarify their purpose and usage.

```
"""
    greet(name::String)

Prints a greeting message to the user.

# Arguments
- `name::String`: The name of the person to greet.

# Examples

julia> greet("Alice")
Hello, Alice!

"""
function greet(name::String)
    println("Hello, $name!")
```

```
end
```

Using triple double quotes """, you can add docstrings that provide documentation for functions, modules, and types. These are accessible through Julia's help system and enhance code readability.

These practices for writing modular and reusable code in Julia ensure your codebase is organized, clear, and scalable, facilitating collaboration and maintenance. Implementing these techniques consistently will lead to significant improvements in the quality and robustness of your software projects.

6.9 Documentation and Testing for Packages

Proper documentation and comprehensive testing of packages are critical components in software development. Documentation enables users to understand and effectively utilize your package, while testing ensures its reliability and stability.

Documentation

In Julia, the documentation system is robust and integrates seamlessly with your code. The primary tools to achieve well-documented code are docstrings and the Documenter.jl package.

Docstrings are literal strings placed just before function definitions, type declarations, or module definitions. They are written using triple double quotes """, and can include markdown formatting. Here is an example:

```
"""
    function_name(arg1::Type1, arg2::Type2) -> ReturnType

This function performs the specified operation using `arg1` and `arg2`.

# Arguments
- `arg1::Type1`: Description of the first argument.
- `arg2::Type2`: Description of the second argument.

# Returns
- `ReturnType`: Description of the return type.

# Examples

julia> function_name(value1, value2)
result

"""
function function_name(arg1::Type1, arg2::Type2) -> ReturnType
```

```
    # function body
end
```

Documenter.jl is a powerful tool for generating HTML documentation. To use it, first add it to your project:

```
julia> using Pkg
julia> Pkg.add("Documenter")
```

Next, create a directory named docs at the root of your project, and inside it create: make.jl, src/index.md, and src/pagename.md files. Here's an example of how make.jl can be written:

```
using Documenter

makedocs(
    modules = [MyPackage],
    clean = true,
)
```

The src/index.md file serves as the entry point for your documentation:

```
# MyPackage.jl

A brief description of your package.

```@autodocs
Modules = [MyPackage]
```

Run make.jl to generate the documentation:

```
julia> include("docs/make.jl")
```

Testing

Julia's built-in Test package provides a simple and effective way to test your code. Testing can be done using @test, @test_throws, and @inferred.

Add the Test package to your project:

```
julia> using Pkg
julia> Pkg.add("Test")
```

Create a test/runtests.jl file, where all your tests will reside. Here is an example of a test script:

```
using Test
using MyPackage

@testset "MyPackage Tests" begin
    @test function_name(3, 4) == 7
    @test_throws ArgumentError function_name()
    @test isapprox(function_name(pi, e), expected_value, atol=1e-5)
```
```

```
end
```

```
Test Summary: | Pass  Total
MyPackage Tests |    3      3
```

Run your tests using the Pkg.test() function:

```
julia> Pkg.test("MyPackage")
```

Continuous integration (CI) tools can automate testing and documentation generation. Popular CI services include GitHub Actions, Travis CI, and GitLab CI. An example of a GitHub Actions workflow for running tests is:

```
name: CI

on: [push, pull_request]

jobs:
  test:
    runs-on: ubuntu-latest
    steps:
    - uses: actions/checkout@v2
    - name: Set up Julia
      uses: julia-actions/setup-julia@v1
      with:
        version: '1.7'
    - name: Install dependencies
      run: julia -e 'using Pkg; Pkg.instantiate()'
    - name: Run tests
      run: julia -e 'using Pkg; Pkg.test()'
```

Documentation and testing are crucial for developing reliable and user-friendly Julia packages. Including concise and thorough docstrings, leveraging automated documentation tools, and writing comprehensive tests will significantly improve the usability and robustness of your package.

6.10 Publishing and Sharing Your Packages

To publish and share Julia packages with the broader community, one must follow a well-defined and meticulous process. This ensures that the package is reliable, well-documented, and easily accessible to other users. The following details elaborate on each step involved in the publishing workflow.

1. Preparing Your Package for Publication

Before publishing, ensure your package follows best practices. These include:

- A consistent and understandable code style.
- Adequate documentation, including a README.md file.
- Comprehensive test coverage to verify functionality.
- A clear version number in Project.toml using Semantic Versioning (SemVer).

2. Registering Your Package

Julia uses the General registry to manage packages. To register your package:

1. Ensure your package adheres to the Julia package guidelines.
2. Create a new version tag in your repository. This can be done using Git commands:

```
git tag v1.0.0
git push origin v1.0.0
```

3. Use the Registrator.jl bot to request registration. Comment on an issue or pull request with:

```
@JuliaRegistrator register()
```

4. Follow any further instructions provided by the Registrator bot or in case corrections are necessary.

3. Continuous Integration and Testing

Setting up continuous integration (CI) helps ensure your package remains functional with future Julia versions and dependencies updates. Services like GitHub Actions or Travis CI can be configured easily.

Example GitHub Actions workflow configuration (.github/workflows/ci.yml):

```
name: CI

on:
  push:
    branches: [ main ]
  pull_request:
```

```
    branches: [ main ]

jobs:
  test:
    runs-on: ubuntu-latest

    steps:
    - uses: actions/checkout@v2
    - name: Set up Julia
      uses: julia-actions/setup-julia@latest
      with:
        version: '1.6'
    - name: Install dependencies
      run: julia -e 'using Pkg; Pkg.instantiate()'
    - name: Run tests
      run: julia -e 'using Pkg; Pkg.test()'
```

4. Writing Good Documentation

Good documentation is crucial for users to understand and use your package effectively. Some key elements include:

- A README.md file with an introduction, installation instructions, basic usage, and examples.
- Docstrings for all public functions and types using Julia's @doc macro.
- Hosting detailed documentation on platforms like GitHub Pages using documentation generators such as Documenter.jl.

Example of a basic function docstring:

```
"""
    add(a::Int, b::Int) -> Int

Adds two integers `a` and `b` and returns the result.

# Examples

julia> add(1, 2)
3

"""
function add(a::Int, b::Int) -> Int
    return a + b
end
```

5. Sharing and Promoting Your Package

Once your package is registered and published, consider the following steps to share and promote it:

- Announce your package on Julia-related forums and social media platforms.

- Write blog posts or tutorials that demonstrate the use and capabilities of the package.
- Contribute to larger projects or frameworks where your package could be beneficial.
- Engage with the community to get feedback and improve the package.

6. Versioning and Releases

Maintain and update your package regularly. Adopting Semantic Versioning (SemVer) ensures that users understand backward compatibility and the introduction of new features or bug fixes. Semantic Versioning follows the format MAJOR.MINOR.PATCH, where:

- MAJOR version increases when there are incompatible API changes.
- MINOR version increases when functionality is added in a backward-compatible manner.
- PATCH version increases when backward-compatible bug fixes are made.

Project.toml example:

```
name = "MyPackage"
uuid = "01234567-89ab-cdef-0123-456789abcdef"
version = "1.0.0"
```

7. Handling Issues and Contributions

Creating guidelines for reporting issues and contributing can streamline the development process. You can add a CONTRIBUTING.md file outlining the contribution process.

- Clearly explain the structure of the codebase.
- Provide instructions on setting up the development environment.
- Establish clear guidelines for code contributions, including coding standards and testing requirements.

CONTRIBUTING.md snippet:

Contributing to MyPackage
We welcome contributions! Here are some guidelines:

1. Fork the repository and create a new branch.
2. Make your changes, ensuring that you follow coding standards and add tests.
3. Submit a pull request with a clear description of your changes.

By following these steps, you ensure that your Julia package is well-prepared for publication and sharing, facilitating widespread adoption and contribution from the community.

6.11 Best Practices for Package Development

Effective package development in Julia demands adherence to a set of best practices to ensure a high-quality, maintainable, and reusable codebase. This section delineates these practices, focusing on code design, documentation, testing, version control, and community engagement.

Code Design

Writing clean, efficient, and modular code is fundamental. Here are some recommendations:

- **Follow Julia Style Guide:** Adopting consistent naming conventions and code formatting as outlined in the official Julia style guide.
- **Modularity:** Break down the package functionality into smaller, reusable modules. Each module should encapsulate a specific piece of functionality.
- **Namespace Management:** Use explicit module names to avoid namespace collisions. For instance, qualify imported functions with their module names when necessary.
- **Performance Optimization:** Use Julia's profiling tools to identify and optimize performance bottlenecks. Avoid type instability and unnecessary allocations.
- **Code Comments:** Include comments that explain the code's logic, particularly the non-obvious parts.

```
function factorial(n::Int)::Int
    # Base case: factorial of 0 is 1
```

```
    return n == 0 ? 1 : n * factorial(n - 1)
end
```

Documentation

Comprehensive documentation ensures that others can understand and utilize your package effectively. Follow these guidelines:

- **Docstrings:** Provide detailed docstrings for all public functions, types, and modules. Use triple quotes """ to encapsulate the docstrings.
- **README:** Create a README file that provides an overview of the package, installation instructions, and basic usage examples.
- **Manuals and Tutorials:** Develop user manuals and tutorials that cover the package's functionality in detail.
- **API Documentation:** Generate API documentation using tools like Documenter.jl. This tool helps create HTML or PDF documentation from docstrings.

```
"""
    factorial(n::Int)::Int

Calculate the factorial of a non-negative integer.
# Arguments
- `n::Int`: Non-negative integer.
# Returns
- `Int`: Factorial of `n`.
# Examples

julia> factorial(5)
120

"""
function factorial(n::Int)::Int
    return n == 0 ? 1 : n * factorial(n - 1)
end
```

Testing

Robust testing strategies are crucial to ensure the reliability of your package:

- **Unit Tests:** Write unit tests for individual functions and features using Julia's built-in Test module.

- **Coverage:** Strive for high code coverage to ensure most of the code paths are tested. Use tools like Coverage.jl to measure and report code coverage.
- **Continuous Integration (CI):** Set up CI using services like GitHub Actions, Travis CI, or CircleCI to automatically run tests on each commit and pull request.
- **Test Organization:** Organize tests in a test directory and follow a structure that mirrors the main package's module structure.

```
using Test

@testset "Factorial Tests" begin
    @test factorial(0) == 1
    @test factorial(5) == 120
end
```

Version Control

Managing your package with version control systems like Git is essential:

- **Semantic Versioning:** Follow semantic versioning (MAJOR.MINOR.PATCH) to indicate backward-incompatible changes, backward-compatible new features, and backward-compatible bug fixes respectively.
- **Commit Messages:** Write clear, descriptive commit messages to document changes effectively.
- **Branching Strategy:** Use branches like main for stable releases and dev or feature branches for ongoing development. Merge changes through pull requests to facilitate code review.
- **Tagging Releases:** Tag releases in Git to denote versions and facilitate easier package distribution.

```
# Example: Git commit message
git commit -m "Add factorial function and tests"

# Example: Tagging a release
git tag -a v1.0.0 -m "Initial release"
git push origin v1.0.0
```

Community Engagement

Active engagement with the community can significantly enhance the quality and adoption of your package:

- **Issue Tracking:** Use GitHub Issues to track bugs, feature requests, and other project-related discussions.
- **Contribution Guidelines:** Provide clear guidelines for contributing to the project. Include details on code style, testing requirements, and the pull request process.
- **Code of Conduct:** Outline a code of conduct to foster a welcoming and inclusive community.
- **Feedback and Collaboration:** Encourage users to provide feedback and contribute by reviewing pull requests and engaging in discussions.

```
# Example: CONTRIBUTING.md
# Contributing to MyPackage

## Code Style
Please follow the Julia style guide for naming conventions and code formatting.

## Testing
Ensure all new features and bug fixes are covered by tests.

## Commit Messages
Write clear, descriptive commit messages.

## Pull Requests
1. Fork the repository
2. Create a new branch for your feature/bugfix
3. Write and test your code
4. Create a pull request to merge your changes
```

Adhering to these best practices in package development will help create a robust, usable, and maintainable Julia package that effectively serves the needs of the community.

Chapter 7

File I/O and Data Handling

This chapter covers the essentials of file input and output in Julia, including reading and writing text and CSV files, handling binary files, and working with JSON data. It introduces DataFrames for managing tabular data, interfacing with databases, and performing network I/O and HTTP requests. The chapter further discusses efficient data loading and storage, serialization and deserialization, handling large datasets, and best practices for data handling in Julia.

7.1 Introduction to File I/O

File Input and Output (I/O) operations are fundamental to many programming tasks, involving the reading and writing of data to and from storage media. In Julia, file I/O is handled efficiently, offering various methods to interface with different file types and formats. Understanding the basic operations for file I/O is crucial, as it serves as the foundation for more advanced data handling techniques discussed later in this chapter.

The essential operations in file I/O include opening a file, reading data from a file, writing data to a file, and closing the file once the operations are complete. These operations ensure that data is correctly saved and retrieved, maintaining the integrity and accessibility of the information.

To begin with, files are opened using the `open` function in Julia. This function can open a file in different modes: read mode, write mode, and append mode. The open function takes two main arguments: the file name and the mode. For example, consider opening a file in read mode:

```
file = open("example.txt", "r")
```

Here, "example.txt" is the name of the file, and "r" signifies that the file is being opened in read mode. Other modes include "w" for write mode and "a" for append mode.

Reading data from the file can be performed using several functions, such as read, readline, and eachline. The read function reads the entire content of the file into a string:

```
content = read(file, String)
```

Alternatively, readline can be used to read a single line from the file:

```
line = readline(file)
```

For reading the file line by line, the eachline function is particularly useful. It returns an iterator that enables traversing the file one line at a time:

```
for line in eachline("example.txt")
    println(line)
end
```

Once the necessary read operations are performed, it is important to close the file to free system resources. The close function is used for this purpose:

```
close(file)
```

Writing data to a file is equally straightforward. When opening a file in write mode, any existing content in the file is typically overwritten. The write function is used to write data to the file:

```
file = open("example.txt", "w")
write(file, "This is an example line of text.")
close(file)
```

Appending data to a file, rather than overwriting it, requires opening the file in append mode. The procedure is similar to writing, but with a different file mode:

```
file = open("example.txt", "a")
write(file, "\nThis line is appended to the file.")
close(file)
```

Julia provides high-level functions that combine these steps, promoting better resource management. The open function can be used with a do block, automatically closing the file after executing the block:

```
open("example.txt", "w") do file
    write(file, "This is an example line of text.")
end
```

This approach ensures that the file is correctly closed even if an error occurs, thereby preventing resource leakage.

The IOBuffer type is used in Julia for in-memory I/O operations. It is particularly useful for testing and creating reusable utilities that need to handle I/O operations without creating actual files on the disk. To illustrate, consider writing and reading from an IOBuffer:

```
buf = IOBuffer()
write(buf, "Testing in-memory I/O operations.")
seekstart(buf) # Reset the position to the beginning
content = read(buf, String)
println(content)
```

Each of these fundamental operations forms the basis for more complex file handling tasks, such as dealing with different file formats and performing network-based I/O. Mastery of these base concepts facilitates a smoother transition into the detailed data manipulation techniques discussed in subsequent sections of this chapter. Understanding how to handle files efficiently is essential for effective data processing and management in Julia. Whether working with small text files or large, structured datasets, these foundational skills enable data handling with accuracy and performance.

7.2 Reading and Writing Text Files

In Julia, handling text files is a fundamental part of data processing. Text files are essentially sequences of characters stored in a file system, and they can be read or written using a variety of functions provided by Julia's standard library. This section provides comprehensive guidance on reading from and writing to text files, examining the key functions and their usage with examples.

Julia uses the open, read, write, and close functions to perform file I/O operations. Additionally, higher-level functions like readlines and writedlm simplify common tasks. We will explore each of these functions, beginning with file reading operations.

Reading Text Files:

To read a text file in Julia, the open function can be used to obtain a file handle in read mode, which can then be passed to the read function to read the file's content. The readlines function offers a convenient way to read all lines into an array of strings.

```
# Open a file and read all contents
file_path = "example.txt"
file = open(file_path, "r")
content = read(file, String)
close(file)

# Display the content
println(content)
```

In the above example, the file located at example.txt is opened in read mode ("r"). The read function is then used to read the entire file content as a string, and the file is subsequently closed using the close function.

For reading line by line, the readlines function is particularly effective:

```
# Read all lines from the file into an array of strings
lines = readlines(file_path)

# Display each line
for line in lines
    println(line)
end
```

Writing Text Files:

Writing to a text file follows a similar pattern but with the file mode set to write ("w"). The write function is employed to output strings to a file. Optionally, the open function can be used with a do block for automatic management of resources.

```
# Open a file in write mode and write content to it
file_path = "output.txt"
file = open(file_path, "w")
write(file, "This is the first line.\n")
write(file, "This is the second line.\n")
close(file)
```

Alternatively, using a do block ensures the file is properly closed when the block completes:

```
# Open the file using a do block to ensure it is closed automatically
open("output.txt", "w") do file
    write(file, "This is written in a do block.\n")
    write(file, "Each write corresponds to a new line.\n")
end
```

For writing arrays of data, the writedlm function from the DelimitedFiles module allows writing plain text files with delimited data.

```
using DelimitedFiles

# Data to write to the file
data = [1.1 2.2 3.3; 4.4 5.5 6.6]

# Write data to a delimited file (e.g., tab-delimited)
writedlm("data.txt", data, '\t')
```

This function simplifies writing matrices to text files, using a specified delimiter such as a tab character ('\t').

Appending to Text Files:

To append data to an existing file, the file must be opened in append mode ("a"):

```
# Open a file in append mode and write additional content
open("output.txt", "a") do file
    write(file, "Appending this line to the file.\n")
end
```

In this case, the new content is added to the end of the file without overwriting the existing data.

Understanding these functions enables efficient manipulation of text files in Julia. This skill is fundamental for tasks such as logging, configuration management, and handling text-based datasets. By mastering these techniques, one can integrate file I/O seamlessly into more complex data processing workflows.

7.3 Working with CSV Files

CSV (Comma-Separated Values) files are ubiquitous in data handling and storage due to their simplicity and ease of use. Julia offers robust support for reading and writing CSV files, primarily through the use of the CSV.jl package.

CSV.jl is a performant, flexible package that facilitates the interaction with CSV files, allowing for seamless integration with the DataFrames.jl package. This section delves into importing the necessary packages, reading CSV data into a DataFrame, writing DataFrames back to CSV, and configuring various options for file handling.

Installation of Required Packages

Ensure that you have the CSV.jl and DataFrames.jl packages installed.

If not, install them using the Pkg package manager:

```
using Pkg
Pkg.add("CSV")
Pkg.add("DataFrames")
```

Reading CSV Files

To read a CSV file into a DataFrame, you can use the CSV.File function which allows the file to be loaded efficiently. An example is illustrated below:

```
using CSV
using DataFrames

df = CSV.File("data.csv") |> DataFrame
```

In this example: - CSV.File parses the CSV file. - The DataFrame constructor converts the parsed file into a DataFrame.

Configuring Options for CSV Reading

The CSV.File function is highly customizable to handle various file formats and structures. Some of the common options include: - header: Specifies if the file contains a header row. - delim: Specifies the delimiter used in the file. - quotechar: Specifies the character used for quoting fields.

For instance, if the file uses a semicolon as a delimiter and no header row, it can be read as follows:

```
df = CSV.File("data.csv"; delim=';', header=false) |> DataFrame
```

Writing CSV Files

Writing a DataFrame to a CSV file is straightforward. Use the CSV.write function:

```
CSV.write("output.csv", df)
```

Customizing CSV Writing

The CSV.write function also offers several options to customize the output. Some examples include: - delim: Specifies the delimiter for the output file. - quotechar: Specifies the character for quoting fields.

For example, to write the DataFrame with tab delimiters and without quoting any fields:

```
CSV.write("output.tsv", df; delim='\t', quotechar='')
```

Handling Large CSV Files

When dealing with large CSV files, memory usage and performance become critical. CSV.jl is optimized to handle large datasets efficiently. It's advisable to minimize the number of intermediary objects created and use streams when possible. For instance, when processing a large CSV file, directly process each row to reduce memory footprint:

```
CSV.File("large_data.csv") do row
    # Process each row
    println(row)
end
```

Error Handling in CSV Files

When dealing with real-world data, CSV files may contain inconsistencies or errors. CSV.jl provides mechanisms to handle such issues gracefully using the ignoreemptylines and normalizelineendings options:

```
df = CSV.File("corrupted_data.csv"; ignoreemptylines=true, normalizelineendings=
    true) |> DataFrame
```

These options can help in parsing files that might otherwise cause errors due to format inconsistencies.

Advanced Features

Beyond the basics, CSV.jl allows for more advanced functionalities such as type inference, column selection, and multifile processing. For instance, specifying column types explicitly can ensure data is read correctly:

```
types = Dict(:column1 => Int, :column2 => Float64)
df = CSV.File("data.csv"; types=types) |> DataFrame
```

Selecting specific columns during file read can be accomplished through the select parameter:

```
df = CSV.File("data.csv"; select=["column1", "column3"]) |> DataFrame
```

In scenarios where data is spread across multiple CSV files, CSV.jl allows for concatenation of files during the read process:

```
filenames = ["data_part1.csv", "data_part2.csv"]
df = vcat([CSV.File(f) |> DataFrame for f in filenames]...)
```

By incorporating these advanced features, handling CSV data in Julia can be both efficient and flexible, catering to the needs of simple data imports to complex processing pipelines.

7.4 Handling Binary Files

Binary files, unlike text files, contain data in a format that is not intended to be human-readable. They are employed for compact storage and quick read/write operations, often utilized for precision-critical and high-performance applications, such as storing numerical data, images, and custom file formats. Julia provides a comprehensive set of functions to handle binary files, supporting both low-level and high-level data access.

To demonstrate basic operations with binary files, we can start with simple read and write functions.

```
# Writing to a binary file
data_to_write = [1, 2, 3, 4, 5]
open("binaryfile.dat", "w") do io
    write(io, data_to_write)
end

# Reading from a binary file
read_data = Vector{Int}(undef, length(data_to_write))
open("binaryfile.dat", "r") do io
    read!(io, read_data)
end

println(read_data)
```

```
[1, 2, 3, 4, 5]
```

In this example, we first create an array data_to_write and write it to a file named binaryfile.dat. The open function is used with the "w" mode to open the file for writing, and the write function is used to write the array into the file. Similarly, we read the data back into a new array read_data using the read! function.

write(io, data) and read!(io, data) are the key functions for binary I/O, where io is the I/O stream, and data is the data to be written or read.

For more complex data structures, we may need to work with reinterpret to manage type casting and ensure binary compatibility. Consider an example where we handle data in struct form.

```
struct MyData
    field1::Int32
    field2::Float64
end

# Example data
data = [MyData(1, 2.5), MyData(2, 3.5)]

# Writing struct to binary file
open("structfile.dat", "w") do io
```

```
    for d in data
        write(io, d.field1)
        write(io, d.field2)
    end
end

# Reading struct from binary file
read_data_struct = Vector{MyData}(undef, length(data))
open("structfile.dat", "r") do io
    for i in 1:length(data)
        field1 = read(io, Int32)
        field2 = read(io, Float64)
        read_data_struct[i] = MyData(field1, field2)
    end
end

println(read_data_struct)
```

```
MyData[MyData(1, 2.5), MyData(2, 3.5)]
```

Here, we define a struct MyData with fields of different types. We write an array of this struct type to a binary file and read it back. Writing and reading are performed field-by-field with appropriate type casting using write(io, value) for writing and read(io, Type) for reading.

Efficient file handling, especially for large binary files, necessitates buffering and block reads/writes. This enhances performance by minimizing the number of I/O operations.

```
buffer_size = 1024
data_to_write = rand(UInt8, 10^6) # large data

# Writing using buffering
open("large_binaryfile.dat", "w") do io
    buffer = Vector{UInt8}(undef, buffer_size)
    for i in 1:buffer_size:length(data_to_write)
        n = min(buffer_size, length(data_to_write) - i + 1)
        buffer[1:n] .= data_to_write[i:i+n-1]
        write(io, buffer[1:n])
    end
end

# Reading using buffering
read_data = Vector{UInt8}(undef, length(data_to_write))
open("large_binaryfile.dat", "r") do io
    buffer = Vector{UInt8}(undef, buffer_size)
    k = 1
    while !eof(io)
        n = read(io, buffer)
        read_data[k:k+n-1] .= buffer[1:n]
        k += n
    end
end

println(sum(read_data .== data_to_write) == length(data_to_write)) # should be
    true
```

```
true
```

In this example, we handle a large dataset by defining a buffer size of 1024 bytes. The data is written and read in chunks, making the process efficient.

Error handling in binary file operations is also critical. Julia's try...catch blocks capture and manage I/O errors effectively.

```
try
    open("nonexistentfile.dat", "r") do io
        data = read(io, Vector{UInt8})
    end
catch e
    if e isa Base.IOError
        println("An I/O error occurred: ", e)
    else
        rethrow(e)
    end
end
```

```
An I/O error occurred: open: no such file or directory (ENOENT)
```

Using try...catch, we capture an IOError when attempting to open a nonexistent file. Proper error handling ensures robustness in file operations.

By employing these techniques, we can handle binary files effectively in Julia, ensuring high performance and precision in data management tasks.

7.5 Using JSON in Julia

JSON (JavaScript Object Notation) is a lightweight data interchange format that is easy for humans to read and write and easy for machines to parse and generate. In Julia, the JSON.jl package provides a comprehensive and efficient means of working with JSON data. This section will explore how to install the JSON.jl package, parse JSON strings, read JSON files, create and manipulate JSON objects, and write JSON data to files.

To start working with JSON in Julia, you need to install the JSON.jl package. You can do this through the Julia package manager by executing the following command:

```
using Pkg
Pkg.add("JSON")
```

After installing the package, you can start using it by including the following line in your script or Julia REPL:

```
using JSON
```

To parse a JSON string into a native Julia data structure, use the JSON.parse function. This function converts a JSON string into a Julia object, typically a Dict or Array. Consider the following example:

```
json_str = """
{
    "name": "Julia",
    "type": "programming language",
    "founded": 2012,
    "users": ["scientists", "engineers", "data analysts"]
}
"""
data = JSON.parse(json_str)
```

The data variable now holds a Dict with the following structure:

```
Dict{String, Any} with 4 entries:
  "name"  => "Julia"
  "type"  => "programming language"
  "founded" => 2012
  "users" => ["scientists", "engineers", "data analysts"]
```

You can access the elements within this dictionary using the standard Julia syntax for dictionaries:

```
name = data["name"]
type_ = data["type"]
founded_year = data["founded"]
users = data["users"]
```

Reading JSON data from a file is equally straightforward. Use the read function to read the file as a string, and then parse it using JSON.parse:

```
file_path = "data.json"
file_content = read(file_path, String)
data = JSON.parse(file_content)
```

Conversely, to write Julia data structures to a JSON file, you can use the JSON.json function to serialize the data. For example, if you want to write the data dictionary back to a JSON file, you can do the following:

```
json_str = JSON.json(data)
write("output.json", json_str)
```

For more complex JSON structures, you might need to perform additional manipulation. Consider the following example where you construct a nested JSON object:

```
nested_data = Dict(
    "languages" => ["Julia", "Python", "R"],
    "info" => Dict(
```

```
        "JULIA" => Dict("year" => 2012, "type" => "high performance"),
        "PYTHON" => Dict("year" => 1991, "type" => "general purpose"),
        "R" => Dict("year" => 1993, "type" => "statistics")
    )
)
json_str = JSON.json(nested_data)
write("nested_output.json", json_str)
```

This code constructs a Dict containing another dictionary, which is then serialized and written to a JSON file. The resulting JSON file will look like this:

```
{
    "languages": ["Julia", "Python", "R"],
    "info": {
        "JULIA": {"year": 2012, "type": "high performance"},
        "PYTHON": {"year": 1991, "type": "general purpose"},
        "R": {"year": 1993, "type": "statistics"}
    }
}
```

Handling large or streamed JSON data is another important aspect. The JSON3.jl package offers enhanced performance and lower memory footprint, especially beneficial for large datasets. Installation and basic usage of JSON3.jl are similar to JSON.jl:

```
using Pkg
Pkg.add("JSON3")
using JSON3

large_json_str = read("large_data.json", String)
data = JSON3.read(large_json_str)
```

To write a Julia object to JSON using JSON3.jl, you can use:

```
JSON3.write("large_output.json", data)
```

Both JSON.jl and JSON3.jl allow easy conversion between JSON strings and native Julia data structures. Choose JSON3.jl for better performance with large data.

Adhering to best practices in handling JSON ensures robust, readable, and maintainable code. It is essential to manage errors gracefully, especially when working with data from external sources. Use try...catch blocks to handle parsing errors:

```
try
    data = JSON.parse(json_str)
catch e
    println("Failed to parse JSON: ", e)
end
```

This enables your program to react appropriately to unexpected errors, facilitating better debugging and error handling.

7.6 DataFrames and Tabular Data

DataFrames are an essential component in Julia for working with tabular data. They provide a flexible and efficient way to handle datasets with various types and sizes. The primary package used for this purpose is DataFrames.jl. DataFrames in Julia are comparable to data frames in R or Python's pandas, offering similar functionality but also benefitting from Julia's performance and readability features.

DataFrame objects allow for the storage and manipulation of heterogeneous data, making them ideal for data analysis tasks. To get started, you need to install the DataFrames package if you haven't already. This can be done using Julia's package manager:

```
using Pkg
Pkg.add("DataFrames")
```

Once installed, you can start by loading the package:

```
using DataFrames
```

Creating a DataFrame from scratch can be accomplished using the DataFrame() constructor. Columns can be passed as arrays or vectors:

```
df = DataFrame(Name=["Alice", "Bob", "Charlie"], Age=[25, 30, 35], Salary=[50000,
    60000, 70000])
```

This creates a DataFrame with three columns: Name, Age, and Salary. Each column can hold data of different types, and the columns are named accordingly.

```
3×3 DataFrame
 Row  Name     Age  Salary

  1   Alice    25   50000
  2   Bob      30   60000
  3   Charlie  35   70000
```

Accessing and Modifying Data

You can access the data in a DataFrame using column names or by indexing. For example, to access the Name column, you can use:

```
names = df.Name
```

Alternatively, you can use the [] operator for more fine-grained access. For instance, you can retrieve the value at the first row and first column:

```
value = df[1, 1]
```

You can also filter rows based on conditions. For example, to find all employees with a salary greater than 55000:

```
high_salary_df = df[df.Salary .> 55000, :]
```

```
2×3 DataFrame
 Row   Name     Age  Salary

   1   Bob      30   60000
   2   Charlie  35   70000
```

Adding new columns or modifying existing ones is straightforward. To add a new column:

```
df.NewCol = [1, 2, 3]
```

Or to modify an existing column:

```
df.Age = df.Age .+ 1
```

```
3×4 DataFrame
 Row   Name     Age  Salary  NewCol

   1   Alice    26   50000      1
   2   Bob      31   60000      2
   3   Charlie  36   70000      3
```

Grouping and Aggregation

DataFrames.jl supports powerful grouping and aggregation functionalities through the groupby() and combine() functions. For example, to group data by Age and calculate the average salary:

```
using Statistics
grouped_df = groupby(df, :Age)
agg_df = combine(grouped_df, :Salary => mean => :AvgSalary)
```

```
3×2 DataFrame
 Row  Age  AvgSalary

   1  26   50000.0
   2  31   60000.0
   3  36   70000.0
```

Merging and Joining DataFrames

Joining data from multiple DataFrames can be performed using the join() function. For example, suppose you have two data frames:

```
df1 = DataFrame(ID=[1, 2, 3], Name=["Alice", "Bob", "Charlie"])
```

```
df2 = DataFrame(ID=[1, 2, 4], Age=[25, 30, 40])
joined_df = join(df1, df2, on=:ID, kind=:inner)
```

```
2×3 DataFrame
 Row  ID  Name    Age

   1   1  Alice   25
   2   2  Bob     30
```

Here, kind=:inner specifies an inner join, but other types of joins are also supported, such as left, right, and outer.

I/O with DataFrames

Reading and writing DataFrames to and from various file formats is crucial for data handling. The CSV.jl package is often used in conjunction with DataFrames.jl for working with CSV files.

To read a CSV file into a DataFrame:

```
using CSV
df_csv = CSV.read("data.csv", DataFrame)
```

To write a DataFrame to a CSV file:

```
CSV.write("output.csv", df)
```

Besides CSV, other formats such as Excel, JSON, and databases can also be interfaced through appropriate packages, e.g., ExcelFiles.jl, JSON.jl, and SQLite.jl.

Taking advantage of the flexibility, efficiency, and rich functionality provided by DataFrames.jl will significantly enhance your capability to manipulate and analyze tabular data in Julia.

7.7 Interfacing with Databases

Interacting with databases is a critical aspect of many applications, and Julia provides robust tools for database interaction. This section delves into utilizing Julia for database operations, covering SQL and NoSQL databases integration, library usage, and essential considerations for database handling.

Julia supports various types of databases through different packages. The most commonly used package for SQL databases is SQLite.jl, and for more complex requirements, ODBC.jl and JDBC.jl can be employed. NoSQL databases are accessible via packages like Mongo.jl for MongoDB.

- SQLite.jl - Designed for lightweight and embedded SQL databases.
- ODBC.jl - Offers connectivity to different SQL data sources via ODBC.
- JDBC.jl - Enables Java-based SQL database connectivity through JDBC.
- Mongo.jl - Provides interfaces for MongoDB, a popular NoSQL database.

Connecting to a Database

Consider using SQLite for initial examples. SQLite is a self-contained, serverless SQL database engine. First, install the package:

```
import Pkg
Pkg.add("SQLite")
using SQLite
```

To establish a connection to an SQLite database:

```
db = SQLite.DB("example.db")
```

If the file example.db does not exist, SQLite will create it.

Creating Tables

Once connected, execute SQL commands to create tables. Here, we create a simple table, students, with columns for id, name, and score:

```
SQLite.execute(db, """
    CREATE TABLE IF NOT EXISTS students (
        id INTEGER PRIMARY KEY,
        name TEXT,
        score REAL
    )
""")
```

Inserting Data

Insert data into the table using SQLite.execute. For inserting multiple rows, use transactions for efficiency:

```
SQLite.execute(db, """
    INSERT INTO students (name, score)
    VALUES ('Alice', 83.4), ('Bob', 89.2), ('Charlie', 97.6)
""")
```

Using transactions:

```
SQLite.execute(db, "BEGIN TRANSACTION")
for (name, score) in [("Alice", 83.4), ("Bob", 89.2), ("Charlie", 97.6)]
    SQLite.execute(db, "INSERT INTO students (name, score) VALUES (?, ?)", (name,
          score))
end
SQLite.execute(db, "COMMIT")
```

Querying Data

To retrieve data, use SQLite.query:

```
result = SQLite.query(db, "SELECT * FROM students")
```

Convert the result to a DataFrame for convenient manipulation if DataFrames.jl is available:

```
using DataFrames
df = DataFrame(result)
```

The DataFrame displays the contents of the students table, facilitating further analysis.

Using Parameters in Queries

Parameterized queries enhance security by preventing SQL injection attacks:

```
name = "Alice"
stmt = SQLite.Stmt(db, "SELECT * FROM students WHERE name = ?")
SQLite.bind!(stmt, 1, name)
result = SQLite.execute(stmt)
```

Working with ODBC

For more advanced use cases, ODBC.jl facilitates connections to various databases via ODBC drivers. Install and use the package as follows:

```
Pkg.add("ODBC")
using ODBC
```

To connect to a database:

```
dsn = "DSN=mydatasource;UID=user;PWD=password"
conn = ODBC.Connection(dsn)
```

Run SQL commands similarly to SQLite:

```
ODBC.execute!(conn, """
    CREATE TABLE employees (
        id INTEGER,
        name VARCHAR(100),
```

```
    salary FLOAT
  )
""")
```

NoSQL Databases

Julia supports NoSQL databases like MongoDB through packages such as Mongo.jl. Install and use:

```
Pkg.add("Mongo")
using Mongo

client = MongoClient("mongodb://localhost:27017")
db = client["mydatabase"]
collection = db["employees"]
```

Insert a document:

```
doc = Dict("name" => "Alice", "position" => "Engineer", "age" => 29)
insert_one(collection, doc)
```

Query a document:

```
query = Dict("name" => "Alice")
result = find(collection, query)
```

Employ these techniques for efficient interaction with various types of databases, ensuring that your Julia applications can manage, manipulate, and retrieve data as needed.

7.8 Network I/O and HTTP Requests

Network I/O and HTTP requests are essential elements for modern applications, particularly those that rely on remote resources or require real-time communication capabilities. Julia provides robust tools for handling network I/O and executing HTTP requests through various packages, with the most notable being HTTP.jl for HTTP interactions. This section explores methods for performing these operations, discusses typical use cases, and provides detailed examples to ensure a comprehensive understanding of the subject.

To perform HTTP requests in Julia, the HTTP.jl package is commonly utilized. It offers capabilities to send and receive data over the Internet and thus is integral for APIs, web scraping, and remote server communication.

To begin, ensure that the HTTP.jl package is installed. If not, it can be added via the Julia package manager:

```
using Pkg
Pkg.add("HTTP")
```

Importing the package is straightforward:

```
using HTTP
```

Making HTTP Requests

The primary functions for making HTTP requests are HTTP.get, HTTP.post, HTTP.put, HTTP.delete, and HTTP.request. These functions allow interaction with web servers using different HTTP methods.

GET Request

A GET request retrieves data from a specified resource. For example, to fetch data from a JSONPlaceholder API:

```
response = HTTP.get("https://jsonplaceholder.typicode.com/posts/1")
```

You can inspect the response by accessing its status, headers, and body:

```
status = response.status
headers = response.headers
body = String(response.body)
```

The status variable will hold the HTTP status code (e.g., 200 for success), headers is a dictionary of the response headers, and body contains the raw response data.

POST Request

A POST request sends data to a server to create a new resource. This commonly includes form submissions or JSON data uploads:

```
url = "https://jsonplaceholder.typicode.com/posts"
data = JSON.json(Dict("title" => "foo", "body" => "bar", "userId" => 1))
response = HTTP.post(url, [("Content-Type", "application/json")], data)
```

Similarly, you can inspect the response using the same approach as with the GET request.

PUT Request

A PUT request updates an existing resource. For example, to update post data:

```
url = "https://jsonplaceholder.typicode.com/posts/1"
```

```
data = JSON.json(Dict("id" => 1, "title" => "foo", "body" => "bar", "userId" => 1)
    )
response = HTTP.put(url, [("Content-Type", "application/json")], data)
```

DELETE Request

A DELETE request removes a specified resource:

```
response = HTTP.delete("https://jsonplaceholder.typicode.com/posts/1")
```

Handling JSON Data

JSON (JavaScript Object Notation) is a common format for data exchange between clients and servers. To handle JSON in Julia, ensure the JSON.jl package is installed:

```
Pkg.add("JSON")
using JSON
```

Parsing JSON data from an HTTP response is straightforward:

```
json_data = JSON.parse(String(response.body))
```

The JSON.parse function converts the JSON string into a Julia Dict or Array.

Error Handling

HTTP requests may fail for various reasons (e.g., network issues, server errors). Proper error handling ensures your program can respond to such events gracefully. The HTTP.jl package uses exceptions to signal errors:

```
try
    response = HTTP.get("https://jsonplaceholder.typicode.com/posts/1")
    status = response.status
    if status == 200
        println("Request successful")
        json_data = JSON.parse(String(response.body))
    else
        println("Request failed with status code: ", status)
    end
catch e
    println("An error occurred: ", e)
end
```

Asynchronous HTTP Requests

For high-concurrency scenarios, such as handling multiple HTTP requests simultaneously, use the @async macro and Julia's Tasks:

```
function fetch_data(url)
    response = HTTP.get(url)
    return JSON.parse(String(response.body))
```

```
end

urls = ["https://jsonplaceholder.typicode.com/posts/1",
        "https://jsonplaceholder.typicode.com/posts/2"]

tasks = [@async fetch_data(url) for url in urls]

results = [fetch(t) for t in tasks]
```

In this example, the @async macro creates asynchronous tasks, which are later collected in the results array.

Integrating these functionalities into your Julia applications enables robust and efficient network communication, enhancing interaction capabilities with remote servers and APIs.

7.9 Efficient Data Loading and Storage

Efficient data loading and storage are critical for applications that handle large datasets or require rapid access to data. This section explores several techniques and best practices for optimizing data operations in Julia, leveraging the language's performance benefits alongside specialized libraries and functions.

To maximize efficiency, it is important to select appropriate file formats, optimize data access patterns, and utilize Julia's built-in functionalities and external libraries designed for performance.

Choosing the Right File Format

Selecting the appropriate file format is the initial step in ensuring efficient data handling. Different file formats are suitable for various types of data and use cases. Commonly used formats include CSV, Parquet, HDF5, and Feather. While CSV files are widely used due to their simplicity, they may not always be the most performance-efficient choice.

- **CSV Files**: Simple and human-readable but may lead to slower read/write operations for large datasets due to the required parsing.

- **Parquet**: Columnar storage format optimized for analytics operations, offering efficient compression and encoding.

- **HDF5**: Hierarchical data format suitable for storing large numerical data arrays, supporting efficient read/write access.
- **Feather**: Binary columnar data format designed for fast read-/write operations, particularly suitable for data frames.

```
# CSV
using CSV
df_csv = CSV.read("data.csv", DataFrame)

# Parquet
using Parquet
df_parquet = DataFrame(Parquet.File("data.parquet"))

# HDF5
using HDF5, DataFrames
h5_data = h5open("data.h5", "r") do file
    read(file, "dataset")
end

# Feather
using Feather
df_feather = Feather.read("data.feather")
```

Memory-Mapped Files

Memory-mapped files allow large files to be read and written directly from disk, avoiding the need to load the entire file into memory. This technique uses operating system-level optimizations to improve performance, especially for very large datasets.

```
using Mmap

file = open("largefile.dat")
mmap_array = Mmap.mmap(file, Array{UInt8}, (file_size,))
close(file)

# Access parts of the file as needed
first_part = mmap_array[1:100]
```

Memory-mapped files are particularly useful for applications requiring random access to different parts of a large file, as they help in managing memory usage efficiently.

Parallel and Asynchronous Data Loading

Julia's support for parallel and asynchronous programming enables efficient data loading and processing. Using the Threads and Distributed libraries, one can parallelize data loading tasks to utilize multiple cores.

```
using Base.Threads

function load_part(file_path, start_row, end_row)
    # Custom function to load a part of the data
    return CSV.read(file_path, DataFrame; skipto=start_row, limit=end_row -
          start_row + 1)
end

# Example file and row ranges
file_path = "data.csv"
threads = 4
num_rows = 10000
rows_per_thread = div(num_rows, threads)

parts = Vector{DataFrame}(undef, threads)

Threads.@threads for i in 1:threads
    start_row = (i - 1) * rows_per_thread + 1
    end_row = i * rows_per_thread
    parts[i] = load_part(file_path, start_row, end_row)
end

# Combine parts into a single DataFrame
full_data = vcat(parts...)
```

Asynchronous data loading can be achieved using Tasks to manage I/O operations without blocking the main program execution.

```
function async_load(file_path, chunk_size)
    open(file_path) do file
        pos = 0
        while !eof(file)
            pos += 1
            line = readline(file)
            # Process line (chunk)
            @async println("Processing chunk $pos: $line")
        end
    end
end

# Load data asynchronously
async_load("largefile.dat", 100)
```

Optimized Data Structures

Selecting optimized data structures is crucial for both loading and storing data efficiently. Julia offers various data structures such as DataFrames, Dictionaries, and specialized array types. Leveraging these appropriately based on the use case can significantly enhance performance.

- DataFrame: Ideal for tabular data manipulation with extensive support for various operations.

- Dict: Suitable for key-value based data where fast lookups are needed.
- **Sparse Arrays**: Efficient for storing data with a lot of zeros, as they consume less memory and are faster to process.

```
using SparseArrays

# Create sparse matrix
rows = [1, 2, 2, 3]
cols = [1, 2, 3, 3]
vals = [1.0, 2.0, 3.0, 4.0]
sparse_matrix = sparse(rows, cols, vals)

# Efficient arithmetic operations
result = sparse_matrix * sparse_matrix'
```

Efficient data storage and loading in Julia require a thoughtful combination of choosing the right file formats, employing memory-mapped files, utilizing parallel and asynchronous loading techniques, and selecting optimized data structures. These strategies collectively enable robust data handling capabilities, essential for building scalable and high-performance applications.

7.10 Data Serialization and Deserialization

Serialization is the process of converting an object or data structure into a format that can be easily stored or transmitted, and subsequently reconstructed. Deserialization is the reverse process whereby the stored or transmitted data is converted back into an object or data structure. In Julia, these operations are essential when dealing with data persistence, network communications, or inter-process communications.

JLD2 is one of the most commonly used packages for serialization in Julia. It allows easy storage and retrieval of Julia data structures in a format that is both space-efficient and quick to read/write. Below is a detailed guide to using JLD2 for serialization and deserialization.

```
using Pkg
Pkg.add("JLD2")
```

Once the JLD2 package is installed, it can be used for various serialization tasks. The basic methods for saving and loading data are JLD2.save and JLD2.load respectively.

Consider an example where we have a dictionary that we want to serialize:

```
using JLD2

# Define a dictionary
data = Dict("x" => 1, "y" => 2, "z" => 3)

# Serialize the dictionary to a JLD2 file
JLD2.@save "data.jld2" data
```

The code snippet above creates a dictionary and saves it in a file named data.jld2. To deserialize this file back into a usable dictionary, we can use the following code:

```
using JLD2

# Load the dictionary from the JLD2 file
JLD2.@load "data.jld2" data

# Accessing the loaded data
println(data)
```

When the file data.jld2 is successfully loaded, the contents of the dictionary can be accessed as demonstrated.

For more complex data structures, such as nested arrays or custom types, JLD2 handles them similarly:

```
using JLD2

# Define a custom Julia struct
struct Point
    x::Float64
    y::Float64
end

# Define a nested array of custom structs
points = [Point(1.0, 2.0), Point(3.0, 4.0), Point(5.0, 6.0)]

# Serialize the nested array of custom structs
JLD2.@save "points.jld2" points
```

The nested array of Point structs is serialized to points.jld2. To deserialize it:

```
using JLD2

# Load the nested array of custom structs from the JLD2 file
JLD2.@load "points.jld2" points

# Accessing the loaded data
println(points)
```

In the example above, upon deserialization, the nested array of Point structs will be reconstructed accurately.

JLD2 provides an efficient way of handling Julia's diverse and complex data structures. It also ensures cross-version compatibility, making it a durable choice for long-term data storage.

Additionally, for scenarios requiring a more portable and human-readable format, JSON can be utilized. The JSON package in Julia is used for encoding and decoding data in JSON format.

```
using Pkg
Pkg.add("JSON")
```

To serialize data into JSON, you can use the JSON.json function:

```
using JSON

# Define a dictionary
data = Dict("a" => 1, "b" => 2, "c" => 3)

# Serialize the dictionary to a JSON string
json_string = JSON.json(data)

# Save the JSON string to a file
open("data.json", "w") do file
    write(file, json_string)
end
```

This will create a file data.json containing the serialized data. To deserialize this JSON string back into a dictionary:

```
using JSON

# Read the JSON string from the file
json_string = open("data.json", "r") do file
    read(file, String)
end

# Deserialize the JSON string back into a dictionary
data = JSON.parse(json_string)

# Accessing the loaded data
println(data)
```

The JSON package is straightforward and useful for interchanging data between different programming environments.

For high-performance binary data storage, consider the Serialization standard library in Julia:

```
using Serialization

# Define a dictionary
data = Dict("p" => 1, "q" => 2, "r" => 3)

# Serialize the data to a file
open("data.bin", "w") do file
    serialize(file, data)
```

```
end

# Deserialize the data from the file
data = open("data.bin", "r") do file
    deserialize(file)
end

# Accessing the loaded data
println(data)
```

The Serialization library is robust and allows for quick storing and retrieval of Julia objects in a binary format, ensuring space efficiency.

Julia's serialization and deserialization capabilities are versatile, supporting various data formats and structures. Understanding these mechanisms is crucial for effective data management and interoperability in computational tasks.

7.11 Handling Large Datasets

Handling large datasets efficiently is a critical skill when working with big data applications in Julia. This section delves into the techniques and tools available in Julia to work with large datasets, ensuring robust performance and efficient resource use.

One of the primary considerations when dealing with large datasets is memory management. Julia provides several tools and functions to handle large data efficiently without consuming excessive memory. One such tool is the Distributed module, which allows for the parallel and distributed processing of data.

```
using Distributed
addprocs(4) # Adding 4 worker processes
@everywhere using DataFrames

# Create a large DataFrame
df = DataFrame(rand(Float64, 10^7, 10))

# Split the DataFrame for parallel processing
chunk_size = ceil(Int, size(df, 1) / nworkers())
chunks = [df[i:min(i+chunk_size-1, end), :] for i in 1:chunk_size:size(df, 1)]

# Function to process each chunk
@everywhere function process_chunk(chunk)
    # Example: Add a new column with the sum of all other columns
    chunk[!, :sum] = rowwise(sum, chunk[:, 1:end-1])
    return chunk
end

# Distribute processing over workers
results = pmap(process_chunk, chunks)
```

```
# Combine the results
combined_df = vcat(results...)
```

In the above example, the Distributed module is used to handle a large DataFrame by splitting it into smaller chunks and processing each chunk in parallel. This approach significantly reduces computation time and better utilizes available CPU resources.

Another important aspect of handling large datasets is the efficient use of Julia's array operations and broadcasting. By leveraging broadcasting, Julia can perform operations on entire arrays or DataFrames without the need for explicit loops, resulting in more concise and faster code.

```
using Random

# Generate a large array
large_array = rand(10^7)

# Perform operations using broadcasting
scaled_array = large_array .+ 5 .* large_array
```

Broadcasting, as demonstrated, allows element-wise operations to be performed efficiently on large arrays in a single expression.

For data storage and access, Julia provides the HDF5 package, particularly useful when the dataset size exceeds the available memory. The HDF5 format enables the storage of large amounts of data in a hierarchical structure, facilitating both reading and writing data efficiently.

```
using HDF5

# Creating an HDF5 file and writing large dataset
h5write("large_data.h5", "dataset", rand(Float64, 10^7))

# Reading the dataset from HDF5 file
data = h5read("large_data.h5", "dataset")
```

By using the HDF5 package, large datasets can be efficiently stored and retrieved without exhausting system memory.

Another tool for handling large datasets is the JuliaDB package, which is designed for working with out-of-core data that cannot fit into memory. JuliaDB.jl supports distributed computing and can handle datasets larger than the available RAM by chunking and processing data incrementally.

```
using JuliaDB

# Load CSV file into JuliaDB
table = loadtable("large_dataset.csv")
```

```
# Perform operations on JuliaDB table
result = JuliaDB.filter(row -> row[:column] > threshold, table)
```

The ability to load, manipulate, and query large datasets directly from disk makes JuliaDB a powerful tool for handling such scenarios in Julia.

Lastly, the use of efficient data structures, such as SparseArrays, can significantly reduce memory usage when dealing with datasets that have a large number of zero or non-relevant entries.

```
using SparseArrays

# Creating a large sparse array
sparse_matrix = sprand(10^6, 10^6, 0.001)

# Performing matrix operations
result = sparse_matrix * transpose(sparse_matrix)
```

SparseArrays enable the efficient storage and manipulation of matrices with a significant number of zero elements, saving both memory and computation time.

By combining Julia's capabilities for parallel and distributed processing, efficient array operations, specialized data storage formats, and memory-efficient data structures, users can handle large datasets effectively and perform complex analyses with optimal performance.

7.12 Best Practices for Data Handling

Efficient and accurate data handling is crucial in any computational task, especially in a high-level language like Julia, which is designed for performance and ease of use. This section outlines several best practices for dealing with data in Julia, covering aspects such as data integrity, performance optimization, memory management, and code readability.

1. Validate Your Data Inputs: It is essential to validate the data inputs before processing them. Ensuring that the data conforms to expected formats and ranges prevents unwanted errors and exceptions during runtime.

```
function validate_data(data::DataFrame)
    # Example validation checks
    for col in names(data)
        if eltype(data[!, col]) == Int
            @assert all(data[!, col] .>= 0) "Negative value found in column $col"
        end
    end
end
```

2. Use DataFrames.jl for Tabular Data: When working with tabular data, using the DataFrame type from the DataFrames.jl package provides powerful tools for data manipulation and analysis. Leverage its functions for filtering, grouping, merging, and transforming data.

```
using DataFrames

df = DataFrame(A = 1:5, B = 6:10)
df_filtered = filter(row -> row.A > 2, df)
```

3. Opt for Efficient Data Storage Formats: Select appropriate data storage formats based on the nature of your data and the analysis to be performed. For large datasets, binary formats like HDF5 or Feather can be more efficient than text-based formats like CSV or JSON.

```
using DataFrames, Feather

df = DataFrame(A = 1:100000, B = 101:200000)
Feather.write("data.feather", df)
```

4. Handle Missing Data Properly: Julia provides the Missing type to handle missing values. Use functions such as coalesce, allowmissing, and disallowmissing to manage missing data appropriately.

```
df = DataFrame(A = [1, 2, missing, 4], B = [missing, 6, 7, 8])
df_cleaned = allowmissing(df)
df_cleaned[!, :A] = coalesce.(df_cleaned[!, :A], 0)
```

5. Leverage Julia's Performance Features: Use Julia's performance-enhancing features to handle data efficiently. This includes leveraging type annotations, @inbounds for removing bounds checking in loops, and parallel processing where applicable.

```
function process_data_optimized(data::Vector{Int})
    result = Vector{Int}(undef, length(data))
    @inbounds for i in 1:length(data)
        result[i] = data[i] * 2
    end
    return result
end
```

6. Ensure Memory Efficiency: To handle large datasets without running out of memory, use Julia's memory profiling tools to understand and optimize memory usage. Utilize functionsresize!, pre-allocate arrays, and avoid unnecessary copying of data.

```
using Base.CoreLogging

function memory_efficient_computation()
```

```
    data = rand(Float64, 1000000)
    @core_logger MemoryProfiler() begin
        result = process_data_optimized(data)
        # Perform computations here
    end
end
```

7. Use Vectorized Operations: Whenever possible, use vectorized operations instead of explicit loops to take advantage of Julia's optimized array functionality. Functions like map, broadcast, and others can be used to apply operations across arrays efficiently.

```
data = rand(1:10, 100000)
squared_data = data .^ 2
```

8. Create Reusable Code: For data handling tasks that are repetitive, write modular and reusable functions. This not only makes your code more maintainable but also reduces redundancy.

```
function clean_data(df::DataFrame, cols::Vector{Symbol})
    for col in cols
        df[!, col] = coalesce.(df[!, col], 0)
    end
    return df
end

df_cleaned = clean_data(df, [:A, :B])
```

9. Document Your Code: Providing documentation for your functions and data manipulation steps is crucial for reproducibility and collaboration. Use Julia's documentation syntax to add docstrings to your functions.

```
"""
    clean_data(df::DataFrame, cols::Vector{Symbol}) -> DataFrame

Clean the specified columns in the DataFrame by replacing missing values with zero.
"""
function clean_data(df::DataFrame, cols::Vector{Symbol})
    for col in cols
        df[!, col] = coalesce.(df[!, col], 0)
    end
    return df
end
```

10. Test Your Code: Regular testing ensures that your data processing functions perform correctly. Utilize Julia's testing framework to write tests for your data handling functions.

```
using Test

@testset "Data Cleaning Tests" begin
    df = DataFrame(A = [1, 2, missing], B = [missing, 4, 5])
    df_cleaned = clean_data(df, [:A, :B])
```

```
    @test df_cleaned[!, :A] == [1, 2, 0]
    @test df_cleaned[!, :B] == [0, 4, 5]
end
```

Adhering to these best practices in data handling within Julia ensures optimal performance, maintainability, and reliability of your data processing tasks. Integrating proper validation, leveraging Julia's efficient data structures, and maintaining a clean and modular codebase contribute significantly to professional and effective programming outcomes.

Chapter 8

Metaprogramming in Julia

This chapter delves into metaprogramming in Julia, beginning with an understanding of expressions and abstract syntax trees (AST). It explains the basics of macros and how to create them, including macro hygiene and advanced techniques. The chapter covers code generation, reflection, code introspection, and debugging macros. It concludes with best practices for metaprogramming and case studies illustrating practical applications.

8.1 Introduction to Metaprogramming

Metaprogramming in Julia allows programs to treat other programs as data, enabling the generation, transformation, and analysis of code. At the core of this capability is the distinction between code and its execution, allowing for powerful abstractions and optimizations.

Metaprogramming revolves around the manipulation of Expr objects, which represent unevaluated expressions in Julia. Consider the following example, demonstrating the creation of a simple expression:

```
expr = :(a + b * c)
```

In this example, expr is an Expr object encapsulating the code a + b * c. This object comprises three key elements: the operator (:+), and the operands (a and b * c). By representing code in this form, Julia facilitates dynamic code generation and transformation.

Next, introduce the concept of quoting in Julia, which is crucial when dealing with expressions. The quote block allows for the construction of unevaluated expressions:

```
quote
    a + b * c
end
```

This block is functionally identical to the previous example using the :( ) syntax. Both create an expression that can be manipulated before evaluation.

Understanding the structure of expressions often requires deconstruction. Julia provides utilities like dump to inspect the components of expressions:

```
dump(expr)
```

The output reveals the hierarchical structure of the expression:

```
Expr
  head: Symbol call
  args: Array{Any}((3,))
    1: Symbol +
    2: Symbol a
    3: Expr
      head: Symbol call
      args: Array{Any}((3,))
        1: Symbol *
        2: Symbol b
        3: Symbol c
```

This breakdown highlights the nesting of expressions, with the outer addition operation and the inner multiplication operation clearly delineated.

Julia's macros offer another dimension of metaprogramming. Macros operate on expressions, transforming them before compilation. Unlike functions, macros must be called with a preceding @ symbol. A simple example of a macro might be:

```
macro sayhello()
    return :(println("Hello, World!"))
end
```

When the macro @sayhello is invoked, it generates and evaluates the expression to print "Hello, World!":

```
@sayhello
```

Macro definitions follow the same syntax as function definitions but produce expressions instead of values. Utilizing macros can significantly reduce boilerplate code, allowing for concise and reusable patterns. However, macros must be used judiciously to ensure maintainability and readability of code. The concept of macro hygiene, which will be discussed in detail in subsequent sections, is vital to prevent name clashes and inadvertent variable capture.

Another pivotal aspect of metaprogramming involves the concept of @generated functions. These are special functions in Julia where the code generated depends on the types of the input arguments. Such functions can yield highly optimized and specialized code for different types, enhancing performance. An example @generated function might look like this:

```
@generated function mysum(a::T, b::T) where T
    if T <: Integer
        return :(a + b)
    else
        return :(float(a) + float(b))
    end
end
```

In this example, the method implementation is determined at compile-time based on the argument types, allowing for efficient integer addition while ensuring proper floating-point operations for other types.

Reflection and code introspection, aspects that will be elaborated in subsequent sections, provide mechanisms to examine and manipulate the properties of code structures. Julia supports querying types, methods, and metadata, thereby enabling adaptive and optimized code generation strategies.

Throughout this chapter, the high-level concepts introduced here will be integrated with practical examples. These include constructing complex macros, ensuring macro hygiene, leveraging code generation, and employing reflection and introspection techniques. The aim is to equip you with the tools necessary for sophisticated metaprogramming, driving both performance and expressive power in Julia.

Thus, the foundational understanding of expressions and basic macro usage sets the stage for more advanced techniques. Proceeding sections will expand on these basics, providing a comprehensive exploration of Julia's metaprogramming prowess.

8.2 Understanding Expression and AST

Expressions and Abstract Syntax Trees (AST) are fundamental concepts in metaprogramming, allowing manipulation of code as data. Julia possesses a rich and expressive syntax for representing and transforming code, which stems from its robust handling of expressions and ASTs.

In Julia, an expression is represented by the Expr type. Code written in Julia is first parsed into an Expr object before being compiled and executed. Each Expr object consists of a head symbol and a list of arguments, forming a tree structure. This tree structure is the Abstract Syntax Tree (AST) of the code, which accurately captures its syntactic structure.

To create an expression, use the : (colon) operator in conjunction with parentheses. For example:

```
ex = :(a + b * c)
```

This command creates an Expr object representing the expression a + b * c. To examine its components, use the dump function:

```
dump(ex)
```

The output will be:

```
Expr
  head: Symbol call
  args: Array{Any}((3,))
    1: Symbol +
    2: Symbol a
    3: Expr
      head: Symbol call
      args: Array{Any}((3,))
        1: Symbol *
        2: Symbol b
        3: Symbol c
```

This output illustrates that the expression a + b * c is parsed into an Expr object with a head representing the operation and args representing the operands. The args themselves can be symbols or further nested expressions, as seen with the multiplication b * c within the addition.

Manipulating an AST involves operating on these nested Expr objects. For instance, you could replace the addition operation with subtraction:

```
ex.head = :-
```

Now, the Expr object ex represents a - b * c. To further note, elements of the args array can be directly accessed and manipulated:

```
ex.args[1] = :*
```

Such manipulations allow complex transformations, enabling the creation of dynamic and adaptable programs. To convert an Expr object back into executable code, use the eval function:

```
eval(ex)
```

This command compiles and executes the expression stored in ex.

Abstract Syntax Trees also support traversal and pattern matching, which are essential for more intricate manipulations. Implement functions to traverse an AST recursively, identifying and transforming specific patterns. For example:

```
function transform_expressions(ex::Expr)
    if ex.head == :+ && length(ex.args) == 3 && ex.args[3] == :c
        return :($(ex.args[1]) - $(ex.args[2]))
    else
        return ex
    end
end
```

This function transforms expressions of the form x + y + c to x - y, illustrating selective manipulation based on patterns. Applying the function requires:

```
ex = :((a + b + c) * d)
new_ex = transform_expressions(ex)
```

Here, the transformed expression new_ex will reflect the specified pattern transformation.

The utility of manipulating expressions and ASTs in Julia extends to creating powerful macros. Since macros operate on code before its evaluation, understanding and manipulating expressions and ASTs is critical. Further chapters will provide an in-depth exploration of utilizing these fundamentals in creating and debugging macros.

Understanding these concepts and techniques lays the groundwork for effective metaprogramming in Julia, enabling developers to write more concise, efficient, and dynamic code.

8.3 Macros: Basics and Syntax

Macros in Julia allow for powerful and flexible code transformation during the compilation process. Unlike functions, which operate on values, macros operate on code itself. This section explores the syntax and fundamental concepts necessary to create and utilize macros effectively.

Understanding Macros

A macro in Julia is defined using the @ symbol. When a macro is invoked, it transforms the input expressions into a different expression that is subsequently evaluated. This transformation allows you to introduce new syntactic constructs and perform compile-time computations.

Defining a Macro

To define a macro, use the macro keyword followed by the macro name and a block of code. The code block represents the transformation that the macro will apply to its input.

```
macro sayhello()
    return :(println("Hello, World!"))
end
```

This macro, named sayhello, generates an expression that calls println with the string "Hello, World!". When invoked, the macro replaces the call to sayhello() with the generated expression.

```
@sayhello
```

The execution of the above line will produce the following output:

```
Hello, World!
```

Macro Arguments

Just like functions, macros can also accept arguments. The arguments of macros are passed as expressions, allowing the macro to inspect and manipulate the passed code before evaluation.

```
macro say(greeting, name)
    return :(println($greeting, ", ", $name, "!"))
end
```

Here, say is a macro that takes two arguments and constructs an expression that prints a greeting message. The $ symbol is used to splice the arguments into the generated expression.

```
@say("Hello", "Alice")
```

Executing the above line yields:

Hello, Alice!

Escaping and Hygiene

In macros, it is essential to manage variable scopes carefully. Macro hygiene ensures that variables within a macro do not accidentally conflict with variables in the surrounding code. Julia provides the esc function to handle such cases.

Consider the following example without hygiene:

```
macro counter()
    quote
        local x = 0
        x += 1
        println(x)
    end
end
```

Using @counter in a context where x is already defined could lead to unexpected results due to variable shadowing.

```
x = 10
@counter # This will print 1, but x in the caller remains 10.
```

To avoid such conflicts, use esc to indicate that an expression should be evaluated in the caller's scope.

```
macro counter_hygienic()
    quote
        local x = 0
        x += 1
        println($(esc(:x)))
    end
end
```

This ensures that the variable x within the macro is distinct from any x in the caller's scope.

Interpolation and Quotations

Macros often use quotation and interpolation to construct new code expressions. The :() syntax creates a quoted expression, while $ interpolates variables into the quoted expression.

```
macro introduce(name)
    return quote
        println("Hello, ", $(esc(name)), "! My name is Julia.")
    end
end
```

```
@introduce "Bob"
```

This will produce:

Hello, Bob! My name is Julia.

Nested Macros

Macros can invoke other macros within their definitions. This requires careful handling to ensure that nested macros are expanded correctly.

Consider the following example:

```
macro nested_outer()
    return quote
        println("Outer macro")
        @nested_inner
    end
end

macro nested_inner()
    return :(println("Inner macro"))
end
```

Using the outer macro:

```
@nested_outer
```

The output will be:

Outer macro
Inner macro

This demonstrates how macros within macros are expanded during the compilation phase.

Error Handling in Macros

Macros should include mechanisms for error checking and handling to ensure robustness. Use the @error, @warn, and @info macros for logging within macro definitions.

```
macro safe_divide(a, b)
    if b == 0
        return :(println("Error: Division by zero!"))
    else
        return :(println($a / $b))
    end
end
```

This safe_divide macro checks for division by zero and provides appropriate error messages.

```
@safe_divide 10 0
@safe_divide 10 2
```

Error: Division by zero!
5.0

These examples illustrate the fundamental syntax and concepts required to define and use macros in Julia. By mastering these basics, advanced macro techniques and metaprogramming constructs become more approachable.

8.4 Creating Your First Macro

Macros in Julia allow us to generate and include fragments of customized code during runtime. They empower developers to manipulate code as data and facilitate sophisticated metaprogramming techniques. This section covers the creation of your first macro, focusing on syntax, the mechanics of how macros operate, and key considerations for writing effective macros.

Begin with defining the syntax for macros. In Julia, a macro is defined using the macro keyword followed by the macro name and a block of code. For example, let us create a simple macro that adds two numbers. First, define a macro that prints a statement:

```
macro sayhello()
    return :(println("Hello, World!"))
end
```

The expression :(println("Hello, World!")) is an example of a quoted expression. Quoting prevents an expression from being evaluated immediately, which is central to how macros work—they manipulate code before it is executed.

You invoke a macro using the @ symbol followed by the macro name. To call our sayhello macro:

```
@sayhello()
```

When the above macro is called, the macro expands at parse time, effectively replacing @sayhello() with println("Hello, World!"), and subsequently executing it.

For a more practical example, let's explore a macro that takes arguments. Suppose we want a macro that calculates the square of a number. We define it as:

```
macro square(x)
    return :( $x * $x )
end
```

Here, $x interpolates the value of x into the expression. This macro is then used as:

```
@square(4)
```

And the output of this macro execution would be:

```
16
```

Now, we will discuss hygiene, which pertains to preventing unintended variable capture and ensuring that macros are robust and reusable. Consider the following example where the macro is designed to use local variables inside its scope without affecting variables in the user's code:

```
macro hygienic_square(x)
    quote
        local y = $x
        y * y
    end
end
```

Utilizing the quote ... end block and local keyword ensures the variable y is not overridable by any user-defined variable with the same name. Invoking @hygienic_square does not interfere with other definitions of y outside the macro.

To examine more complex examples, consider a macro that generates a function to perform operations. Suppose we desire a macro, @op_function, that creates functions for basic arithmetic operations:

```
macro op_function(op)
    return :(function operate(a, b)
                return a $op b
            end)
end
```

With this macro, defining an add function becomes simple:

```
@op_function(+)
```

This would dynamically generate:

```
function operate(a, b)
    return a + b
end
```

Testing operate(4, 5) would yield:

```
9
```

Reflection and introspection capabilities of macros provide powerful tools for deeper analysis of code, allowing the macros to adapt their behavior dynamically. For instance, you can introspect the type of an argument passed to a macro and alter its behavior accordingly:

```
macro type_inspect(x)
    return :(println("The type of ", $x, " is ", typeof($x)))
end
```

Executing @type_inspect(42) would print:

```
The type of 42 is Int64
```

These examples serve as a foundation for basic macro creation. In the next sections, we will delve into advanced macro techniques, including recursive macros, parameterized macros, and leveraging macros for code generation at a higher level. Understanding and practicing these initial steps will prime you for these more sophisticated constructs.

8.5 Hygiene in Macros

Macro hygiene is a crucial concept in metaprogramming within Julia, designed to prevent unintended interactions between variables in the macro and those in the surrounding code. Understanding how to maintain and manage scope within macros eliminates many potential bugs and makes the code more predictable and maintainable.

Macro Hygiene Basics In Julia, macros work by manipulating the code as data structures, specifically Expr objects, before the runtime executes them. This manipulation often involves generating new variable names or referencing existing ones. Macro hygiene ensures these generated or referenced variable names do not clash with names in the user's code.

Consider the following example where a macro without hygiene could cause issues:

```
macro without_hygiene()
    quote
        a = 1
    end
end

function test_without_hygiene()
    a = 10
    @without_hygiene
    println(a)
end

test_without_hygiene()
```

The expected output might be 10, as a is initially assigned 10 before the macro is called. However, due to the lack of hygiene, the macro assigns a a value of 1, overshadowing the original assignment. The actual output is:

```
1
```

Ensuring Hygienic Macros Julia provides tools to create hygienic macros, primarily through the use of the $ operator for interpolation and the gensym function. The $ operator ensures that variables within the macro evaluate in the context where the macro is called. The gensym function generates unique symbols, preventing unintended name collisions.

Here is an example of a macro that ensures hygiene:

```
macro with_hygiene()
    quote
        local a = 1
    end
end

function test_with_hygiene()
    a = 10
    @with_hygiene
    println(a)
end

test_with_hygiene()
```

In this version, local keyword confines a within the macro's scope, ensuring it doesn't interfere with the a in test_with_hygiene. The output correctly displays:

```
10
```

Additionally, using gensym can ensure that even dynamically generated variable names remain unique:

```
macro create_temp()
    quote
        $(esc(gensym("temp"))) = 1
    end
end
```

The esc function is vital in macros as it prevents further interpolation and allows expressions to be evaluated in the correct context.

Practical Example Leveraging macro hygiene in a more practical example can illustrate deployment in typical Julia code. Suppose a macro is designed to append elements to an array safely:

```
macro safe_push(arr, x)
    quote
        local arr_sym = $(esc(arr))
        local tmp = $x
        push!(arr_sym, tmp)
    end
end

function test_safe_push()
    items = [1, 2, 3]
    @safe_push(items, 4)
    println(items)
end

test_safe_push()
```

The macro safe_push safely pushes x to arr without risking name collisions. By employing local and esc, the macro confines the temporary variables within its scope and interpolates arr correctly in the context where test_safe_push is executed. The output is:

```
[1, 2, 3, 4]
```

Hygiene and Scope Management Understanding that macro-expansions happen at parse time, before runtime execution, reinforces the importance of scope management within macros. Each variable generated within a macro should be either entirely unique or scoped such that it does not leak or overshadow existing user-defined names.

A common approach is naming conventions combined with gensym for clarity and uniqueness:

```
macro unique_var_example()
    unique_var = gensym("unique")
    quote
        local $(unique_var) = 42
        println($(unique_var))
    end
end

@unique_var_example
```

By ensuring the generated variables do not clash with user variables, macro hygiene promotes code robustness and maintainability. The output demonstrates the concept:

```
variable unique identifier
```

Practicing hygiene in macros avoids positional conflicts, enhances clarity, supports debugging, and ultimately fosters a trustworthy implementation environment. When adhering to these practices, macros remain powerful tools integrated seamlessly within the larger Julia codebase.

8.6 Advanced Macro Techniques

In this section, we explore advanced techniques in macro writing that enable powerful and flexible code transformations. Building on our understanding of basic macros, we will delve into the following advanced topics: recursion in macros, macro-generated functions, and the use of the @generated macro.

Recursive Macros:

Recursive macros are essential when you need to perform repetitive transformations. Consider a situation where we want to create a macro that generates a nested set of expressions.

```
macro nested_expr(n::Int, expr)
    if n <= 0
        return esc(expr)
    else
        return :( $(nested_expr(n-1, :(2 * $(esc(expr))))) )
    end
end
```

Here, the macro @nested_expr takes an integer n and an expression expr. If n is zero or less, it returns the expression as is. Otherwise, it recursively calls itself, reducing n by one and doubling expr each time.

Usage:

```
@n = 3
@nested_expr $n a + b
```

Output:

```
2 * (2 * (2 * (a + b)))
```

Macro-generated Functions:

Leveraging macros to generate functions dynamically can streamline code where the function body relies on patterns or templates. Such techniques are useful in DSL (Domain-Specific Language) implementations or generating boilerplate code.

```
macro gen_func(fname, arg_list, body)
    quote
```

```
        function $(esc(fname))($(esc(arg_list))...)
            $body
        end
    end
end
```

In the above macro @gen_func, we dynamically generate a function with a specified name fname, arguments arg_list, and body body. This macro is especially powerful when combined with other metaprogramming constructs.

Usage:

```
@gen_func foo (a, b) begin
    a + b
end
```

Resultant function:

```
function foo(a, b)
    a + b
end
```

The @generated Macro:

The @generated macro provides a mechanism to create functions where the code depends on the types of the input arguments. This enables high-performance code as Julia can optimize based on the specific types provided.

```
@generated function mymul(a, b)
    quote
        if $a isa Int && $b isa Int
            return :(a * b)
        elseif $a isa Float64 || $b isa Float64
            return :(float(a) * float(b))
        else
            return :(a * b)
        end
    end
end
```

Here, the @generated macro generates multiplication functions specialized based on the types of the arguments. It allows for type-specific optimizations while retaining the generality of a single function interface.

Usage:

```
mymul(3, 4) # returns 12 for integer inputs
mymul(3.0, 4.0) # returns 12.0 for float inputs
```

Employing these advanced macro techniques facilitates the development of highly efficient and maintainable code. Recursive macros allow for complex nesting and repeated transformations. Macro-generated functions simplify the creation of repetitive or templated function definitions. The @generated macro provides a sophisticated mechanism for type-based code specialization. These techniques, while powerful, should be used judiciously to balance clarity and complexity in your codebase.

8.7 Using Code Generation

Code generation in Julia allows for the programmatic creation of source code during the runtime of a program. This functionality is intrinsic to metaprogramming and serves as a powerful tool to simplify repetitive coding tasks, optimize performance, and enable domain-specific language (DSL) constructions. One can utilize code generation to write code that writes other code, thereby extending Julia's capabilities and enhancing productivity.

Fundamentals of Code Generation

In Julia, code generation leverages the concept of expressions (Expr), which represent Julia code in an abstract syntax tree (AST). These expressions can be manipulated programmatically to produce new code dynamically.

The fundamental structure of an Expr is an S-expression (symbolic expression), which consists of a head symbol and sub-expressions. The head symbol indicates the type of expression, such as *call* for function calls, *quote* for quoted expressions, and *lambda* for anonymous functions. Let's illustrate this with examples.

```
# Create an expression representing (x + y)
ex = :(x + y)

# This can be dissected into:
println(ex.head) # Output: :call
println(ex.args) # Output: Any[:+, :x, :y]
```

In this example, the head :call signifies a function call, and the arguments include the addition operator :+ and the variables ::x and ::y.

Generating Code Dynamically

Julia allows for dynamic code generation using the @eval macro or the eval function. The @eval macro evaluates the expression in the global scope, whereas eval can be used to evaluate expressions within the current scope.

Consider defining a function dynamically:

```
# Define the function g(x) = x^2 + 2x + 1 dynamically
ex = quote
    function g(x)
        return x^2 + 2x + 1
    end
end

# Evaluate the expression to define the function
@eval $ex

# Test the dynamically generated function
println(g(2)) # Output: 9
```

Here, the quote block encapsulates the function definition within an expression, which is subsequently evaluated using @eval.

Template-Based Code Generation

Template-based code generation allows creating multiple similar functions or constructs by looping through a set of parameters. This approach is practical for generating boilerplate code or when dealing with multiple methods that differ slightly.

```
# Generate multiple functions f_1, f_2, ..., f_n where each function adds a constant
for i in 1:5
    ex = quote
        function $(Symbol("f_", i))(x)
            return x + $i
        end
    end
    @eval $ex
end

# Testing the generated functions
println(f_1(5)) # Output: 6
println(f_3(5)) # Output: 8
```

In this code snippet, a loop generates functions f_1, f_2, f_3, etc., each adding a different constant to the input.

Performance Considerations

Code generation should be used judiciously, as it can introduce complexity and maintenance challenges. However, it can also lead to significant performance improvements. By generating specialized functions, one can reduce overhead and improve execution time, especially in performance-critical applications.

Consider generating specialized functions for element-wise operations on arrays:

```
# Template for generating element-wise multiplication functions for different types
types = [Int, Float64, Complex{Float64}]

for T in types
    ex = quote
        function $(Symbol("mul_elements_", T))(a::Vector{$T}, b::Vector{$T})::Vector
            {$T}
            return [a[i] * b[i] for i in 1:length(a)]
        end
    end
    @eval $ex
end

# Testing the specialized functions
println(mul_elements_Int([1, 2, 3], [4, 5, 6])) # Output: [4, 10, 18]
println(mul_elements_Float64([1.0, 2.0, 3.0], [4.0, 5.0, 6.0])) # Output: [4.0, 10.0, 18.0]
```

Using this technique, we create specialized versions of the mul_elements function for different data types, reducing type conversion overhead.

Combining Reflection and Code Introspection

Reflection and code introspection can be employed in tandem with code generation to handle more sophisticated use cases. These methods allow examining and modifying the structure and behavior of code at runtime, enabling advanced dynamic behaviors.

For instance, generating accessor methods for struct fields:

```
# Define a struct
struct MyStruct
    a::Int
    b::Float64
    c::String
end

# Generate accessor methods for each field of MyStruct
fields = fieldnames(MyStruct)
for field in fields
    ex = quote
        function $(Symbol("get_", field))(s::MyStruct)
            return getfield(s, $(QuoteNode(field)))
        end
    end
    @eval $ex
end

# Testing the generated accessor methods
s = MyStruct(10, 15.5, "hello")
println(get_a(s)) # Output: 10
println(get_b(s)) # Output: 15.5
println(get_c(s)) # Output: hello
```

This example demonstrates reflection by leveraging fieldnames and getfield to generate accessor methods dynamically, thus simplifying code maintenance.

Employing code generation strategically can lead to cleaner, more maintainable, and efficient code. It reduces redundancy and enhances flexibility, making it an invaluable tool in a Julia programmer's toolkit.

8.8 Reflection and Code Introspection

Reflection and code introspection are powerful tools in Julia that enable developers to analyze and manipulate code during runtime. These techniques allow a program to inspect its own structure, and adapt its behavior based on its components. This section explores the essential aspects of reflection and code introspection, providing a thorough understanding of how to leverage these features effectively.

Reflection refers to the ability of a program to examine and modify its own structure and behavior at runtime. Julia's dynamic nature facilitates reflection by providing a rich set of facilities to query and manipulate various aspects of code, such as types, functions, and modules.

Code introspection involves examining code entities' properties, such as the names of methods within a function or the fields of a type. Introspection is particularly useful for debugging, optimization, and metaprogramming, where understanding the internal structure of code can lead to more efficient and robust programs.

Using typeof, whos, and methods for Type and Method Introspection

Julia provides several built-in functions to facilitate introspection. One of the fundamental functions for type introspection is typeof, which returns the type of an expression. Consider the following example:

```
x = 42
ty = typeof(x)
println(ty)
```

```
Int64
```

For introspecting the available names and their corresponding types in the current scope, the whos() function can be utilized. This function lists all the variables and their types:

```
using InteractiveUtils
whos()
```

To inspect the methods associated with a particular function, the methods function is employed:

```
methods(println)
```

```
# 5 methods for generic function "println":
[1] println() in Base
[2] println(x...) in Base at coreio.jl:4
[3] println(io::IO) in Base at coreio.jl:5
[4] println(io::IO, x...) in Base at io.jl:73
[5] println(io::IO, x::UInt128) in Base at int.jl:680
```

Inspecting Modules and Fields with names and fieldnames

To examine the symbols exported by a module or present in a particular namespace, use the names function:

```
names(Base)
```

To delve deeper into type structures and introspect their fields, the fieldnames function is valuable:

```
type MyType
    a::Int
    b::String
end
fieldnames(MyType)
```

```
(:a, :b)
```

Reflection with @code_llvm, @code_native, and @code_typed

Julia also supports more advanced reflection capabilities that enable developers to inspect the lower-level representations of code. For instance, the @code_llvm macro displays the LLVM intermediate representation of a function, providing insights into the optimization and compilation processes:

```
@code_llvm sqrt(2.0)
```

Similarly, the @code_native macro reveals the native assembly code generated for a function:

```
@code_native sqrt(2.0)
```

For examining the typed Julia intermediate representation (IR), the @code_typed macro is useful:

```
@code_typed sqrt(2.0)
```

Practical Application of Reflection and Introspection in Macros

Reflection and code introspection are particularly advantageous when developing macros. Macros can generate code that adapts based on the properties of their input expressions or current state of the program.

Consider a macro that automatically generates getter functions for all fields of a given type:

```
macro generate_getters(T)
    field_names = fieldnames(T)
    quote
        $(Expr(:block, [:(get_$fname(t::$T) = t.$fname) for fname in field_names]...))
    end
end

@macroexpand @generate_getters MyType
```

```
quote
   get_a(t::MyType) = t.a
   get_b(t::MyType) = t.b
end
```

In this example, the macro uses fieldnames to dynamically generate getter functions for all fields of MyType at compile time.

Reflection and code introspection provide Julia developers with the tools to create flexible, adaptive, and efficient programs. By utilizing functions such as typeof, methods, names, and fieldnames, developers can gain deep insights into the structure and behavior of their code. Advanced reflection capabilities with @code_llvm, @code_native, and @code_typed enable examination of the lower-level details of the code generation process, facilitating optimization and debugging. These techniques are particularly powerful in the context of metaprogramming, allowing for sophisticated code generation and adaptive program behavior.

8.9 Debugging Macros

Debugging macros in Julia can be a challenging task due to the complexity and abstraction level of metaprogramming. However, with systematic approaches and Julia's intrinsic tools, the process becomes manageable. The most effective techniques for debugging macros include expanding macros manually, using the @macroexpand and @macroexpand1 functions, employing the @show macro, and adhering to best practices for writing readable and maintainable macros.

To debug a macro, it is essential to first understand how macros transform code. Macros in Julia return an expression that gets evaluated in the context where the macro is called. Thus, the primary task in debugging is ensuring that the macro returns the expected expression.

```
macro mymacro(x)
    return :(println($x^2))
end
```

Suppose the above macro, mymacro, does not provide the desired output. The first step is to expand the macro to understand what expression it generates.

```
@macroexpand mymacro(3+2)
```

The output will be:

```
:(println(3 + 2 ^ 2))
```

The @macroexpand function provides the fully expanded form of the macro. This helps in visualizing the exact transformation applied by the macro. Notice in the example that the expression 3 + 2 is not correctly enclosed in parentheses, which results in the wrong sequence of operations. To debug this, one could define the macro with additional parentheses.

```
macro mymacro(x)
    return :(println(($x)^2))
end
```

Re-expanding the macro:

```
@macroexpand mymacro(3+2)
```

The output should now be:

```
:(println((3 + 2) ^ 2))
```

This ensures the correct interpretation of the expression within the macro.

When a macro expands into another macro, @macroexpand1 can be used to expand only the outermost macro.

```
macro outer(x)
    return :(@inner($x))
end

macro inner(x)
    return :($x + 1)
end

@macroexpand1 outer(2)
```

The output will be:

```
@inner(2)
```

To fully expand all nested macros, use:

```
@macroexpand outer(2)
```

The resulting output:

```
2 + 1
```

Another useful technique for inspecting values during macro execution is embedding @show within the macro definition. This displays intermediate values during expansion.

```
macro debugmacro(x)
    @show x
    return :(println($x^2))
end
```

When calling debugmacro:

```
debugmacro(3+2)
```

The output in the REPL will display:

```
x = 3 + 2
```

This reveals how the macro processes its input before returning the final expression.

Additionally, one should be cautious about macro hygiene to avoid unintentional variable capture. The esc function should encapsulate variables that are evaluated in the macro's caller context.

Refactoring larger macros into smaller, testable functions can also ease debugging. Consider breaking down complex logic within the macro into separate helper functions and testing each independently.

```
macro complexmacro(x, y)
    result = helperfunction(x, y)
    return :(println($result))
end

function helperfunction(a, b)
    return a * b
end
```

By separating concerns, one can independently verify the correctness of helperfunction before integrating it into the macro.

Comprehensive debugging also involves writing extensive tests for macros. Create diverse test cases covering various scenarios to ensure robust macro performance under different conditions.

An illustrative test case for complexmacro:

```
@testset "Testing complexmacro" begin
    @test @macroexpand complexmacro(2, 3) == :($(2*3))
    @test macrosan(2, "3") == "Input error"
end
```

By systematically applying these techniques, one can effectively debug and validate Julia macros, ensuring their correctness and reliability.

8.10 Best Practices for Metaprogramming

When engaging in metaprogramming within Julia, it is imperative to adhere to best practices to ensure that your code is maintainable, efficient, and accurate. Here, we explore several guidelines that will help you create robust metaprogramming solutions.

Understanding the Scope and Limitations: Before delving into metaprogramming, it is crucial to comprehend why and when to use it. Metaprogramming should be employed to eliminate boilerplate, enforce compile-time checks, or perform code transformations that are otherwise cumbersome or error-prone. Overusing metaprogramming can lead to complex and difficult-to-debug code.

Macro Hygiene: Hygiene in macros means preventing accidental variable name clashes between the macro's context and the caller's context. Non-hygienic macros can lead to subtle bugs that are hard to detect. In Julia, use the esc function to return expressions intended to be evaluated in the macro caller's scope.

```
macro example_hygienic(expr)
    esc(quote
        x = $expr + 1
        println("Result: $x")
    end)
end

x = 10
@example_hygienic(x)
```

In this example, the use of esc ensures that the variable x inside the macro result does not interfere with x in the caller's scope.

Limiting Macro Complexity: Macros should be simple and perform minimal transformations. If a transformation is highly complex, consider refactoring it into Julia functions instead. This separation of concerns makes the code more readable and easier to test.

Proper Documentation: Always document macros adequately. Describe what the macro does, its arguments, and any side effects it may have. Users of your macro should clearly understand its purpose and usage without delving into its implementation.

Consistent Naming Conventions: Use consistent and descriptive naming conventions for macros to distinguish them from regular functions. A common practice is to prefix macro names with the @ symbol, e.g., @timeit, @debug.

Testing Macros: Macros can be tested by embedding unit tests that check for expected behaviors and outputs. Use Julia's Test module for writing such tests. Ensure that macros adhere to intended use cases and handle edge cases gracefully.

```
using Test

macro double_it(x)
    esc(:($x * 2))
end

@test @double_it(4) == 8
@test @double_it(-3) == -6
```

Code Generation: When generating code within macros, ensure that the generated code adheres to Julia's syntax and best practices standards. Static analysis tools can be beneficial in verifying the correctness of generated code.

Avoiding Side Effects: Macros should ideally be free of side effects. Any mutable state or side-effect-producing operations should be implemented in regular functions rather than within macros. This approach helps maintain macro idempotency, ensuring consistent and predictable behavior.

Reflection and Introspection Caution: While reflection and code introspection is powerful, their use should be judicious. Overusing introspection can lead to performance overhead and complications in understanding the flow of the program. For example, using @eval inside macros should be carefully managed.

Backward Compatibility: When updating macros, ensure backward compatibility in your codebase if older code depends on them. Use versioning and deprecation warnings to guide users through transitions smoothly.

Error Handling: Macros should include comprehensive error handling mechanisms to report issues clearly. Use informative error messages to assist users in diagnosing problems quickly. For instance, validate input expressions before transforming them.

```
macro safe_divide(a, b)
    :(($b == 0) ? throw(ArgumentError("Division by zero")) : $a / $b)
end

@safe_divide(10, 0) # This will generate a division by zero error
```

This macro checks for a division by zero scenario and throws an appropriate error message. Such validations ensure that macros behave safely under erroneous conditions.

Reproducibility and Debugging: Develop macros with reproducibility in mind. Print or log intermediate steps when debugging complex macros. Tools like @macroexpand can help visualize expanded macro expressions, making it easier to debug and understand the transformation process.

```
macro my_macro(expr)
    println("Macro called with: ", expr)
    expanded_expr = esc(expr)
    println("Expanded expression: ", expanded_expr)
    expanded_expr
end

@my_macro(1 + 2)
```

This example illustrates a logging mechanism to inspect macro invocation and its resulting expanded expression.

- Use @macroexpand for visualizing and debugging expanded macros.

- Consider logging intermediary states for complex transformations.
- Validate inputs rigorously to prevent runtime errors.
- Maintain backward compatibility and document changes thoroughly.

8.11 Case Studies and Examples

Case Study 1: Simplifying Repetitive Code Patterns

In many scientific computing tasks, one often encounters repetitive code patterns that can be simplified using macros. Let us consider a scenario in numerical analysis where we need to apply a series of mathematical transformations to several matrices. Instead of writing separate code for each transformation, we can write a macro to automate this process.

```
macro apply_transformations(mat, transformations...)
    quote
        for transform in $transformations
            $mat = transform($mat)
        end
        $mat
    end
end
```

In the provided macro, apply_transformations takes a matrix and a list of transformation functions. It generates code to apply each transformation function in sequence to the matrix. Here is how you can use it:

```
A = [1 2; 3 4]
transform1(x) = x * 2
transform2(x) = x .+ 1

@apply_transformations(A, transform1, transform2)
```

Output:

```
2×2 Array{Int64,2}:
 3  5
 7  9
```

This macro dramatically reduces the boilerplate code, making the codebase more readable and maintainable.

Case Study 2: Metaprogramming for Domain-Specific Languages (DSLs)

Julia's ability to handle metaprogramming makes it ideal for creating domain-specific languages. Consider a hypothetical DSL designed for specifying and solving optimization problems.

```
macro constraint(expr)
    :(push!(constraints, $expr))
end
```

This macro allows users to succinctly add constraints to an optimization problem:

```
constraints = []

@constraint(x + y <= 10)
@constraint(2x - y == 3)
@constraint(x >= 0)
@constraint(y >= 0)
```

Output:

```
4-element Array{Expr,1}:
 :(x + y <= 10)
 :(2x - y == 3)
 :(x >= 0)
 :(y >= 0)
```

`constraints` now contains the specified constraints, which can then be passed to an optimization solver.

Case Study 3: Performance Optimization using Generate-Time Computation

In computational tasks where performance is critical, metaprogramming can optimize certain computations by executing code at generate-time instead of run-time. Consider a polynomial evaluation that can be optimized by generating specific code paths based on the polynomial's degree.

```
macro eval_poly(coeffs, x)
    degree = length(coeffs) - 1
    ex = :(0)
    for i in 0:degree
        ex = :($ex + $(coeffs[i+1]) * $x^$i)
    end
    return ex
end
```

The `eval_poly` macro generates the polynomial evaluation code at compile-time, ensuring optimal performance. Here is an example usage:

```
coefficients = [1, -3, 2] # Represents 1 - 3x + 2x^2
x = 5
```

```
@eval_poly(coefficients, x)
```

Output:

```
36
```

This macro's generated code is compact and efficient, providing performance benefits over a more generic implementation.

Case Study 4: Reflection and Debugging Support

For robust software development, reflection capabilities and debugging support are invaluable. Macros can be used to provide enhanced logging and debugging facilities.

```
macro log_and_execute(expr)
    quote
        println("Executing: ", $(string(expr)))
        result = $expr
        println("Result: ", result)
        result
    end
end
```

This macro logs the expression being evaluated and its result, which aids in debugging:

```
a = 10
b = 20

@log_and_execute(a + b)
```

Output:

```
Executing: a + b
Result: 30
```

Such macros prove especially useful in complex applications where understanding intermediate results is critical for debugging.

These case studies illustrate the power and versatility of metaprogramming in Julia. The techniques discussed can greatly simplify code, improve performance, and facilitate the creation of domain-specific languages and comprehensive debugging tools. These examples serve as a foundation for exploring deeper applications of metaprogramming, encouraging the development of innovative solutions in scientific and technical computing.

Chapter 9

Performance and Optimization

This chapter addresses key aspects of optimizing performance in Julia, starting with profiling code and ensuring type stability. It explores memory management, garbage collection, and optimizing mathematical computations. The chapter includes parallel computing, multithreading, in-place operations, and using SIMD for performance gains. It also covers benchmarking tools and best practices for writing high-performance code, supplemented by case studies and performance tuning examples.

9.1 Introduction to Performance in Julia

Performance optimization is critical to leveraging the full potential of the Julia programming language. Julia's design philosophy centers around providing high-level abstractions while maintaining the performance characteristic of low-level languages. This section delves into the foundational aspects of performance in Julia, exploring the features and mechanisms that allow developers to write efficient and performant code.

The performance in Julia is achieved through several mechanisms:

- Just-In-Time (JIT) Compilation

- Type Inference and Multiple Dispatch
- Efficient memory management
- Native support for parallel and concurrent programming

Just-In-Time (JIT) Compilation: Julia utilizes the LLVM framework for Just-In-Time (JIT) compilation, converting high-level Julia code into efficient machine code at runtime. This process enables Julia to run as fast as statically-typed languages like C or Fortran, with the advantage of writing code in a high-level, interactive environment. The JIT compilation pipeline not only performs standard compilation tasks but also includes aggressive optimizations, such as inlining functions, eliminating dead code, and optimizing loops.

Type Inference and Multiple Dispatch: Julia makes extensive use of type inference, which is the process of automatically deducing the types of expressions. This capability allows Julia to generate optimized machine code, as knowing explicit types at compile-time reduces the overhead associated with dynamic typing. Multiple dispatch leverages type inference by allowing functions to have different implementations based on the combination of argument types. This not only facilitates generic programming but also enhances performance by selecting the most efficient method for a given set of argument types.

Example code demonstrating multiple dispatch:

```
function add(x::Int64, y::Int64)
    return x + y
end

function add(x::Float64, y::Float64)
    return x + y
end

# Calling add with different types
result_int = add(10, 20)
result_float = add(10.5, 20.5)
```

Output:

```
result_int = 30
result_float = 31.0
```

This example illustrates that the function add is dispatched based on the types of its arguments, allowing the compiler to generate efficient code for integer and floating-point additions separately.

Efficient Memory Management: Julia employs a sophisticated memory management system, including garbage collection, to efficiently manage and allocate memory. This system minimizes memory leaks and fragmentation, crucial for long-running applications and large datasets. Julia's garbage collector is a mark-and-sweep collector enhanced with generational collection, which optimizes the reclamation of short-lived objects while efficiently handling long-lived objects.

To understand the impact of memory management on performance, consider the following example where we measure the performance of code with and without unnecessary memory allocations.

Example code with unnecessary memory allocations:

```
function allocate_example(n)
    total = 0.0
    for i in 1:n
        arr = [rand() for _ in 1:1000]
        total += sum(arr)
    end
    return total
end

# Call the function
time_allocated = @elapsed allocate_example(1000)
```

Output:

```
time_allocated = 0.5674321
```

Example code optimized to minimize memory allocations:

```
function allocate_example_optimized(n)
    total = 0.0
    arr = Vector{Float64}(undef, 1000)
    for i in 1:n
        for j in 1:1000
            arr[j] = rand()
        end
        total += sum(arr)
    end
    return total
end

# Call the optimized function
time_optimized = @elapsed allocate_example_optimized(1000)
```

Output:

```
time_optimized = 0.1234567
```

In this refined example, we allocate the array arr once outside the loop and reuse it within the loop. This reduces memory allocations, decreasing the computational time significantly.

Native Support for Parallel and Concurrent Programming: Julia provides native support for parallel and concurrent programming, making it easier to exploit multi-core processors and distributed computing environments. The language includes constructs for multi-threading, distributed computing, and asynchronous I/O operations.

Example code using parallel computing:

```
using Distributed

# Add worker processes
addprocs(4)

# Parallel computation function
@everywhere function parallel_sum(n::Int)
    return sum(1:n)
end

# Perform the computation in parallel
result_parallel = @distributed (+) for i in 1:4
    parallel_sum(250000000)
end
```

Output:

```
result_parallel = 125000000500000000
```

In this example, we utilize the Distributed module to add worker processes and distribute the workload of summing a large range of integers across multiple processors. Julia's parallel computing facilities automatically handle the distribution of data and the collection of results, streamlining the parallelization process.

Understanding these foundational aspects of Julia's performance-critical features provides the necessary context for more advanced optimization techniques discussed in subsequent sections. Competence in JIT compilation, type inference, memory management, and parallel computing forms the backbone of writing high-performance Julia code.

9.2 Profiling Julia Code

Performance optimization begins with identifying the bottlenecks in code execution. Profiling helps ascertain where the program spends most of its time, enabling targeted improvements. Julia provides robust tools for profiling and performance analysis, notably the @profile macro and the Profile standard library.

To use the @profile macro, simply precede the function or code block you aim to profile with it. For example,

```
using Profile
```

```
function compute_distances(points)
    n = length(points)
    distances = zeros(n, n)
    for i in 1:n
        for j in 1:n
            distances[i, j] = sqrt(sum((points[i] .- points[j]).^2))
        end
    end
    return distances
end

points = rand(3, 1000)
@profile compute_distances(points)
```

In this example, the @profile macro profiles the compute_distances function, which calculates the pairwise Euclidean distances between points. On executing the code, Julia collects profiling data.

To visualize and analyze the collected profiling data, the Profile standard library includes the Profile.print and ProfileView for graphical display. The command

```
Profile.print()
```

displays a textual summary of the profiling data, showing which lines of code consumed the most execution time. For a more intuitive visual analysis, ProfileView can be used:

```
using ProfileView
ProfileView.view()
```

By offering a flame graph, ProfileView makes it easier to perceive the hierarchical nature of function calls and locate performance bottlenecks.

After identifying the bottleneck, the next step involves investigating potential reasons and devising solutions. Common reasons include type instability, redundant allocations, and suboptimal algorithm implementations. For instance, consider type instability within the code:

```
function sum_numbers(arr)
    s = 0 # starts as an Int
    for num in arr
        s += num # num might be Float64 or Int
    end
    return s
end
```

In the above example, if arr contains a mixture of Int and Float64 numbers, s may change types during the iterations, leading to significant performance degradation due to type instability.

Julia's @code_warntype macro helps detect such issues by showing the inferred types of variables. Using @code_warntype, the function call appears as:

```
@code_warntype sum_numbers([1, 2.0, 3])
```

The output will indicate if variables change types, allowing focused corrections.

Using BenchmarkTools.jl, the @btime macro provides more accurate timing results by conducting multiple evaluations and accounting for fluctuations:

```
using BenchmarkTools
@btime sum_numbers([1, 2.0, 3])
@btime sum_numbers([1.0, 2.0, 3.0])
```

Considering execution time consistency is crucial. Sometimes, parts of the code might execute quickly in isolation but cause significant performance hits when part of larger systems, due to issues like cache misses or resource contention.

When optimizing, always compare against baseline measurements. Profiling data can guide incremental improvements, systematically analyzing each change's impact. Start with high-level algorithm choices and proceed to lower-level details like types and memory allocation strategies. Profiling is an iterative process, each stage revealing new insights and areas for potential refinement.

9.3 Type Stability and Performance

Understanding the concept of type stability is crucial for writing high-performance Julia code. Type stability occurs when the type of a function's output is determined solely based on the types of its inputs. Performing type-stable operations facilitates numerous compiler optimizations, leading to faster and more efficient code. This section delves into how type stability can be achieved, why it is important, and how you can use Julia's tools to ensure type stability in your code.

Type inference is the process where the Julia compiler predicts the types of variables and expressions in the program. The @code_warntype macro in Julia helps in analyzing the type stability of functions. All types should ideally be concrete for optimized performance. If the types are abstract, the compiler cannot generate optimized machine code.

Consider a simple function where type inference is crucial:

```
function add_numbers(a, b)
    return a + b
end
```

To inspect the type stability of this function, use the @code_warntype macro:

```
@code_warntype add_numbers(1, 2)
```

Executing this will provide an annotated version of the code indicating any type instability. The output will look like:

```
Variables
  #self#::Core.Const(add_numbers)
  a::Int64
  b::Int64

Body::Int64
1  %1 = (a + b)::Int64
       return %1
```

Here, the inferred type, represented after ::, suggests the function is type stable when both inputs are Int64. However, consider the following example where type stability is not ensured:

```
function add_mixed(a, b)
    if rand() > 0.5
        return a + b
    else
        return "error"
    end
end
```

Inspecting this function's type stability:

```
@code_warntype add_mixed(1, 2)
```

Here, the output may reveal type instability:

```
Variables
  #self#::Core.Const(add_mixed)
  a::Int64
  b::Int64

Body::Union{Int64, String}
1  %1 = Main.rand()::Float64
   %2 = (%1 > 0.5)::Bool
        goto %4 if not %2
2  %4 = (a + b)::Int64
        return %4
3  %5 = "error"::Core.Const("error")
        return %5
```

The Union{Int64, String} type in the output points towards type instability as it represents multiple possible types. This causes the Julia compiler to generate less efficient code.

Achieving type stability often involves ensuring function return types are predictable and consistent. Use explicit type annotations and avoid heterogeneous return types within conditional blocks.

For example:

```
function better_add_mixed(a::Int, b::Int)::Union{Int,Nothing}
    if rand() > 0.5
        return a + b
    else
        return nothing
    end
end
```

Perform a type stability check:

```
@code_warntype better_add_mixed(1, 2)
```

Analyzing complex and nested types often comes with challenges. Structures like arrays, dictionaries or custom-defined types should ideally have consistent element types for optimized performance. For example:

```
struct User
    name::String
    age::Int
end

function get_user_attributes(users::Vector{User})
    attributes = []
    for user in users
        push!(attributes, (user.name, user.age))
    end
    return attributes
end
```

Here, attributes is an array of heterogeneous tuples. Using a type-annotated array improves performance:

```
function get_user_attributes(users::Vector{User})::Vector{Tuple{String,Int}}
    attributes = Vector{Tuple{String,Int}}()
    for user in users
        push!(attributes, (user.name, user.age))
    end
    return attributes
end
```

Julia's typing system is powerful and flexible. Leveraging parametric types and type aliases can provide further performance enhancements without compromising code generality.

```
struct Point{T}
    x::T
```

```
    y::T
end

function distance(p1::Point{T}, p2::Point{T}) where T
    return sqrt((p1.x - p2.x)^2 + (p2.y - p2.y)^2)
end
```

The use of parametric types Point{T} ensures type stability across different types of numerical computations. This avoids performance pitfalls associated with type instability.

Maintaining type stability in Julia is critical for achieving optimal performance. The use of tools such as @code_warntype, along with careful design of function outputs, type annotations, and the use of parametric and concrete types, can significantly impact the execution efficiency of your Julia programs, enabling high-performance computing solutions.

9.4 Memory Management and Garbage Collection

Effective memory management is a foundational aspect of high-performance computing in Julia. This section delves into how Julia manages memory, the mechanisms behind garbage collection, and strategies to optimize memory usage.

Julia utilizes a garbage-collected runtime, which automates the process of freeing memory that is no longer in use. This enables developers to write code more efficiently without being overly concerned with manual memory management, which can be error-prone and complex.

The primary memory allocation in Julia happens in the Mutable data structures such as arrays, dictionaries, and custom structs. Allocation involves reserving a segment of memory where data is stored. The garbage collector (GC) in Julia takes care of deallocating memory that is no longer in use, thus preventing memory leaks. However, to achieve optimal performance, understanding and minimizing unnecessary allocations is crucial.

```
function example_function()
    x = []
    for i in 1:10^6
        push!(x, i)
    end
    return sum(x)
end
```

For the above code snippet, every invocation of push! leads to an allocation when the array x grows beyond its initial capacity. If memory allocation is not managed carefully, such operations can significantly slow down the program. By pre-allocating memory for the array, one can mitigate this issue.

```
function optimized_function()
    x = Vector{Int}(undef, 10^6)
    for i in 1:10^6
        x[i] = i
    end
    return sum(x)
end
```

Memory allocation in Julia can occur in either the stack or the heap. Stack allocation is preferable due to its lower overhead and faster access times. However, complex data structures and objects that require a longer lifespan are allocated on the heap.

Garbage collection in Julia is split into several phases:

- Mark phase: The GC traverses all live objects starting from the roots (such as global variables and the stack). It marks the objects as live.
- Sweep phase: The GC reclaims unmarked objects by deallocating their memory.
- Incremental and Generational collection: Julia employs an incremental GC to reduce pause times and a generational strategy to optimize the frequent reclamation of short-lived objects.

While Julia's memory management is automated, developers can monitor and manually influence GC behavior to enhance performance. Commands like GC.@preserve, GC.gc(), and GC.enable()/GC.disable() provide some level of control over garbage collection.

```
# Manually trigger garbage collection
GC.gc()
```

Optimizing memory usage often involves reducing the number of allocations and keeping memory access patterns cache-friendly. Understanding the allocation patterns in your code can be achieved using profiling tools like @time, @allocated, and Profile. Analyzing the allocation graph can help identify parts of the code that trigger frequent allocations, which can then be optimized.

```
function memory_intensive_function()
```

```
    a = rand(10^6)
    b = a .+ 1
    return sum(b)
end

@time memory_intensive_function()
```

The output will indicate the time taken and memory allocated during the function execution. Reducing unnecessary allocations often involves using in-place operations—operations that reuse existing memory rather than allocating new memory.

```
function optimized_memory_function()
    a = rand(10^6)
    @. a += 1
    return sum(a)
end

@time optimized_memory_function()
```

In-place operations, indicated by the .@ macro, significantly reduce memory allocations, thereby improving performance.

Developers must also be aware of type stability to ensure efficient memory usage. Type instability can lead to excessive and slow heap allocations. Utilizing Julia's powerful type system to specify function return types and enforcing type stability can enhance both performance and memory management.

Understanding and optimizing memory management and garbage collection is integral to developing high-performance Julia applications. Effective strategies to minimize allocations, leverage in-place operations, and manage the garbage collector can result in significant performance improvements.

9.5 Optimizing Mathematical Computations

Optimizing mathematical computations in Julia requires understanding and leveraging both Julia's language features and its extensive library ecosystem. By focusing on computational efficiency, we aim to reduce execution time and memory overhead, essential for applications demanding high performance such as simulations, scientific computations, and data analysis.

Avoiding Global Variables: Global variables in Julia hamper performance due to their dynamic type nature. Instead, use local variables, passed parameters, or closures which help the compiler determine types at compile time, enhancing optimization. Consider the following example:

```
# Using a global variable (inefficient)
x = 10
function square_global()
    return x * x
end
@time square_global()

# Avoiding global variable (efficient)
function square_local(x)
    return x * x
end
@time square_local(10)
```

Leveraging Built-in Functions: Julia offers built-in functions optimized for performance. Exploit functions like sum, prod, and maximum which are implemented efficiently in Julia's core and often outperform custom loops due to their low-level optimizations.

```
# Using built-in sum function
array = rand(10^6)
@time sum(array)

# Custom summation (typically less efficient)
function custom_sum(arr)
    total = 0.0
    for x in arr
        total += x
    end
    return total
end
@time custom_sum(array)
```

Vectorization: Vectorized operations operate on entire arrays rather than element-wise, taking advantage of low-level optimizations and memory access patterns. Avoid writing loops for array operations whenever possible.

```
# Using vectorized operations
a = rand(10^6)
b = rand(10^6)

@time c = a .+ b

# Using a loop (less efficient)
function add_arrays(a, b)
    c = similar(a)
    for i in 1:length(a)
        c[i] = a[i] + b[i]
    end
    return c
end
@time c = add_arrays(a, b)
```

In-place Operations: In-place operations modify existing arrays without allocating new memory, which can significantly reduce overhead. Use the ! suffix convention in function names to indicate in-place modifications.

```
# In-place addition
@time .+= a, b

# Non in-place addition (allocates new array)
@time d = a + b
```

Using Specific Data Types: Leveraging appropriate data types can yield substantial performance improvements. For instance, use Float32 instead of Float64 when double precision is unnecessary, as Float32 operations are typically faster and consume less memory.

```
# Using Float32
arr_float32 = rand(Float32, 10^6)
@time sum(arr_float32)

# Using Float64 (default)
arr_float64 = rand(10^6)
@time sum(arr_float64)
```

Loop Unrolling: Julia's compiler optimizes simple for-loops, but for more complex operations, manually unrolling loops can sometimes enhance performance by reducing the loop overhead.

```
# Loop unrolling example
function unrolled_sum(arr)
    total = 0.0
    n = length(arr)
    for i in 1:4:n-3
        total += arr[i] + arr[i+1] + arr[i+2] + arr[i+3]
    end
    for i in n-n%4+1:n
        total += arr[i]
    end
    return total
end
```

Reduce Memory Allocations: Minimizing memory allocations directly impacts performance. Preallocate memory outside of loops and use functions like view() to create subarrays without copying data, thus reducing unnecessary allocations.

```
# Using view to avoid allocations
matrix = rand(1000, 1000)
sub_matrix = view(matrix, 1:500, 1:500)
@time sum(sub_matrix)
```

Utilizing Libraries: Leverage Julia's rich ecosystem of libraries such as LoopVectorization.jl for loop optimizations and Tullio.jl for array operations. These libraries provide highly optimized implementations of common mathematical operations.

```
using LoopVectorization, Tullio

# LoopVectorization for element-wise addition
@turbo c = a + b

# Tullio for efficient summation
@tullio d = sum(a[i] * b[i])
```

This approach ensures that mathematical computations are executed as efficiently as possible, providing significant performance improvements essential for computationally intensive applications.

9.6 Parallel Computing and Multithreading

Parallel computing and multithreading are essential techniques for maximizing the performance of computationally intensive applications in Julia. Understanding how to effectively distribute tasks across multiple processing cores can significantly enhance the execution speed of your programs. Julia provides a rich set of tools to facilitate parallel computing and multithreading, allowing users to write high-performance, scalable code.

Parallel Computing in Julia

Julia's parallel computing capabilities are largely centered around its primitive constructs: @spawn, @distributed, @sync, and @async. These constructs enable the concurrent execution of tasks, distributing the computational load across multiple processors.

To execute a simple parallel computation using @spawn, consider the following example:

```
futures = []
for i in 1:10
    push!(futures, @spawn fib(i))
end

results = [fetch(f) for f in futures]
```

This code snippet spawns multiple futures, each computing the Fibonacci sequence of a different number. The fetch function retrieves the result of each future, effectively synchronizing the concurrent tasks. The @spawn macro allows the execution of tasks on any available worker, facilitating distributed computation.

The @distributed macro

The @distributed macro is a higher-level construct for parallel computing that simplifies the parallel execution of loops. It can be particularly useful for operations that are inherently parallelizable, such as numerical simulations or data processing tasks. An example of using @distributed is shown below:

```
using Distributed
addprocs(4) # Adds 4 worker processes

@distributed (v = 0.0) for i in 1:100
    v += my_function(i)
end
```

In the example above, the iterations of the loop are distributed across the available worker processes, and the results are combined using the specified operation (in this case, summation).

Synchronization with @sync and @async

Julia's @sync and @async constructs manage the synchronization and execution of asynchronous tasks. The @async macro creates a new task to be executed concurrently, while @sync ensures that the parent task waits for all spawned tasks to complete before proceeding.

Consider the following example code:

```
@sync begin
    for i in 1:10
        @async begin
            println("Task $i starts")
            sleep(2)
            println("Task $i ends")
        end
    end
end
```

In this code, @async creates multiple tasks that run concurrently, while @sync ensures that the main program waits for all tasks to complete.

Multithreading in Julia

In addition to parallel computing, multithreading can be used to achieve concurrency within a single process. Multithreading in Julia is accomplished using the Threads.@threads macro, which parallelizes the execution of loops over multiple threads.

The following example demonstrates the usage of Threads.@threads:

```
using Base.Threads

threaded_sum = 0
```

```
Threads.@threads for i in 1:1000
    threaded_sum += i
end

println("Sum: $threaded_sum")
```

This code parallelizes the summation loop across multiple threads, potentially increasing the execution speed compared to a single-threaded version. Note that care must be taken to avoid race conditions and ensure thread safety when using multithreading.

Thread Safety and Race Conditions

When writing multithreaded code, it is crucial to ensure that shared resources are accessed in a thread-safe manner. Race conditions occur when multiple threads access and modify shared data concurrently, leading to unpredictable results. To prevent race conditions, synchronization mechanisms such as locks or atomic operations should be used.

For example, using an atomic operation to safely increment a counter:

```
using Base.Threads

atomic_sum = Atomic{Int}(0)

Threads.@threads for i in 1:1000
    atomic_add!(atomic_sum, i)
end

println("Atomic sum: $(atomic_sum[])")
```

In this example, atomic_add! ensures that the summation operation is thread-safe, avoiding race conditions that could corrupt the final sum.

Optimizing Task Parallelism

On multi-core systems, optimizing task parallelism involves balancing the workload across available resources to minimize idle time. Julia provides tools like Folds, which offer efficient parallel and sequential reduction operations across collections.

Consider the reduce function from the Folds package, which leverages multi-core processors effectively:

```
using Folds

data = rand(1000)
result = Folds.reduce(+, data)

println("Folded sum: $result")
```

This parallel reduction operation may outperform a conventional reduction on large data sets by exploiting multiple cores.

To write efficient, parallel and concurrent code in Julia, understanding and applying these constructs and best practices is paramount. Mastery of parallel computing and multithreading enables leveraging Julia's full potential for high-performance computing applications.

9.7 In-place Operations and Avoiding Allocations

In computational tasks, minimizing memory allocations can lead to significant performance gains. Allocations are often a major source of overhead in numerical computations. By performing operations in-place, we reduce the need for memory management and improve cache performance, leading to faster execution times.

In Julia, many functions have two forms: an out-of-place version which returns a new array or matrix and an in-place version which modifies the input argument. The convention for in-place functions is to add a ! at the end of the function name. For example, the out-of-place addition for arrays A and B would look like:

```
C = A + B
```

This operation allocates memory for the new array C. In contrast, the in-place addition uses the $.+=$ operator:

```
A .+= B
```

This modifies A directly without allocating additional memory for the result. Similar in-place versions exist for many other operations. Here, we delve into more details on how and when to use in-place operations effectively.

Matrix Multiplication:

Consider a matrix multiplication example:

```
C = A * B
```

This operation allocates memory for a new matrix C. For large matrices, these allocations can be significant. Instead, we can use the $\mathrm{mul!}$ function, which performs the multiplication in-place:

```
mul!(C, A, B)
```

Here, C must be pre-allocated with the appropriate dimensions. It's updated with the result of $A * B$.

Dot Product:

The out-of-place operation for the dot product of vectors a and b is straightforward:

```
d = dot(a, b)
```

An in-place variant isn't necessary for the dot product since it returns a scalar value and does not create significant overhead.

Element-wise Functions:

For element-wise operations, in-place versions are generally more performant. For example, adding two arrays element-wise:

```
A .+= B
```

This avoids the allocation of a new array.

Broadcasting:

Julia's broadcasting system allows for the application of functions over entire collections of data. For example, applying the sine function to all elements of an array:

```
B = sin.(A)
```

This broadcasts $\sin$ over all elements of A, allocating a new array B. To perform this in-place, use:

```
sin!.(A)
```

This modifies A directly.

Advanced Example: Matrix Inversion

Matrix inversion is typically an expensive operation. Using the inv function:

```
B = inv(A)
```

This computes the inverse of A and allocates a new matrix B. Alternatively, using in-place methods, we can avoid this allocation:

```
using LinearAlgebra
```

```
A_inv = Matrix{Float64}(undef, size(A)...)
LinearAlgebra.BLAS.gesv!(A, A_inv)
```

Here, A_inv is pre-allocated and filled with the inverse of A.

Optimizing Loops:

Efficient use of in-place operations within loops can greatly improve performance. Consider a loop performing repeated updates:

```
for i in 1:n
    x = A*x + b
end
```

This continuously allocates new memory for x. Instead, we can do:

```
for i in 1:n
    mul!(x, A, x)
    x .+= b
end
```

This modifies x directly each iteration, avoiding unnecessary allocations.

Avoiding allocations through in-place operations fundamentally optimizes performance-critical tasks. This requires careful pre-allocation and understanding of in-place function variants in the Julia ecosystem. Efficient memory management and minimized allocations are key to unlocking the full potential of Julia's performance capabilities.

9.8 Using SIMD for Performance

Single Instruction, Multiple Data (SIMD) is a parallel computing method that enables performance gains by allowing a single instruction to process multiple data points simultaneously. In Julia, leveraging SIMD can lead to significant improvements in computational efficiency, particularly for operations involving vectors and arrays.

To utilize SIMD in Julia, it is essential to understand how to write code that the compiler can easily vectorize. This involves specific considerations and techniques, such as ensuring loop vectorization and aligning data in memory.

Loop Vectorization: Loop vectorization is the process by which the compiler converts scalar operations in a loop into vector operations. In Julia, writing type-stable and simple loops can often allow the compiler to automatically apply SIMD. Consider the following example where we aim to perform element-wise addition of two arrays.

```
function array_addition!(C::Vector{Float64}, A::Vector{Float64}, B::Vector{Float64})
    @inbounds for i in eachindex(C, A, B)
        C[i] = A[i] + B[i]
    end
end
```

The @inbounds macro is used here to skip bounds checking within the loop, which can provide a marginal performance benefit. When compiled, Julia attempts to apply SIMD to the loop. To ensure that the SIMD instructions are applied, one can use the @simd macro explicitly:

```
function array_addition_simd!(C::Vector{Float64}, A::Vector{Float64}, B::Vector{
        Float64})
    @inbounds @simd for i in eachindex(C, A, B)
        C[i] = A[i] + B[i]
    end
end
```

Verifying SIMD Usage: To verify that SIMD instructions are being used, one can inspect the generated assembly code. This can be achieved using the @code_native macro.

```
@code_native array_addition_simd!(zeros(10), ones(10), ones(10))
```

The output will show SIMD instructions such as vmovapd, vaddpd, which confirm that the vectorized additions are being performed.

Memory Alignment: Memory alignment ensures that data is stored at properly aligned addresses, which can impact performance. Modern CPUs typically require specific alignment (e.g., 16-byte boundaries for 128-bit SIMD registers). While Julia handles most alignment issues internally, ensuring proper alignment can help attain optimal performance.

Using The LoopVectorization.jl Package: Manual SIMD optimization can be complex. Julia simplifies this through the LoopVectorization.jl package, which automatically applies SIMD optimization to loops. The package significantly reduces the need for explicit vectorization instructions.

First, install the package:

```
using Pkg
Pkg.add("LoopVectorization")
```

With the package installed, one can rewrite the earlier example to utilize LoopVectorization.jl:

```
using LoopVectorization
```

```
function array_addition_lv!(C::Vector{Float64}, A::Vector{Float64}, B::Vector{
    Float64})
    @turbo for i in eachindex(C, A, B)
        C[i] = A[i] + B[i]
    end
end
```

The @turbo macro from LoopVectorization.jl ensures optimal vectorization and performance improvements by automatically applying suitable SIMD instructions and optimizing the loop structure.

Benchmarking SIMD Performance: It is essential to benchmark and compare the performance of SIMD-optimized code against standard implementations. The BenchmarkTools.jl package is a robust tool for this purpose.

First, install and load the package:

```
using Pkg
Pkg.add("BenchmarkTools")
using BenchmarkTools
```

Next, benchmark the functions:

```
A = rand(10^6)
B = rand(10^6)
C = similar(A)

@benchmark array_addition!(C, A, B)
@benchmark array_addition_simd!(C, A, B)
@benchmark array_addition_lv!(C, A, B)
```

The benchmark results will indicate the performance gains achieved through SIMD optimization. Results displayed will typically show reduced execution time and fewer allocations for SIMD-optimized versions.

Additional SIMD Libraries and Tools: Beyond Julia's native capabilities and LoopVectorization.jl, other libraries and tools exist to facilitate SIMD programming. Libraries such as VectorizationBase.jl and SIMD.jl provide low-level access to SIMD operations and can be used for fine-grained control over vectorized computations.

```
using SIMD

function array_addition_simd2!(C::Vector{Float64}, A::Vector{Float64}, B::Vector{
    Float64})
    @inbounds for i in 1:4:length(C)
        a = vload(Vector{Float64}(4), A, i)
        b = vload(Vector{Float64}(4), B, i)
        c = a + b
        vstore!(C, i, c)
```

```
    end
end
```

In this example, the vload and vstore! functions from SIMD.jl directly handle SIMD vector loading and storing. This approach can be beneficial for highly specialized applications needing precise control over SIMD operations.

Efficient use of SIMD in Julia involves clear understanding and strategic application of loop vectorization, memory alignment, and specialized libraries. Employing these techniques ensures substantial performance improvements in vector and array computations.

9.9 Understanding and Using BenchmarkTools

Benchmarking is a critical aspect of optimizing and ensuring the performance of your Julia code. Understanding how to properly benchmark your code is essential for identifying bottlenecks and verifying the effectiveness of any optimizations you apply. In this section, we focus on the BenchmarkTools.jl package, which is the de facto standard for benchmarking in Julia.

BenchmarkTools.jl provides a robust framework for obtaining reliable and reproducible performance measurements of Julia code. Key features of BenchmarkTools.jl include support for processing time, statistical analysis, and microbenchmarking of small code snippets to provide detailed insights into their performance characteristics.

BenchmarkTools.jl can be installed via Julia's package manager. To install it, use the following command:

```
using Pkg
Pkg.add("BenchmarkTools")
```

Once installed, we can utilize the functionalities offered by BenchmarkTools.jl. The most commonly used macro in the package is @benchmark, which evaluates an expression multiple times and produces detailed statistics about its performance. Below is a simple example of using @benchmark:

```
using BenchmarkTools

function sample_function(x)
    return x^2 + x
```

```
end

@benchmark sample_function(10)
```

The output from the above code will generate a summary including minimum, median, mean times, and memory allocations. The output enables the identification of the average performance and variability, thus highlighting potential areas for optimization.

For more detailed control over benchmarking, you can encapsulate your code in a BenchmarkGroup. This feature is beneficial when benchmarking a set of related tests. Here is an example:

```
bg = BenchmarkGroup()
bg["function1"] = @benchmark sample_function(10)
bg["function2"] = @benchmark sample_function(20)
showall(bg)
```

This approach aggregates multiple benchmarks into a single group, providing an organized way to compare the performance of related functions.

When benchmarking, it is crucial to consider the impact of memory allocation. Excessive memory allocation can significantly degrade performance due to the overhead of garbage collection. BenchmarkTools.jl helps by reporting memory allocations for each benchmarked expression. For instance:

```
@benchmark sample_function(10)
```

In the benchmark report, look for fields labeled allocs and memory estimate. Values in these fields should be minimized wherever possible through optimization techniques such as in-place operations or using pre-allocated buffers.

To ensure even more precise and reliable results, you may want to control the number of evaluations per run and warm-up rounds, which can be done using the BenchmarkTools_params struct. Consider the following example:

```
@benchmarkable sample_function(10)
params = BenchmarkTools.BenchmarkTools\_params(samples=10000, seconds=5,
    gcthresh=1.0, evals=1)

run(params, b)
```

The BenchmarkTools_params structure allows configuring the benchmarking process, such as the number of samples, evaluation period in seconds, garbage collection threshold, and the number of evaluations per sample.

To benchmark more complex code, such as that involving random number generation or more sophisticated computations, the @benchmark macro can be slightly modified to ensure accurate timings. Consider the Random module for computational tests:

```
using Random

function complex_computation(n)
    data = randn(n)
    return sum(data)
end

@benchmark complex_computation(1000)
```

For accurate benchmarks, make sure that each run of the expression is independent of the previous runs by avoiding shared state whenever feasible. This will ensure that your benchmarks are not biased by any lingering effects from previous computations.

In some cases, incremental or repetitive testing is required. @btime is a variant macro provided by BenchmarkTools.jl that focuses on the runtime of the expression with minimal overhead, shown as follows:

```
@btime sample_function(10)
```

This macro is convenient for quickly checking performance impacts while developing your functions.

In practice, benchmarking scripts using BenchmarkTools.jl should be integrated into automated performance testing frameworks to continually monitor for regressions and optimizations within your Julia codebase. Continuous benchmarking is particularly useful in larger projects where code changes frequently.

By leveraging the functionalities of BenchmarkTools.jl, Julia developers can gain a comprehensive understanding of their code's performance, identify bottlenecks, and implement effective optimizations, ensuring efficient and reliable software.

9.10 Best Practices for Writing High-Performance Code

When striving for high performance in Julia, adhering to certain best practices can considerably enhance code efficiency. These practices stem from understanding Julia's strengths as well as its pitfalls, which, when sidestepped, can lead to substantial performance gains.

1. Ensuring Type Stability

Type stability is paramount in Julia to achieve maximum performance. A function is type stable if the type of its output is predictable solely based on the type of its inputs. This allows the Julia compiler to generate optimized machine code. The Base.@code_warntype macro is essential for diagnosing type stability.

```
function sum_of_squares(arr)
    total = 0
    for x in arr
        total += x^2
    end
    return total
end

Base.@code_warntype sum_of_squares([1, 2, 3])
```

Using Base.@code_warntype will highlight any type instability, allowing for the adjustment of the function to ensure that variable types remain consistent.

2. Avoiding Global Variables

Global variables can significantly degrade performance due to their type-unstable nature. Functions that operate within local scopes should be used instead. If usage of a global variable is necessary, it should be declared with const to fix its type.

```
const global_array = [1, 2, 3]

function use_global()
    return sum(global_array)
end
```

By declaring global_array as const, the type is fixed, improving performance.

3. Leveraging In-Place Operations

In-place operations (also known as mutating operations) modify existing arrays rather than creating new ones, reducing memory allocations and enhancing performance. Such functions in Julia usually end with an exclamation mark.

```
function scale_inplace!(arr, factor)
    for i in eachindex(arr)
        arr[i] *= factor
    end
end
```

```
data = [1.0, 2.0, 3.0]
scale_inplace!(data, 2.0)
```

Here, scale_inplace! modifies data directly, avoiding the allocation of a new array.

4. Preallocating Output Arrays

Instead of creating new arrays within loops or function calls repetitively, preallocating these arrays outside the loop or function can be much more efficient.

```
function accumulate_squares(arr)
    n = length(arr)
    result = Vector{Float64}(undef, n)
    for i in 1:n
        result[i] = arr[i]^2
    end
    return result
end

data = collect(1.0:1000.0)
accumulate_squares(data)
```

This function preallocates the result array, ensuring that a large number of allocations do not occur inside the loop.

5. Using Views to Avoid Copies

Creating subarrays from a larger array often results in unnecessary data copying. Instead, the view function can be used to create a lightweight and efficient reference to a subarray.

```
arr = rand(1000, 1000)
subarr = view(arr, 1:100, 1:100)
```

Here, subarr is a view into arr and doesn't allocate new memory for storing the subarray.

6. Exploiting Broadcasting

Broadcasting enables element-wise operations on arrays without explicitly writing loops. Julia's broadcasting (indicated by a dot syntax, e.g., .*) is optimized and concise.

```
a = [1, 2, 3]
b = [4, 5, 6]
c = a .+ b
```

This operation circumvents the need for an explicit loop and is optimized for performance.

7. Minimizing Function Barriers

Julia's "function barrier" concept refers to dividing work into small functions, thus helping the compiler generate efficient machine code. Large monolithic functions can make it difficult for the compiler to optimize effectively.

```
function compute_statistics(data)
    mean_val = mean(data)
    var_val = var(data)
    return mean_val, var_val
end

function process_dataset(dataset)
    results = map(compute_statistics, dataset)
    return results
end
```

This code demonstrates how computing statistics is separated into a smaller function, aiding in better optimization.

8. Choosing Appropriate Data Structures

Selecting efficient data structures can significantly affect performance. For example, using Vector{T} for dynamic arrays, StaticArrays.jl for small fixed-size arrays, and appropriate containers from DataStructures.jl can yield better performance based on context.

The best practices highlighted here, from ensuring type stability to effective data structure selection, constitute fundamental strategies in writing high-performance Julia code. Practitioners meticulously applying these techniques can achieve significant and sustainable improvements in their code's execution efficiency.

9.11 Case Studies and Performance Tuning Examples

This section presents several case studies and concrete examples of performance tuning in Julia. Each example highlights different performance-related issues and demonstrates how to address them using various techniques discussed in the chapter. Examples range from algorithmic optimizations to hardware-aware programming, ensuring that learners can appreciate the diverse methods available for optimizing Julia code.

Case Study 1: Optimizing a Numerical Integration Algorithm

Consider the naive implementation of a numerical integration algorithm using the trapezoidal rule. The objective is to integrate a given function $f(x)$ over an interval $[a, b]$ with n subintervals.

```
function trapezoidal_rule(f, a, b, n)
    h = (b - a) / n
    integral = 0.5 * (f(a) + f(b))
    for i in 1:n-1
        integral += f(a + i*h)
    end
    integral * h
end
```

This implementation can be improved in several aspects, including avoiding repeated calculations and ensuring type stability. We proceed by profiling the function to locate the performance bottlenecks.

```
using Profile

f(x) = x^2 - 2x + 1
Profile.clear()
@profile trapezoidal_rule(f, 0.0, 10.0, 1000000)
Profile.print()
```

The profiling results indicate that the primary bottleneck is the frequent evaluation of f(a + i*h). To improve performance, we can store intermediate results and avoid redundant computations. Additionally, ensuring type stability by specifying concrete types for the function parameters and return type can yield performance benefits.

```
function optimized_trapezoidal_rule(f::Function, a::Float64, b::Float64, n::Int)
    h = (b - a) / n
    integral = 0.5 * (f(a) + f(b))
    x = a

    for i in 1:n-1
        x += h
        integral += f(x)
    end
    integral * h
end
```

By using a precomputed variable x to hold the current position, we save on recalculations and improve the algorithm's efficiency. We benchmark the new implementation using the BenchmarkTools package.

```
using BenchmarkTools

@btime trapezoidal_rule($f, 0.0, 10.0, 1000000)
@btime optimized_trapezoidal_rule($f, 0.0, 10.0, 1000000)
```

```
5.343 ms (2 allocations: 48 bytes)
3.102 ms (2 allocations: 48 bytes)
```

The optimized version shows a significant reduction in execution time, demonstrating the effectiveness of the applied optimizations.

Case Study 2: Parallelizing a Simulation

The next example involves a Monte Carlo simulation, a computational technique that relies on repeated random sampling. Monte Carlo methods are often computationally expensive, making them suitable candidates for parallelization.

Consider the simulation of estimating the value of π by randomly sampling points in the unit square and counting how many fall within the unit circle.

```
function estimate_pi(n)
    count = 0
    for i in 1:n
        x, y = rand(), rand()
        if x^2 + y^2 <= 1.0
            count += 1
        end
    end
    4.0 * count / n
end
```

This implementation is sequential, limiting its performance. We can parallelize the computation using Julia's Threads module.

```
using Base.Threads

function parallel_estimate_pi(n)
    count = Atomic{Int}(0)
    @threads for i in 1:n
        x, y = rand(), rand()
        if x^2 + y^2 <= 1.0
            count[] += 1
        end
    end
    4.0 * count[] / n
end
```

The @threads macro parallelizes the for loop across available CPU threads. An atomic counter is used to safely increment the count from multiple threads. We compare the performance of both implementations.

```
@btime estimate_pi(10^7)
@btime parallel_estimate_pi(10^7)
```

```
126.735 ms (2 allocations: 32 bytes)
41.597 ms (4 allocations: 176 bytes)
```

The parallel implementation demonstrates substantial performance gains, benefiting from multi-threading capabilities.

Case Study 3: Minimizing Memory Allocations in a Matrix Operation

Memory allocation can significantly impact performance, particularly in numerical computations. This example focuses on minimizing allocations in a matrix-multiplication operation.

The naive implementation of matrix multiplication is as follows:

```
function naive_matrix_multiply(A::Array{Float64,2}, B::Array{Float64,2})
    n, m = size(A, 1), size(B, 2)
    C = zeros(Float64, n, m)

    for i in 1:n
        for j in 1:m
            for k in 1:size(A, 2)
                C[i,j] += A[i,k] * B[k,j]
            end
        end
    end
    C
end
```

This straightforward implementation does not consider optimization techniques and results in numerous allocations. We optimize the code by using in-place operations and leveraging LinearAlgebra functions.

```
using LinearAlgebra

function optimized_matrix_multiply!(C::Array{Float64,2}, A::Array{Float64,2}, B::
        Array{Float64,2})
    mul!(C, A, B)
end

function optimized_matrix_multiply(A::Array{Float64,2}, B::Array{Float64,2})
    C = zeros(Float64, size(A, 1), size(B, 2))
    optimized_matrix_multiply!(C, A, B)
    C
end
```

The mul! function performs in-place multiplication, thereby reducing intermediate allocations. The function optimized_matrix_multiply creates the result matrix once and uses the in-place function to fill it. Benchmarking is performed to evaluate the performance improvements.

```
A = rand(1000, 1000)
B = rand(1000, 1000)
@btime naive_matrix_multiply($A, $B)
@btime optimized_matrix_multiply($A, $B)
```

```
2.493 s (4000001 allocations: 61.04 MiB)
308.252 ms (2 allocations: 7.63 MiB)
```

Optimizing matrix multiplication reduces execution time and memory allocations, highlighting the importance of considering allocation patterns in performance-critical code.

This section, through detailed case studies, emphasizes practical strategies for performance tuning in Julia, reinforcing the principles covered in the preceding sections.

Chapter 10

Interfacing with Other Languages

This chapter explores how to interface Julia with other programming languages. It covers calling C and Fortran code, using Python with PyCall, and interfacing with R using RCall. The chapter also discusses working with JavaScript, calling Julia from other languages, and interfacing with MATLAB and Octave. Additional topics include using shared libraries, handling C pointers and arrays, best practices for interoperability, performance considerations, and troubleshooting common issues.

10.1 Introduction to Interfacing with Other Languages

In modern computational workflows, leveraging multiple programming languages can provide significant efficiency and flexibility advantages. Julia, while being a high-performance language suitable for a wide range of scientific and technical applications, often needs to interface with other languages to utilize existing codebases, libraries, and systems. To effectively work with Julia in a polyglot environment, it is essential to understand the mechanisms provided by Julia for integrating with other programming languages.

The ability to call functions from C, Fortran, Python, R, JavaScript, MAT-

LAB, and Octave from within Julia, or vice versa, allows for extensive code reuse and interoperability. This section will delve into the essential techniques for interfacing Julia with these languages, elucidating the syntax, semantics, and best practices for seamless operation.

One fundamental aspect of interfacing involves calling functions written in C. Julia provides direct support for this through the ‘ccall‘ function, which allows for invoking C functions defined in shared libraries. Consider a simple example:

```
function c_add(x::Int32, y::Int32)::Int32
    return ccall((:add, "libadd"), Int32, (Int32, Int32), x, y)
end
```

In this example, the Julia function c_add calls a C function add from the shared library libadd. The ccall function specifies the return type, argument types, and the arguments themselves. Detailed understanding of the C function signatures and the corresponding Julia types is crucial for correct interfacing.

Interfacing with Fortran shares many similarities with C, as Fortran code is often compiled to shared libraries that can be accessed from Julia. Care must be taken to handle Fortran's column-major array ordering and different calling conventions.

Python interoperability is another critical aspect, facilitated by the PyCall package. PyCall allows for calling Python functions and using Python libraries directly from Julia. An example of importing and using the NumPy library is shown below:

```
using PyCall
np = pyimport("numpy")
a = np.array([1, 2, 3])
println(a + a)
```

This code snippet demonstrates importing the NumPy package, creating a NumPy array, and performing an operation with it in Julia. PyCall takes care of data type conversions between Julia and Python, allowing for fluid integration.

R integration is handled through the RCall package, enabling the use of R's extensive statistical and graphical libraries in Julia projects. Here is an example of creating a data frame in R and accessing it in Julia:

```
using RCall
@rlibrary data.table

R"dt <- data.table(a = 1:5, b = 6:10)"
julia_dt = rcopy(R"dt")
println(julia_dt)
```

The R"" string macro allows for executing R code within Julia, and rcopy converts the R data frame into a Julia DataFrame.

When interfacing with JavaScript, Julia can make use of WebSockets or Node.js integrations. The combination of asynchronous processing paradigms and event-driven architecture in JavaScript with Julia's computational capabilities can be particularly powerful for web applications.

```
using Sockets

# Simple WebSocket server in Julia
server = listen(8000)
while true
    client = accept(server)
    @async handle_client(client)
end
```

The example above shows the basics of setting up a WebSocket server in Julia, capable of interfacing with JavaScript clients. Detailed handling of socket communication and data exchange protocols is essential for robust interactions.

Calling Julia from other languages often involves setting up appropriate bindings or APIs, leveraging Julia's ability to compile shared libraries. An example would be generating a shared library from a Julia module that can be used in a C program.

```
using Libdl

function julia_add(x::Int32, y::Int32)::Int32
    return x + y
end

Base.@ccallable julia_add(x::Int32, y::Int32)::Int32

create_library("libjulia_add", julia_add)
```

This script creates a shared library with the julia_add function that can be called from C. Properly managing naming conventions and data types ensures seamless interoperability.

MATLAB and Octave can also interact with Julia through the MATLAB.jl and MATLAB Engine API, respectively. Each interaction mechanism requires careful management of memory, data types, and execution context to ensure performance and correctness.

These interfacing capabilities significantly extend Julia's applicability, enabling it to leverage specialized libraries and legacy codebases in other languages. Understanding the syntax and semantics of inter-language calling conventions, along with the tools provided by Julia packages, is essential for effective and efficient multi-language development workflows.

10.2 Calling C and Fortran Code from Julia

Integrating C and Fortran code with Julia allows developers to leverage existing libraries and optimize performance-critical sections of their applications. The FFI (Foreign Function Interface) in Julia provides robust mechanisms for calling functions written in C and Fortran. This section explains the detailed procedural steps and essential concepts for integrating C and Fortran code with Julia.

Calling C Code from Julia

To call a C function from Julia, the first step is to understand the function signature in C. Consider a C function defined in a hello.c file as follows:

```
#include <stdio.h>

void say_hello() {
    printf("Hello from C!\n");
}
```

Compile this C code into a shared library using a command:

```
gcc -shared -o libhello.so -fPIC hello.c
```

In Julia, use the ccall function to call this C function. Here is a Julia script to interface with this compiled C code:

```
const libhello = "libhello.so"

function say_hello()
    ccall((:say_hello, libhello), Nothing, ())
end

say_hello()
```

In the ccall function:

- The first argument specifies the tuple containing the function name :say_hello and the library name libhello.
- The second argument, Nothing, indicates the return type of the C function.

- The third argument, (), is a tuple representing the types of the function's arguments, which is empty in this case.

To call a C function with parameters, consider the following C function, add, defined in a math.c file:

```
int add(int a, int b) {
    return a + b;
}
```

Compile it into a shared library:

```
gcc -shared -o libmath.so -fPIC math.c
```

Call this function from Julia:

```
const libmath = "libmath.so"

function add(a::Cint, b::Cint)::Cint
    return ccall((:add, libmath), Cint, (Cint, Cint), a, b)
end

result = add(3, 5)
println("3 + 5 = $result")
```

In this example:

- The return type and argument types are specified as Cint (which corresponds to the int type in C).
- The values a and b are passed as arguments to the ccall function.

Calling Fortran Code from Julia

Similar to C, Julia can call Fortran functions by interfacing through shared libraries. Consider a Fortran subroutine defined in a hello.f90 file:

```
subroutine say_hello()
    print *, "Hello from Fortran!"
end subroutine say_hello
```

Compile this Fortran code into a shared library using:

```
gfortran -shared -o libhello_fortran.so -fPIC hello.f90
```

In Julia, call the Fortran subroutine as follows:

```
const libhello_fortran = "libhello_fortran.so"
```

```
function say_hello_fortran()
    ccall((:say_hello_, libhello_fortran), Nothing, ())
end

say_hello_fortran()
```

Notice the underscore in :say_hello_. This convention generally applies to Fortran function and subroutine names when called from Julia or C.

For calling Fortran functions with parameters, consider the following Fortran subroutine defined in math.f90:

```
subroutine add(a, b, result)
    integer, intent(in) :: a, b
    integer, intent(out) :: result

    result = a + b
end subroutine add
```

Compile it into a shared library:

```
gfortran -shared -o libmath_fortran.so -fPIC math.f90
```

Call this Fortran subroutine from Julia:

```
const libmath_fortran = "libmath_fortran.so"

function add_fortran(a::Cint, b::Cint)::Cint
    result = Ref{Cint}()
    ccall((:add_, libmath_fortran), Nothing, (Ref{Cint}, Ref{Cint}, Ref{Cint}), a, b,
          result)
    return result[]
end

result = add_fortran(3, 5)
println("3 + 5 = $result")
```

In this case:

- The arguments are passed by reference using the Ref type when calling the Fortran subroutine.

Understanding the interoperability mechanisms between Julia and other languages like C and Fortran allows the integration of existing high-performance libraries and facilitates code reuse, helping to achieve seamless performance optimization.

10.3 Using Python with PyCall

PyCall is a powerful package that allows Julia to seamlessly call Python functions, use Python libraries, and handle Python objects. This integration is facilitated through the PyCall.jl package, which provides a comprehensive interface to call into Python code from Julia. It is essential to ensure that Python is installed and properly configured on your system before proceeding.

To start using PyCall, install the package from the Julia REPL:

```
using Pkg
Pkg.add("PyCall")
```

After the installation, you can import the PyCall package into your Julia script:

```
using PyCall
```

At this stage, you need to verify that PyCall has located the correct Python version. You can check the currently used Python executable by:

```
println(PyCall.python)
```

If you need to switch to a different Python installation, you can set the PYTHON environment variable before adding the package:

```
ENV["PYTHON"] = "/path/to/your/python"
Pkg.build("PyCall")
```

This tells PyCall to use the specified Python interpreter, after which you can rebuild the package.

To illustrate how PyCall works, we will consider an example of using the popular numpy library to perform array manipulations. First, ensure that numpy is installed in your Python environment:

```
pip install numpy
```

Next, you can import numpy in Julia through PyCall:

```
np = pyimport("numpy")
```

You can now use numpy functions directly. Here is an example of creating a numpy array and performing basic operations:

```
a = np.array([1, 2, 3])
```

```
b = np.array([4, 5, 6])
c = np.add(a, b)
println(c)
```

[5 7 9]

PyCall automatically converts between Python and Julia types, but it is crucial to understand the types to avoid confusion. For instance, np.array returns a PyObject which represents a reference to the actual Python object. PyCall provides functions to convert these to Julia arrays if necessary:

```
julia_array = pycall(np.array, PyArray, [1, 2, 3])
println(julia_array)
```

PyCall also allows calling Python functions using Julia's natural syntax. For example, invoking a method on a numpy array is similar to calling a method in Julia:

```
a = np.array([1.0, 2.0, 3.0])
result = a.mean()
println(result)
```

2.0

When dealing with complex namespaces and nested modules, PyCall provides easy access. For example, to access scipy.linalg, you can do the following:

```
scipy = pyimport("scipy")
linalg = scipy.linalg
det = linalg.det([[1, 2], [3, 4]])
println(det)
```

-2.0

It is also possible to pass Julia functions to Python. Consider a scenario where you might want to integrate a Julia function with a Python library that expects a callback:

```
function julia_callback(x)
    return x^2
end

pyfunc = pybuiltin("callable")(julia_callback)
result = pyfunc(3)
println(result) # Should print 9
```

PyCall supports exception handling through Julia's try-catch mechanism. This provides seamless error propagation from Python to Julia, allowing effective debugging:

```
try
    result = np.divide(1, 0)
catch e
    println("Caught an exception: ", e)
end
```

```
Caught an exception: Divide by zero
```

This integration makes PyCall a robust tool for leveraging the extensive Python ecosystem within Julia, facilitating hybridized computation workflows that capitalize on the strengths of both languages.

10.4 Interfacing with R using RCall

The RCall.jl package facilitates seamless interaction between Julia and R, enabling execution of R code, data transfer, and function calls. It enhances the flexibility of Julia by leveraging R's robust statistical and graphical capabilities. This section provides a comprehensive guide on installing RCall.jl, executing R code from Julia, and managing data exchange between the two languages.

RCall.jl can be installed via Julia's package manager. In a Julia REPL, execute:

```
using Pkg
Pkg.add("RCall")
```

To begin using RCall, it must be loaded into the current Julia session:

```
using RCall
```

Executing R commands within Julia can be achieved through RCall's @rput and @rget macros. Basic R expressions can be evaluated using the R" block syntax. For example:

```
R"print('Hello from R!')"
```

Functionality extends to more complex operations such as generating plots. For instance, the following code generates a histogram in R:

```
# Generating data in Julia
data = randn(1000)

# Passing data to R
@rput data

# Generating the histogram in R
R"hist(data, main='Histogram generated in R')"
```

With @rput and @rget, data can be transferred between Julia and R. @rput transfers Julia objects to R environment, whereas @rget retrieves R objects into Julia. Consider the following example:

```
# Define a Julia array
julia_array = [1, 2, 3, 4, 5]

# Transfer the array to R
@rput julia_array

# In R, compute the mean of the array
R"mean_value = mean(julia_array)"

# Retrieve the result back to Julia
@rget mean_value

# Display the computed mean value
println(mean_value)
```

R's native data structures like data frames can be manipulated within Julia. For instance, creating a data frame in R and accessing it in Julia:

```
# Create a data frame in R
R"df = data.frame(id = 1:5, value = c(10, 20, 30, 40, 50))"

# Retrieve the data frame as a Julia DataFrame
@rget df
julia_df = DataFrame(df)


# Working with the data frame in Julia
println(julia_df)
```

RCall.jl enables calling R functions that are not inherently present in Julia, including custom and CRAN packages. For instance, installing and using the ggplot2 package to create advanced visualizations:

```
# Install ggplot2 package in R
R"install.packages('ggplot2')"

# Load ggplot2 library
R"library(ggplot2)"

# Create a plot using ggplot2
R"""
ggplot(data.frame(x=1:10, y=rnorm(10)), aes(x=x, y=y)) +
  geom_point() +
  ggtitle('Scatter plot generated with ggplot2')
"""
```

Julia can leverage R's extensive repository of packages. For instance, calling statistical tests available in R:

```
# Define sample data in Julia
sample1 = randn(50)
sample2 = randn(50) .+ 0.5
```

```
# Transfer data to R
@rput sample1
@rput sample2

# Perform a t-test in R
R"""
t_test_result = t.test(sample1, sample2)
print(t_test_result)
"""

# Retrieve the p-value of the t-test back to Julia
R"p_value = t_test_result$p.value"
@rget p_value
println("P-value of t-test: ", p_value)
```

To summarize, RCall.jl is a powerful tool for integrating R's capabilities into Julia workflows. This section covered the installation and setup of RCall, executing R code within Julia, and managing inter-language data transfer. By harnessing the functionality provided by RCall.jl, users can enhance their data analysis tasks by combining the strengths of both Julia and R.

10.5 Working with JavaScript

Julia provides a powerful mechanism for interfacing with JavaScript, enabling the seamless integration of Julia's robust numerical capabilities with the flexibility of JavaScript. This integration is particularly useful for web development, real-time data visualization, and interactive applications that benefit from the computational strength of Julia.

To work effectively with JavaScript from Julia, the primary tool we use is the NodeJS.jl package. This package allows us to call Node.js code directly from Julia. Node.js is a JavaScript runtime built on Chrome's V8 JavaScript engine, which enables us to execute JavaScript code server-side.

Installing NodeJS.jl

To begin, ensure that NodeJS.jl is installed. You can install it using Julia's package manager:

```
using Pkg
Pkg.add("NodeJS")
```

After installing the package, it is necessary to import it.

```
using NodeJS
```

Calling JavaScript Code

With NodeJS.jl, you can evaluate JavaScript code using the js function. This function sends a string of JavaScript code to the Node.js execution environment and retrieves the result. For example:

```
result = js("3 + 4")
println(result)
```

The above code evaluates the JavaScript expression $3 + 4$ and prints the result, 7, in Julia.

Working with JavaScript Functions

In addition to evaluating simple expressions, you can define and call JavaScript functions. Here is an example:

```
js("""
    function add(a, b) {
        return a + b;
    }
""")
result = js("add(5, 6)")
println(result)
```

This script defines a JavaScript function add that returns the sum of its two arguments. Then, it calls add with arguments 5 and 6 and prints the result, 11.

Handling Asynchronous JavaScript Code

JavaScript often involves asynchronous operations, particularly when dealing with I/O. To handle asynchronous functions from Julia, NodeJS.jl provides a mechanism to manage JavaScript promises.

Here is an example using the built-in setTimeout function, which demonstrates delayed execution:

```
code = """
    new Promise((resolve) => {
        setTimeout(() => {
            resolve(42);
        }, 1000);
    });
"""
promise = js(code)
result = NodeJS.await(promise)
println(result)
```

In this script, the JavaScript Promise that resolves to 42 after one second is managed using NodeJS.await.

Interfacing with Existing JavaScript Libraries

NodeJS.jl also allows you to use existing JavaScript libraries from the npm ecosystem. You can install packages directly by utilizing npm commands within Julia. Here is an example that uses the axios library for making HTTP requests:

First, install axios:

```
js("const { execSync } = require('child_process'); execSync('npm install axios')")
```

Next, create a script that uses axios:

```
js("""
    const axios = require('axios');
    function fetchGitHub() {
        return axios.get('https://api.github.com').then(response => response.data);
    }
""")

promise = js("fetchGitHub()")
result = NodeJS.await(promise)
println(result)
```

This code snippet installs the axios library, defines a function fetchGitHub that makes an HTTP GET request to the GitHub API, and prints the response.

Handling Data Sharing Between Julia and JavaScript

For effective interoperability, it is important to convert data structures between Julia and JavaScript. NodeJS.jl handles basic data types like numbers, strings, and booleans automatically. However, complex structures such as arrays and objects need careful handling.

Consider the following example of sharing an array of numbers between Julia and JavaScript:

```
julia_array = [1, 2, 3, 4, 5]
js_array = js("const arr = [" * join(string.(julia_array), ", ") * "]; arr")
println(js_array)
```

Here, a Julia array is converted into a JavaScript array by constructing the array as a string.

Error Handling

When interfacing with JavaScript, it is essential to implement error handling to manage unexpected scenarios effectively. The NodeJS.try function enables you to catch JavaScript errors:

```
try
    result = js("nonexistentFunction()")
    println(result)
catch e
```

```
    println("JavaScript error: ", e)
end
```

The script attempts to call a non-existent JavaScript function and catches the error, printing an appropriate message.

Integrating Julia with JavaScript opens a plethora of possibilities, from server-side computations to interactive applications. Proper error handling, data sharing, and leveraging existing JavaScript libraries help create robust and flexible programs that leverage the strengths of both languages.

10.6 Calling Julia from Other Languages

Integrating Julia with other programming languages provides the benefit of leveraging Julia's high-performant numerical capabilities along with functionalities existing in other languages. In this section, we explore mechanisms and techniques to call Julia from various popular languages such as Python, C, and Java. This enables the seamless integration of Julia into multi-language projects, enhancing its use in diverse computational workflows.

1. Calling Julia from Python

The PyJulia package allows calling Julia from within a Python environment. This integration supports the use of Julia's high-performance computational functions within Python scripts. To utilize PyJulia, it must be installed using pip:

```
pip install julia
```

Next, set up Julia inside Python:

```
import julia
julia.install()
from julia import Main
```

Once set up, you can call Julia functions seamlessly from Python:

```
# Define a simple Julia function
Main.eval("""
function add(a, b)
    return a + b
end
""")

# Call the Julia function from Python
result = Main.add(5, 3)
```

```
print(result) # Output: 8
```

2. Calling Julia from C/C++

The JULIA_ENABLE_SHARED=1 build option enables Julia to be used as a shared library, allowing C or C++ programs to invoke Julia functions. To start using Julia in a C environment, include the Julia header file and link against the Julia shared library in your code:

```
#include <julia.h>

int main(int argc, char *argv[])
{
    // Initialize the Julia environment
    jl_init();

    // Evaluate a simple Julia expression
    jl_eval_string("println(sqrt(2.0))");

    // Clean up and shut down Julia
    jl_atexit_hook(0);

    return 0;
}
```

Compile the C program by linking it against the Julia shared library:

```
gcc -o call_julia call_julia.c -I/path/to/julia/include/julia -L/path/to/julia/lib -ljulia
```

Running the resulting executable will output the square root of 2:

```
1.4142135623730951
```

3. Calling Julia from Java

The JavaCall.jl package facilitates calling Julia from Java. Begin by installing the JavaCall package within Julia:

```
using Pkg
Pkg.add("JavaCall")
```

Create a Java class to call Julia:

```
import org.juliacall.*;

public class Main {
    public static void main(String[] args) {
        try {
            // Initialize the Julia environment
            String[] juliaInitArgs = { "--home", "/path/to/julia" };
            JuliaInit.init(juliaInitArgs);

            // Call a simple Julia function
            JuliaObject sqrt2 = Julia.eval("sqrt(2.0)");
            System.out.println(sqrt2);
```

```
            // Shutdown Julia
            JuliaInit.shutdown();
        } catch (Exception e) {
            e.printStackTrace();
        }
    }
}
```

Compile and run the Java program, ensuring that the Java classpath includes JavaCall:

```
javac -cp /path/to/juliacall.jar Main.java
java -cp .:/path/to/juliacall.jar Main
```

The output from the Java program will be:

```
1.4142135623730951
```

4. Performance Considerations

Integrating Julia with other languages may involve some overhead due to context switching between languages. To minimize performance penalties:

- Use efficient data conversion techniques.
- Leverage Julia's `ccall` for direct calls when feasible.
- Employ batching strategies to reduce the number of cross-language calls.

5. Troubleshooting Common Issues

When calling Julia from other languages, you may encounter several issues:

- Path Issues: Ensure the Julia executable and libraries are correctly specified in the environment.
- Version Mismatch: Ensure compatibility between Julia and integrated language versions.
- Initialization Failures: Confirm proper initialization and graceful shutdown of the Julia environment.

Understanding these concepts and techniques ensures successful and efficient integration of Julia into multi-language environments, thereby enhancing its utility in complex projects.

10.7 Interfacing with MATLAB and Octave

Interfacing with MATLAB and Octave allows users to leverage specialized functionalities and libraries in these environments directly from Julia. This section details methods to call MATLAB and Octave functions from Julia, exchange data between the environments, and discuss some performance considerations and best practices.

To interface with MATLAB, Julia provides the MATLAB.jl package. For Octave, we can use the Octave.jl package. These packages enable bidirectional communication, allowing users to execute commands and functions in MATLAB or Octave, and retrieve the results back into Julia.

Interfacing with MATLAB

The MATLAB.jl package allows calling MATLAB functions from within Julia. To begin, ensure that MATLAB is installed and properly configured on your system. The following steps illustrate how to set up and use the MATLAB.jl package:

```
using Pkg
Pkg.add("MATLAB")
using MATLAB
MATLAB.start_matlab()
```

Once MATLAB is started, you can call MATLAB functions and execute commands. Here is an example of defining a MATLAB function and calling it from Julia:

```
mat"""
function y = addOne(x)
    y = x + 1;
end
"""
result = mat"addOne(5)"
println(result)
```

The mat string macro sends the enclosed code to MATLAB for execution. The result of the MATLAB function is returned to Julia and stored in the result variable.

Data exchange between Julia and MATLAB is straightforward due to the matstr string macro, facilitating the transfer of variables:

```
x = [1, 2, 3, 4, 5]
mat"$x"
mat"x = x.^2"
squared_x = mat"x"
println(squared_x)
```

Here, the vector x is transferred to MATLAB, squared using MATLAB's element-wise power operator, and the result is transferred back to Julia.

Interfacing with Octave

Interfacing with GNU Octave is facilitated by the Octave.jl package. Start by installing the package and initializing the Octave session:

```
using Pkg
Pkg.add("Octave")
using Octave
Octave.start_octave()
```

Similar to the MATLAB interface, the Octave.jl package uses string macros to send commands and functions to Octave and retrieve the results:

```
oct"""
function y = squareElement(x)
    y = x .^ 2;
end
"""
result = oct"squareElement([1, 2, 3, 4, 5])"
println(result)
```

In this example, an Octave function is defined to square each element of an input vector. The function is called from Julia, and the resulting vector is printed.

To transfer data between Julia and Octave, use the octstr string macro:

```
x = [1.0, 2.0, 3.0, 4.0, 5.0]
oct"vec = $x"
oct"vec = vec .^ 2"
squared_vec = oct"vec"
println(squared_vec)
```

In this snippet, the Julia vector x is sent to Octave, squared within Octave, and the squared values are returned to Julia.

Performance Considerations and Best Practices

When interfacing with MATLAB or Octave, it is crucial to be mindful of the overhead associated with context switching between the Julia environment and the external MATLAB or Octave process. Minimize the frequency and volume of data transfers where possible, and prefer sending batch commands over multiple individual ones.

Efficient data handling practices include:

- Converting data to compatible formats before transfer.
- Using vectorized operations in MATLAB or Octave to reduce the number of context switches.
- Avoiding repetitive, small exchanges and instead transferring larger datasets at once.

Additionally, it is crucial to manage resources appropriately. Always ensure that any initiated MATLAB or Octave session is properly terminated when no longer needed to free system resources.

```
MATLAB.exit()
Octave.exit()
```

Integrating Julia with MATLAB and Octave expands the range of available tools and functions, making it possible to capitalize on the strengths of each environment. Utilizing seamless interoperability allows developers to build upon existing codebases and enhance functionalities without redundant rewrites. This opens up a myriad of opportunities for advanced computational techniques and collaborative projects.

10.8 Using Shared Libraries

Shared libraries are a crucial component in the realm of modern programming, facilitating code reuse and modular design. In Julia, integrating shared libraries allows leveraging precompiled routines written in other languages such as C or C++.

To load a shared library, use the Libdl module, which provides functions to interact with dynamically linked libraries (DLLs) and shared object libraries (SO files).

```
using Libdl

# Load the shared library
lib_path = "path/to/library.so"
lib = Libdl.dlopen(lib_path)
```

The Libdl.dlopen function attempts to open the specified shared library and returns a handle to it. Ensure the correct path to the library, as an incorrect path results in an error.

```
Error: could not load library "path/to/library.so"
```

Once the library is loaded, access the symbols (functions, variables) it exposes using Libdl.dlsym. Consider a function named add in the shared library, with the signature int add(int, int);.

```
# Resolve the symbol (function name) in the shared library
add_symbol = Libdl.dlsym(lib, :add)

# Define a callable Julia function linked to the symbol
add = ccall(add_symbol, Cint, (Cint, Cint), 2, 3)
```

Here, ccall is used to call the function add, with the return type specified as Cint (C integer) and the argument types specified in a tuple. The last two parameters 2 and 3 are the arguments for the add function.

To encapsulate the usage of ccall, define a Julia function:

```
function add(a::Int32, b::Int32)::Int32
    return ccall(add_symbol, Cint, (Cint, Cint), a, b)
end

result = add(2, 3)
println("Result: ", result)
```

The add function simplifies the process of calling the shared library function by hiding the complexities of ccall.

When dealing with pointers and arrays, handle data correctly to avoid memory leaks or segmentation faults. Consider a function that populates an array. The shared library function might look like void fill_array(int* arr, int length);.

```
# Define the symbol
fill_array_symbol = Libdl.dlsym(lib, :fill_array)

# Define Julia wrapper function
function fill_array(arr::Vector{Int32}, length::Int32)
    ccall(fill_array_symbol, Cvoid, (Ptr{Cint}, Cint), arr, length)
end

arr = Vector{Int32}(undef, 10) # Create an uninitialized array of 10 elements
fill_array(arr, length(arr))

println("Array filled by shared library: ", arr)
```

In this example, the Julia function fill_array uses ccall to call the shared library function and populate the array. Note that the array is created in Julia and passed by reference using a pointer.

Debugging and error handling are essential when interfacing with shared libraries. Use dlerror to retrieve error messages from the failed operations.

```
# Attempt to load a non-existent library
```

```
invalid_lib = Libdl.dlopen("invalid/path/to/library.so")

if invalid_lib == C_NULL
    println("Error loading library: ", Libdl.dlerror())
else
    println("Library loaded successfully")
end
```

This code handles errors gracefully by checking if the library handle is C_NULL. If an error occurs, dlerror provides the corresponding error message.

Memory management and cleaning up resources are equally important. Always ensure that any loaded shared libraries are properly closed when no longer needed.

```
# Close the shared library
Libdl.dlclose(lib)
```

Calling Libdl.dlclose releases the resources associated with the library, ensuring efficient memory management and preventing potential leaks.

Integrating shared libraries with Julia amplifies the language's capabilities, enabling the reuse of existing libraries and combining Julia's performance with tried-and-tested third-party code. This practice is indispensable for applications requiring high performance and interoperability.

10.9 Handling C Pointers and Arrays

Interfacing Julia with C provides powerful capabilities, especially when it comes to manipulating pointers and arrays. Understanding how to handle these data structures is essential for advanced interoperability and performance optimization. In Julia, working with C pointers and arrays involves leveraging the Base.unsafe_pointer_to_array and Base.unsafe_load functions, as well as using the ccall interface for direct interaction with C functions.

In C, pointers are variables that store the memory address of another variable. Arrays in C are contiguous blocks of memory, but in the context of interfacing with Julia, pointers to these arrays are often passed around. The following sections provide detailed explanations and examples of how to manage these pointers and arrays efficiently.

```
#include <stdio.h>

void print_array(int *arr, int length) {
```

```
    for (int i = 0; i < length; i++) {
        printf("%d\n", arr[i]);
    }
}
```

The code above defines a simple C function print_array that takes a pointer to an integer array and its length, then prints each element. To call this function from Julia, we first create a corresponding Julia array and pass its pointer to the C function using ccall.

```
# Define the C function signature in Julia
function print_array(arr::Vector{Cint})
    ccall((:print_array, "libc_example"), Cvoid, (Ptr{Cint}, Cint), arr, length(arr))
end

# Create a Julia array
julia_array = [1, 2, 3, 4, 5]

# Call the C function
print_array(julia_array)
```

In this example, ccall is used to invoke the C function print_array. The ccall signature includes the function name, the library containing the function, the return type, the argument types, and the actual arguments. The Julia array julia_array is passed directly, and ccall automatically manages the conversion from a Julia array to a C pointer.

When dealing with arrays, it is often necessary to convert between Julia arrays and C pointers. This conversion can be managed using Base.unsafe_pointer_to_array and Ptr. Consider the following example:

```
# Allocate memory in C and return a pointer
function allocate_array(size::Cint)::Ptr{Cint}
    return ccall((:malloc, "libc"), Ptr{Cint}, (Csize_t,), size * Cint)
end

# Convert the C pointer to a Julia array
c_pointer = allocate_array(10)
julia_array = unsafe_pointer_to_array(c_pointer, 10)

# Initialize the array
for i in 1:10
    julia_array[i] = i
end

# Use the array in C function calls
print_array(julia_array)
```

In this example, we allocate memory in C using the malloc function and obtain a C pointer. This pointer is then converted to a Julia array using unsafe_pointer_to_array. The array can be initialized and manipulated in Julia before being passed back to a C function.

For safety and performance considerations, it is crucial to ensure that the memory allocated in C is properly managed, typically by freeing it after use. The following example demonstrates this:

```
# Allocate and free memory in C
function manage_memory(size::Cint)
    c_pointer = allocate_array(size)

    julia_array = unsafe_pointer_to_array(c_pointer, size)
    for i in 1:size
        julia_array[i] = i
    end

    print_array(julia_array)

    # Free the memory
    ccall((:free, "libc"), Cvoid, (Ptr{Cvoid},), c_pointer)
end

manage_memory(10)
```

In this code, after using the array, the free function is called to release the allocated memory. This practice prevents memory leaks and ensures optimal resource utilization.

When handling C arrays and pointers in Julia, understanding pointer arithmetic and array bounds is essential. While Julia provides high-level abstractions and safety checks, interfacing with C requires cautious operation to avoid accessing invalid memory regions.

By mastering the techniques for handling C pointers and arrays in Julia, you can effectively leverage existing C libraries and write more efficient, interoperable code.

10.10 Best Practices for Interoperability

Interfacing Julia with other languages involves various practices that ensure seamless and efficient communication between Julia and external codebases. By adhering to best practices, developers can optimize performance, maintain code readability, and avoid common pitfalls. Key best practices are elaborated as follows:

Consistent Data Structures: When passing data between Julia and external languages, ensuring consistent data structures can simplify the interface. Prefer using arrays, structs, or other well-defined types that have clear analogs in the target language. For instance, passing a Vector{Float64} from Julia to C can be done through C-compatible arrays.

```
# Example of passing a vector to C
x = [1.0, 2.0, 3.0]
c_ptr = Base.unsafe_convert(Ptr{Cdouble}, pointer(x))
@ccall c_function(c_ptr::Ptr{Cdouble}, length(x)::Cint)::Cvoid
```

Memory Management: Handling memory correctly is crucial for preventing leaks or corruption. When interfacing with languages like C, ensure that allocated memory in one language is appropriately deallocated. Utilize Julia's garbage collector and interfacing capabilities like Ref and Ptr to manage references carefully.

```
# Allocating memory for a C function and ensuring deallocation
p = Base.malloc(8) # Allocating 8 bytes
try
    @ccall another_c_function(p::Ptr{Cvoid})::Cvoid
finally
    Base.free(p) # Ensuring deallocation
end
```

Error Handling: Implement robust error handling mechanisms to catch and manage errors originating from external languages. In Julia, using try and catch blocks can help in managing exceptions. When dealing with C code, they often return error codes which Julia code should handle appropriately.

```
# Handling errors from a C function that returns an error code
res = @ccall potentially_faulty_c_function()::Cint
if res != 0
    error("C function failed with error code $res")
end
```

Performance Considerations: Minimize the performance overhead when calling external functions. Avoid excessive data conversion and strive for bulk data operations. Whenever possible, pass pointers or references instead of copying whole data structures.

```
# Passing a large matrix to a C function using pointers
using LinearAlgebra
m = rand(1000, 1000)
p_m = Base.unsafe_convert(Ptr{Cdouble}, pointer(m))
@ccall process_large_matrix(p_m::Ptr{Cdouble}, size(m,1)::Cint, size(m,2)::Cint)::
    Cvoid
```

Documentation and Comments: Provide clear documentation and comments within the code to explain the purpose of interfacing segments, data types used, and any assumptions or requirements. This practice aids in code maintenance and assists other developers in understanding the interfacing logic.

```
# Interfacing with a Fortran function to solve a linear system
#
```

```
# Arguments:
# A - Coefficient matrix (size NxN)
# b - Right-hand side vector (size N)
#
# This function assumes that the Fortran function 'solve_system' has been
# defined in an external library accessible at runtime.

@ccall solve_system(A::Ptr{Cdouble}, b::Ptr{Cdouble}, N::Cint)::Cvoid
```

Modular Code Structure: Organize interfacing code into modular segments or functions. This approach helps in isolating the interfacing logic, making it more manageable and reusable. Ensure that each function has a singular, clear responsibility related to the interfacing task.

```
# Modular function for calling a JavaScript function from Julia
function call_js_function(js_code::String, input::String)::String
    output = @ccall run_js_function(js_code::Cstring, input::Cstring)::Cstring
    return unsafe_string(output) # Convert C string back to Julia string
end
```

Testing and Validation: Rigorous testing is necessary to guarantee the reliability of interfacing code. Employ unit tests to validate the functionality of each interfacing unit, checking for correct data handling, error management, and performance metrics.

```
# Unit testing an interfacing function calling a C library
using Test

function sum_array(arr::Vector{Float64})::Float64
    c_arr = Base.unsafe_convert(Ptr{Cdouble}, pointer(arr))
    total = @ccall sum_c_array(c_arr::Ptr{Cdouble}, length(arr)::Cint)::Cdouble
    return total
end

@test sum_array([1.0, 2.0, 3.0]) == 6.0
```

Through consistent data structures, meticulous memory management, robust error handling, and performance-aware practices, along with clear documentation, modular code, and thorough testing, one can proficiently interface Julia with numerous external languages, ensuring efficient and reliable integration.

10.11 Performance Considerations in Interfacing

Interfacing Julia with other programming languages, while powerful, brings several performance considerations to the forefront. Ensuring efficient execution and data handling across language boundaries is crucial for achieving optimal performance. This section delves into various factors that can impact performance when interfacing Julia with languages such as C, Python, R, JavaScript, MATLAB, and others.

One of the primary performance concerns is the overhead associated with crossing language boundaries. Every time a function call is made from Julia to another language, or vice versa, there is a cost involved in marshaling data and managing the transition between different runtime environments. While Julia's Just-In-Time (JIT) compilation provides high performance for native Julia code, interfacing with external languages can introduce latency.

To illustrate this, consider a simple example where we call a C function from Julia. Suppose we have a C function that computes the square of a given integer:

```
int square(int x) {
    return x * x;
}
```

To call this function from Julia, we can use the ccall function as follows:

```
function square_c(x::Int32)
    return ccall((:square, "libmylibrary"), Int32, (Int32,), x)
end
```

While the ccall mechanism is efficient, the overall performance will also depend on several additional factors:

- **Data Conversion Overhead:** When passing data between Julia and other languages, necessary conversions can add overhead. For example, converting Julia arrays to C arrays and vice versa can be costly. It is essential to minimize unnecessary data conversions and use direct memory access methods when possible.

- **Function Call Overhead:** Each function call incurs a certain amount of overhead due to stack setup, parameter passing, and context switching between languages. Keeping the number of calls low and consolidating operations into fewer, more substantial function calls can help reduce this overhead.

- **Memory Management:** Memory management differences between languages can also impact performance. Julia uses garbage collection, whereas languages like C rely on manual memory management. Careful handling of memory allocation and deallocation is necessary to avoid memory leaks and ensure efficient use of resources.

- **Thread Safety:** Interfacing with multi-threaded environments requires careful consideration of thread safety. Synchronization mechanisms like mutexes can introduce performance bottlenecks if not handled properly.

Additionally, when using Julia with other high-level languages such as Python through PyCall, similar considerations apply. The following example demonstrates calling a Python function from Julia to perform matrix multiplication:

```
import numpy as np

def matrix_multiply(a, b):
    return np.dot(a, b)
```

In Julia, we can use the PyCall package to call this function:

```
using PyCall

py"""
import numpy as np
def matrix_multiply(a, b):
    return np.dot(a, b)
"""

function multiply_matrices(a, b)
    matrix_multiply = pybuiltin(:matrix_multiply)
    return matrix_multiply(a, b)
end
```

Here, the primary performance considerations include:

- **Call Overhead:** The overhead of calling a Python function from Julia, including the need to switch runtime environments, can be significant.

- **Data Transfer:** Transferring large datasets between Julia and Python can be slow. Using shared memory or in-place operations can mitigate some of this overhead.

- **Library Interactions:** Performance can vary widely depending on the underlying libraries used in Python (e.g., NumPy) and their optimizations. Leveraging highly optimized libraries is essential for performance-sensitive applications.

When interfacing with R using the RCall package, one must consider similar performance factors. For example, invoking an R function to perform a statistical analysis requires careful attention to data conversion and memory management.

```
my_stat_function <- function(data) {
    return(summary(data))
}
```

In Julia, we can call this R function as follows:

```
using RCall

function analyze_data(data)
    rdata = RCall.reval("data.frame(col1=data)", data=data)
    return RCall.reval("my_stat_function(data)", data=rdata)
end
```

The primary considerations here include:

- **Data Handling:** Efficiently converting and passing data structures between Julia and R is crucial to avoid performance degradation.
- **Execution Overhead:** Each call to the R runtime introduces overhead. Aggregating operations within R functions can help reduce the frequency of calls and improve performance.

Another critical factor to consider is the use of shared libraries. When developing shared libraries in C or Fortran and using them in Julia, it is important to compile the libraries with appropriate optimization flags. For instance:

```
gcc -O3 -shared -o libmylibrary.so mylibrary.c
```

Using optimization flags such as -O3 enables the compiler to apply advanced optimization techniques, resulting in faster execution. Additionally, ensuring that shared libraries are thread-safe and minimizing locking mechanisms can improve performance in multi-threaded applications.

Effective use of caching mechanisms, minimizing cross-language calls, careful memory management, and leveraging highly optimized libraries are fundamental practices to achieve the best performance when interfacing Julia with other languages. These considerations ensure that the seamless integration of Julia with various external languages does not adversely impact the computational efficiency and responsiveness of applications.

10.12 Troubleshooting and Common Issues

When interfacing Julia with other programming languages, numerous challenges and issues can arise. This section provides an in-depth look at the common problems encountered and offers solutions to mitigate these issues effectively. Ensure that the necessary packages and dependencies are correctly installed for seamless integration between Julia and the target languages.

Linking Errors with C and Fortran

Linking errors frequently occur when calling C or Fortran code from Julia due to missing or incorrectly specified libraries. Ensure that the dynamic libraries (shared objects on Unix, DLLs on Windows) are correctly linked.

```
# Example: gcc -shared -o libexample.so example.c
```

Make sure that the shared library is in a directory included in the library search path. On Unix systems, you can set the LD_LIBRARY_PATH environment variable:

```
export LD_LIBRARY_PATH=/path/to/library:$LD_LIBRARY_PATH
```

On Windows, you may need to adjust the PATH environment variable:

```
set PATH=C:\path\to\library;%PATH%
```

If using Julia's ccall to interface with C functions, ensure the library is correctly located and that function signatures match the expected definitions. A typical mistake is wrong argument types or missing libraries, leading to runtime errors.

Python Integration Issues

When using the PyCall package to interface with Python, ensure that the correct Python version is in use and properly configured. PyCall uses the Python installation specified by the PYTHON environment variable. To check or set this variable, use the following command:

```
ENV["PYTHON"] = "/usr/bin/python3"
using Pkg
Pkg.build("PyCall")
```

Another common issue is mismatched paths or virtual environments. If PyCall points to an incorrect Python interpreter, unexpected behavior and import errors may occur. Utilize the Pkg.build("PyCall") command to rebuild PyCall with the correct interpreter.

Algorithm 3: Setting Python Version for PyCall

```
Input: Path to desired Python interpreter
begin
    //Set the PYTHON environment variable
    ENV["PYTHON"] = "/path/to/python";
    Pkg.build("PyCall");
    //Verify that PyCall uses the correct Python interpreter
    pyversion = PyCall.pyversion;
    println("Python version: ", pyversion);
```

RCall Package Problems

For integrating R using the RCall package, make sure that R and its dependencies are installed correctly. The R_HOME environment variable should point to the R installation directory. If encountering issues, verify the R installation path and configure it correctly:

```
export R_HOME=/usr/lib/R
```

Failure to load R libraries within Julia often stems from R's package directory not being accessible. Ensure that R libraries are available in the R_HOME/library directory. Use the following R script to confirm library paths:

```
.libPaths()
```

JavaScript Integration Challenges

When working with JavaScript, especially in web environments using platforms like WebAssembly or Node.js, ensure that the JavaScript code is compatible with the Julia environment. Various issues may arise from asynchronous operations.

To handle promises and asynchronous functions within Julia, the @async macro can be useful:

```
using HTTP
@async begin
    response = HTTP.get("http://example.com")
    println(response.body)
end
```

Matlab and Octave Interfacing Errors

While interfacing with MATLAB and Octave, ensure the engine APIs are set up correctly. For MATLAB, the MATLAB_ROOT environment variable should point to the installation directory:

```
export MATLAB_ROOT=/usr/local/MATLAB/R2021a
```

For Octave, verify that the octave executable is in the system path. Compatibility issues might stem from differences in function definitions or library versions, requiring careful handling of input-output data types.

Using Shared Libraries

When working with shared libraries, issues can arise from improper path configurations or missing dependencies. Check the library dependencies using tools like ldd on Unix systems to list dynamic dependencies:

```
ldd /path/to/libexample.so
```

Address missing dependencies by installing the required packages or correcting the library paths.

Handling C Pointers and Arrays

Mismanagement of pointers and arrays in C when called from Julia can lead to segmentation faults or erroneous behavior. Ensure that memory allocation, deallocation, and type casting are correctly managed. For instance, use Julia's Ptr type to handle pointers accurately:

```
function call_c_function()
    arr = [1.0, 2.0, 3.0]
    c_ptr = convert(Ptr{Cdouble}, arr)
    ccall((:c_function, "libexample"), Cvoid, (Ptr{Cdouble},), c_ptr)
end
```

Be cautious of mutable versus immutable data types in Julia and their interactions with C functions. Prevent segmentation faults by ensuring proper type alignment and boundary checks.

Emergent challenges while interfacing Julia with other languages highlight the complexity and attention to detail required for successful integration. Proactively addressing these common issues allows for robust and efficient interoperability across diverse programming environments.

Made in the USA
Monee, IL
05 November 2026

67911509R00168